Christos Tsiolkas and the Fiction of Critique

Christos Tsiolkas and the Fiction of Critique

Politics, Obscenity, Celebrity

Andrew McCann

ANTHEM PRESS

Anthem Press
An imprint of Wimbledon Publishing Company
www.anthempress.com

This edition first published in UK and USA 2015
by ANTHEM PRESS
75–76 Blackfriars Road, London SE1 8HA, UK
or PO Box 9779, London SW19 7ZG, UK
and
244 Madison Ave #116, New York, NY 10016, USA

British Library Cataloguing-in-Publication Data
A catalogue record for this book is available from the British Library.

Library of Congress Cataloging-in-Publication Data
McCann, Andrew (Andrew Lachlan), author.
Christos Tsiolkas and the fiction of critique : politics, obscenity,
celebrity / Andrew McCann.
pages cm
ISBN 978-1-78308-403-6 (hard back : alk. paper) – ISBN 978-1-78308-404-3
(paper back : alk. paper) – ISBN 978-1-78308-405-0
(pdf ebook) – ISBN 978-1-78308-448-7 (epub ebook)
1. Tsiolkas, Christos, 1965—Criticism and interpretation.   I. Title.
PR9619.3.T786Z75 2015
823'.914–dc23
2015007534

ISBN-13: 978 1 78308 403 6 (Hbk)
ISBN-10: 1 78308 403 0 (Hbk)

ISBN-13: 978 1 78308 404 3 (Pbk)
ISBN-10: 1 78308 404 9 (Pbk)

Cover image by Zoe Ali.

This title is also available as an ebook.

CONTENTS

ACKNOWLEDGEMENTS

Some parts of this book have already appeared in journal articles. Parts of chapter 3 have appeared in "Christos Tsiolkas and the Pornographic Logic of Commodity Capitalism," *Australian Literary Studies*, 25.1 (May 2010) and in "Discrepant Cosmopolitanism and Contemporary Fiction: Reading the Inhuman in Christos Tsiolkas's *Dead Europe* and Roberto Bolaño's *2666*," *Antipodes*, 24.2 (December 2010). Parts of chapter 4 have appeared in "Professing the Popular: Political Fiction circa 2006," *Australian Literary Studies*, 32.2 (2007). I am grateful to both journals and their editors (Leigh Dale and Nick Burns) for permission to use that material here. I am also grateful to Christos Tsiolkas for his permission to reproduce the entirety of the poem "Pasolini's Ashes," from *Jump Cuts* (Milsons Points, NSW: Random House, 1996), in my introduction.

PREFACE

According to Tom Shone, Christos Tsiolkas was "plucked from semi-obscurity and set on the literary rock-star track by his fourth novel, *The Slap*." This fairly innocuous comment appeared near the opening of a *Sunday Times* article that Shone had based on an interview with Tsiolkas, conducted in New York in 2010. The setting is important. Shone and Tsiolkas are on the roof deck of the "quirky" and "boutique" Roger Smith Hotel on Lexington Avenue. Tsiolkas is apparently awed by the Manhattan skyline. He is also fiddling with his cell phone and juggling other commitments in a way befitting for someone in the middle of an American book tour.

The article is fairly typical of the manner in which literary journalism introduces, or frames, an ostensibly new writer: the implicit approval of the marketplace is registered in an attention to the trappings of celebrity, while the distance between Manhattan and the suburbs of Melbourne, in which *The Slap* was set, also tells a story about international circulation that is a crucial part of a writer's claim on our attention. As Pascale Casanova has suggested, literary value can be as much a matter of geography as it is textuality, and like it or not, Australia is still one of the suburbs of world literature. In fairness to Shone, his article does make passing mention of *Loaded* and *Dead Europe*, and it does list some of their themes: "history, migration, blood, belonging, poverty, refuge, anti-Semitism."[1] The idea of plucking Tsiolkas from "semi-obscurity" might have made sense to a British or North American readership, but to anyone who had paid even fleeting attention to the Australian literary scene over the preceding fifteen years, during which time Tsiolkas's fiction had become a staple of critical discussion, it was likely to be jarring. Nevertheless, the comment did highlight one of the most salient aspects of Tsiolkas's career: even after the enormous Australian interest generated by his 2005 novel *Dead Europe*, he had a very limited international profile. In the divide between the local and the global—between the apparently insular Australian market and the market *per se*—*The Slap* seemed to appear *ex nihilo*, and Tsiolkas himself was somehow disembodied and decontextualized in a way that would have been unthinkable to anyone familiar with the political vehemence and visceral extremism of his earlier work.

I am dwelling on Shone's article because it was at the moment I read it that I decided I wanted to write a monograph about Christos Tsiolkas. I had already experienced the difficulty of getting literary and academic communities outside of Australia interested in Australian writers. When I began working in the United States about a decade ago, some of my American colleagues had never heard of Peter Carey. And some had never heard of Patrick White. Confronting this merely reminds one that Australia is still, culturally speaking, a relatively small part of a global, Anglophone formation. From the perspective of the northern hemisphere, its literature tends to be either opaque or invisible. The dynamics of the field of literary studies have not helped. Scholars are professionally rewarded for working in established, and well trafficked, areas of predominantly British and American literature where relatively large academic constituencies facilitate citation and circulation. At the same time notions of cultural capital in the American liberal arts still orient to traditionally defined periods and the canonical texts that constitute them. Yet as Tsiolkas worked his way along the east coast of the United States, he seemed to be gaining a level of exposure that produced both visibility and a certain kind of legibility. People had heard him interviewed on National Public Radio. He seemed to be topical, and topicality, of course, is one of the things that a critic looks for as a way of justifying a project. But related to this was the feeling that his celebrity was raising some genuinely pressing questions about the fate of radical writing in the era of global capitalism. "I had no idea [*The Slap*] was going to take me to Lexington Avenue," Tsiolkas tells Shone. "Trying to stand back, I'm interested in why it has proved so popular. I wonder what it says about contemporary writing—can you be popular without being populist?"[2] The composure of the self-questioning in this comment is quite different from the way in which Tsiolkas was speaking about global circulation earlier in his career. A passage from the 1996 *Jump Cuts*, a series of dialogues with Sasha Soldatow that forms a sort of joint autobiography, seems to question exactly the sort of success Tsiolkas was now experiencing: "Writing for the world is exciting, tempting, but I think it is an imperialist dream. There are people who can't read, people who don't much want to read, there are people who read in different ways to me."[3] The comment echoes one he made at the Melbourne Writers Festival in 1995. Partly reflecting on the distance between his work and the milieu of his Greek-speaking parents, he said,

> I do not believe there is a writing that speaks to everyone. I write in English, and my parents cannot read my work. And even if they could, my work is dependent on the cultural practices of queer, of experimental

writing, of a popular culture and music which makes little attempt to speak to them.[1]

Of course, coming up with an international bestseller is not "writing for the world," or producing "writing that speaks to everyone," but one still cannot help sensing a certain tension between the *Sunday Times*'s vision of Tsiolkas gazing over the New York skyline, realizing his arrival at the heart of global capitalism, and this earlier distance from a globalizing ambition that seems sufficiently implicit in the act of writing that one might want to disavow it.

If there is a tension here—and perhaps there is only the semblance of a tension—it is one that occurs outside the ambit of authorial control or agency. Literary careers, strung between the private and the public, the interior and the exterior, are as much about an involuntary surrender to (or capture by) the dynamics of the public sphere as they are about the austere self-discipline of creativity. I imagine a great many writers routinely wake up to find themselves hopelessly misrepresented by the forms of publicity that are central to their commercial viability. Nevertheless, the distance between the vision of Tsiolkas that I had assimilated from my repeated readings of *Jump Cuts*, with its painful, puzzling, but also inspired attempts to embody a radicalized subjectivity, and Shone's vision of the "literary rock star" seemed like an invitation. What, exactly, has to happen for a writer like Tsiolkas—a writer whose work is as explicit in its depictions of transgressive sexuality as it is in its loathing of neoliberalism—to make the leap from the local to the global? The terms "politics," "obscenity" and "celebrity" were already suggesting themselves as the points of a triangle, and yet the idea that success in the marketplace (celebrity) was somehow at odds with what the terms "politics" and "obscenity" implied seemed completely inadequate. Wasn't there a way in which the Tsiolkas gazing over the Manhattan skyline, cell phone in hand, was also in the process of gaining the sort of readership that might give his politics popular traction? Wasn't the flipside of celebrity the possibility of speaking as a genuinely public intellectual on the global stage? But what sort of public intellectual has written so nakedly about the violence of his own fantasies? And what sort of intellectual project can be founded on the volatile collision of politics and sexual transgression that lies at the center of much of Tsiolkas's work? As I intend to show in this book, the relationships between these terms—politics, obscenity and celebrity—are complex and extremely unpredictable. Tsiolkas's career sets all of these terms in motion, such that each of them qualifies and animates each of the others. Tsiolkas's status today as a recognizable, best-selling author—one of "Australia's most glittering literary treasures," as publicity from Melbourne's Wheeler Centre[5] cloyingly put it—gives him access to a wide public, but it also threatens to integrate him into the sort of middlebrow niche that, at moments in his career, he has railed against. His interest in obscenity is a central part of his political vision, yet it also has the ability to sabotage politics by limiting it to the libidinal. At the same time, however, the confluence of the political and the obscene has produced an iconoclastic form of writing that is central to both Tsiolkas's involvement in working-class theater and his recuperation by the marketplace. These dynamics clearly cannot be reduced to a series of oppositions. Celebrity does not nullify the political any more than obscenity impedes one's access to a popular readership. On the contrary, these terms (politics, obscenity and celebrity) form a series of dialectical relationships; they simultaneously enable and limit each other.

The complexity of these relationships is undergirded by the range of contexts in which Tsiolkas appears nowadays. He is not only a novelist, but also a playwright, a producer, an essayist and a film critic. His work crosses the boundaries between what are thought of as very different media environments and very different visions of the public sphere. Of Tsiolkas's five novels to date, three of them have been adapted for either television or the cinema. At the same time, the starkness of *The Slap*'s realism refers, at least implicitly, to the banality of soap operas like *Neighbours* and *Home and Away*, which were no doubt central to the reception of the novel in the United Kingdom. In this respect, at least, the success of the novel probably owes as much to forms of circulation established by the international marketing of Australian television as it does to the dynamics of a more specifically literary field. If the television adaptation of *The Slap* suggests a proximity to the market technologies of the culture industry, we also need to bear in mind Tsiolkas's involvement with the Melbourne Workers Theatre, a very different, emphatically counter-hegemonic sphere of cultural production, and his repeated pleas for the counter-cultural autonomy of the writer. That Tsiolkas's work can circulate as both mainstream television and radical theater suggests another series of questions about the relationship between the literary text and other, ostensibly more popular, forms of cultural production, though exactly what the term "popular" means in these contexts is open to debate. Of course, a text seldom becomes popular without being embedded in a series of discourses that effectively circulate it. In this respect, I am also interested in ephemeral genres such as entertainment and lifestyle journalism that increasingly frame literary production once it reaches a threshold of public recognition and visibility. How a writer manages to model his own identity, let alone his own politics, in the midst of these forces and the often unpredictable forms of affect and identification they imply is one of the issues I want to foreground.

Of course, there is a certain sort of absurdity in writing a book about a figure who is still only "mid-career," to draw on the language of grant applications.

I do feel that quite acutely. No doubt this study will be superseded, or require revision, before too long. Yet I also think Tsiolkas's career is sufficiently advanced to reveal at least a provisional narrative, an arc that links his beginnings to his moment of international acceptance, the local to the global, the immediacy of *Loaded* to the more measured, perhaps self-consciously "topical" orientation of *The Slap* and *Barracuda*. The variable ways in which the organizing terms of this book inform each other will be the key to describing the development of Tsiolkas's career across very different contexts of production and reception. Yet this is not simply a book about the career of an individual. It is also one that tries to think through some of the processes and dynamics that inform the field of contemporary literature. That field can often seem amorphous. It forces us to rethink national literary traditions and spaces in terms of a broader set of relationships involving regional and transnational formations that, to some extent, displace the national. It is also a field increasingly informed by different media (film, television and the digital) that circulate and translate literary texts in ways that force us to rethink assumptions about the autonomy of literary production. Tsiolkas's work, I want to argue, explores these processes and registers their impact on the possibility of a radical cultural politics that has only become more urgent as the disparities produced by global capitalism become more extreme.

None of this is without its difficulties. *Barracuda*, Tsiolkas's fifth novel, was published as I was writing a first draft of this book. The way its reception will impact his career is still in play, as is my own conflicted response to the novel. *Merciless Gods*, a superb collection of short stories spanning a twenty-year period, appeared just as I was beginning final revisions. This is one of the problems of writing about a contemporary figure; one's object is never stable, and things are constantly in flux. At the same time though, the early part of Tsiolkas's career is already overdetermined by categories of identification that run the risk of speaking in place of his work and of flattening its complexity. His public interviews, which are unusually candid and verge on the confessional, have made his own life an integral part of the framework around his writing. The 2013 publication of John Vasilakakos's *Christos Tsiolkas: The Untold Story*, which includes over 150 pages of exhaustive, and extremely useful, interview material, has underlined this aspect of his career. In fact, we could say that the interview itself has become a curiously fetishized critical mode in regard to Tsiolkas. The result is that we know a great deal about his life. Details that another kind of writer might choose to keep private are now routinely rehearsed across a wide range of popular media forms. Most, if not all, of Tsiolkas's readers will know that he is openly gay, that he is Greek-Australian and that he is from a working-class, immigrant background. These forms of identification are evident in the novels themselves and have been underlined by marketing strategies and book reviews. But even minimally attentive readers have access to a wide range of more personal details and anecdotes that evoke these identifications on a much more intimate, molecular level. They are also likely to know the name of his long-term partner, that he worked in a veterinary clinic while writing *Dead Europe*, that he barracks for Richmond Football Club, that he lives in Melbourne's inner north, and that he studied political science at the University of Melbourne, where he also edited the student newspaper *Farrago*. It would be easy enough to use the overt forms of political and sexual identification contained in the biography as a way of organizing a book like this one. My decision not to stems from the sense that, on the one hand, none of these forms of identification emerge unproblematically from his work, and that, on the other, the terms they imply (gay, immigrant, working-class) are already so obviously central to the matrix of Tsiolkas's public legibility that they demand as much scrutiny as the novels they help us understand. One of the things that has guided my interest in Tsiolkas is the rigor of his critical intelligence, which produces a constantly adversarial relationship to prevailing political and cultural pieties. His work attacks the insularity of nationalism and of the Anglo-Australian middle class, but it also forces us to scrutinize the lazy embrace of transnationalism, cosmopolitanism and liberalized sexuality that loom as easy alternatives. The fact that Tsiolkas's public persona has a lot to do with the degree to which he embodies multiple forms of difference means that difference itself has to be treated not as a given, but as part of the framework that mediates the production and circulation of his work.

Finally, I should admit to a certain ambivalence in my own relationship to Tsiolkas's writing. His work can sometimes feel dependent on the stereotypes it works so hard to displace. His characters and narrators also frequently speak in a demotic idiom that an Australian reader is more likely to recognize than a North American reader. Part of what is at stake here is the way in which particular forms of incivility, woven into fairly ordinary forms of discourse, are recognizable as expressions of a class-based identity (or the collapse of one). But part of it stems from the ethos of rebelliousness that Tsiolkas himself seems to temper as his work develops. As James Ley put it, the writing can be "blunt to the point of brutality," but "when the tension slips the bluntness can seem puerile and sordid." As Ley goes on to say, however, the distinction here is "largely in the eye of the beholder," which is why the writing is often so polarizing.[6] Notions of taste, tact and propriety are at stake, but so are forms of aesthetic education that, as Pierre Bourdieu has argued, reflect deep class divisions. The result is that critics sympathetic to Tsiolkas's work often have to approach it by suspending that kind of "appreciation" that is a staple of literary journalism. No one should be reading Tsiolkas to experience the joys of stylistic refinement or just to be entertained. His topicality consists in the

ways in which his work brings the political and the aesthetic into a proximity
that produces an openness to critical dialogue and reflection. At the same time,
his often terrifically articulate commentaries on contemporary political life in
Australia, particularly on the emergence of a New Right committed to an
anachronistic vision of Anglo-Celtic cultural hegemony, have started to define
the way in which we read novels that are often much more conflicted than these
views suggest. I am skeptical as well about the claims that are now routinely
made around novels like *The Slap* and *Barracuda*: the author as a "vivisector"
with an "unflinching and all-seeing eye," or the novel as a "mirror" held up
to contemporary Australia. These tropes—mirrors, reflections, omnipotent
or endoscopic vision—turn on a fantasy of recognition that seems to have a
narcotic effect on critical consciousness. It is as if the most that a novel can
achieve is to let us see ourselves. Whether this process is about consciousness-
raising or the narcissism of the marketplace is a question that, as I write this
preface, is genuinely undecidable. Tsiolkas's own doubles, as we will see, are a
good deal more complex than this framework suggests.

Introduction

PASOLINI'S ASHES

The autobiographical dimension of Christos Tsiolkas's early fiction is not terribly hard to trace. If we read his first two novels—*Loaded* and *The Jesus Man*—alongside obviously autobiographical works like *Jump Cuts* or his book on *The Devil's Playground*, which charts a very personal experience of Fred Schepisi's film, we can see that the conflicts and tensions that he foregrounds in his vision of his own life are also those of his principal characters. This only becomes clearer when we look at interviews and newspaper articles that focus heavily, if not overwhelmingly, on Tsiolkas's life and family background. However, the term "autobiographical" is misleading in this context. If we understand it as establishing the relationship between a life and a written work, between a lived experience and a work of literature, then we also need to acknowledge that the term opens itself to a certain kind of arbitrariness. How one imagines one's own life, in other words, is conditioned by narrative conventions and conceptual frameworks that organize it in a certain way, that shape it around conflicts, oppositions, hopes and disappointments that are all materially determined. In this context, the notion of *experience* is worth dwelling upon for a moment, if only to highlight its constantly contested and inherently volatile character. Critical theory, for instance, insists that the quality and texture of our experience is one of the things most at stake in our integration into capitalist modernity. Walter Benjamin's famous discussion of shock, to take one leading example, hinges on the distinction between a localized, visceral moment of lived experience (*Erlebnis*) and a more robust order of consciousness bound up with memory, temporality and futurity (*Erfahrung*).[1] For a long line of critical theorists working in the Frankfurt School tradition, this second sense of experience is precisely what capitalist ideology disorganizes. As Miriam Hansen puts it, *Erfahrung* implies something that is "mnemonic, mimetic, and collective"; it thus also offers a kind of emancipatory potential absent in the immediate experience of everyday life.[2] In contrast, what Oskar Negt and Alexander Kluge call the "context of commodity fetishism" constitutes experience in a way that is inherently mystified, erodes its collective possibilities and reorients it to a sequence of "private interests."[3]

As we can gather from these comments, neither side of the *Erlebnis/Erfahrung* opposition escapes social mediation, and in fact mediation (the mediation of cultural forms or physical spaces, for instance) is probably most emphatically and corrosively present at those very moments that seem most spontaneous. Most of us at least intuitively assume a distinction between personal or private experience and the much more abstract and obviously mediated experiences of history and of politics. We all have access to a range of experiences that strike us as immediately our own. By contrast, the experiences of a community, a political collective, a trade union or a nation are shared, and sometimes can only come into being with a good amount of institutional or organizational help. These decidedly social experiences, in other words, strike us as culturally conditioned. They depend on contexts and cultural forms that demand of us that we broaden a sense of ourselves beyond the immediate facticity of the private. And yet those experiences that we might want to consider private—the experience of sexual intimacy, of childbirth and child-rearing or of illness, for instance—are also framed by structures and institutions that intrude into our lives with different degrees of explicitness depending on who and where we are. Critical theory invites us to see the very idea of a distinction between private and public spheres as indicative of broader relations of production.[1] The distinction, it insists, is both tenuous and historically mutable. This is evident in any number of ways. How we imagine our private space is fundamentally anchored in property relations and the variable constitution of the workplace. The law impacts upon our bodies and regulates our capacity for pleasure. Our access to health care informs our ability to manage sickness. How we raise children is subject to the scrutiny of the state. Changes in the media landscape since the end of the Second World War have also had a profound impact on how we encounter the relationship between private and public experience. With the rise of mass media forms like television, video, digitalization and now social networking, these boundaries have been constantly shifting in a way that makes traditional distinctions between the private and the public increasingly difficult to draw. In fact, as Oskar Negt and Alexander Kluge point out, with the proliferation of new media forms "the consciousness and programming industry" is able to circumvent the "intermediate realm of the traditional public sphere (the seasonal public sphere of elections, the formation of public opinion)" and seek "direct access to the private sphere of the individual."[5] In something as innocuous as watching television, private experience is directly informed, if not constructed by, cultural processes and market technologies, sometimes in a manner that disables the possibility of experience in the sense of *Erfahrung*, but sometimes in a manner that facilitates it.

The way in which critical theory worries the category of experience forces us to rethink the apparent immediacy of the autobiographical. It suggests that what we know and understand of ourselves is undergirded by processes and forces that are exterior to us, even as they penetrate our innermost depths. This problem, I want to argue, is one of the crucial preoccupations of Tsiolkas's work. To the extent that his work channels aspects of his own life, it does so with a conceptual rigor that traces the precarious relationship between the private and the public, and between the body and the culture that constructs it. If this sometimes lacks the conceptual clarity of an opposition between lived experience and the reflective, mnemonic quality of historical experience, it is because Tsiolkas's investment in the libidinal also scrambles the values attaching to each of these formulations. The confrontational nature of those early novels, *The Jesus Man* especially, stems from the fact that the body is the crucial site from which Tsiolkas's thinking and writing seem to emerge. In this respect Tsiolkas is immediately at odds with an Enlightenment sense of the political as a rational, disembodied process, organized around an abstract sense of a subject comfortably alienated from the scandal of the flesh as a site of both pleasure and abjection. By the same token, the tension between the idealized, sanitized body of consumer culture and the actuality of embodied experience drives an ambiguously recuperative impulse in which the appearance of the body is itself an affront to the mediated, falsified experience of ideology. At the center of much of Tsiolkas's early work is this tension between the body and the surfaces of a culture that both figure and disfigure it. Hence the anti-aesthetic or anti-cultural impulse that we can detect in *Jump Cuts*, as well as in *Loaded* and *The Jesus Man*—the sense of cultural forms as an intrusion onto or into something that pre-exists them:

> I don't want to deconstruct culture, I want to destroy culture. It is coming between us, a wedge that should illuminate has now turned superficial. In the process we lose tenderness and insight. We have lost our bodies to fashion, our eyes to images, our smell to deodorants, our ears to recordings, our mouths to plastic food, our teeth to rot, our hair to be coloured, our faces lifted, our lungs corroded, our hearts bypassed, veins sacrificed, feelings to be mutilated till we feel no more.[6]

There is, of course, a lurking essentialism in this sort of passage: the idea that we once had bodies unmarked by cultural processes, natural bodies obeying their own proclivities independently of the forms of figuration, disfiguration, prosthesis and repression that we experience with the fall into modernity. This very issue has preoccupied theorists over the last two decades. It is no coincidence that the early part of Tsiolkas's career coincides with the most sophisticated attempts to think through our fraught relationship with the body and its subordination to cultural, political and historical forces.

In the work of theorists like Judith Butler and Elizabeth Grosz, these issues loom large. Both show us, in the words of Pheng Cheah, that "the body, not just consciousness, is a crucial link in the circuit of social production and reproduction, both constituted by and also constituting a given social order."[7] While the emphasis here is away from the sense of the body (and by implication the experience of sexuality) as something natural that exists outside of history, there is also an acknowledgement that simply to see the body as socially mediated, or constructed, concedes too much to processes of social control. This is especially true in feminist and queer theory, where the experience of the body is also a crucial resource in the displacement of patriarchal, heterosexual norms.

Consider, in this light, Tsiolkas's essay on *The Devil's Playground*, which charts in an acutely confessional manner one instance of the relationship between the body and the media that surround it. At the center of Tsiolkas's first reaction to the film, which he saw around about 1978, probably as a twelve-year old, is his identification with Schepisi's central character, a student at a Catholic seminary in country Victoria: "Like Tom, the film's young protagonist, I too was determined to follow a Christian God into good works and self-sacrifice. Also like Tom, I too was clutching at a permanent erection."[8] The film clearly models the tension between culture and the body in a way that reflects, and perhaps clarifies, Tsiolkas's own experiences: "Whether it was God or home or even something called masculinity, I felt close to the innocent Tom, trying to be a good boy but betrayed always by my cock, my fantasies, my daydreams and my wish for freedom. Until I had the means and the capabilities for this freedom, the dark caverns of movie houses became its closest approximation."[9] The cinema acts as a form of incitement, an invitation, an anticipation of an experience of the body somehow in excess of what Tsiolkas feels able to achieve in isolation. It seems to usher an immediate experience of the sexual toward something more emphatic and, potentially at least, politically invested. Tom's "pagan body" anticipated "a future not dominated by authoritarian or ascetic or tyrannical morality."[10] It is abundantly clear at this point that Tsiolkas's early experience of his own sexuality was virtually indistinguishable from his experience of cinema:

> The rendering of flesh on the giant screen is one of the primal attractions of cinema. Instinctively we understand the pleasures of voyeurism and the eroticism of the moving celluloid image. The sensuality is not only about photographing flesh. If I think back to my initial responses to film, to becoming enamoured with film, I remember moments of swooning, truly orgasmic motion.[11]

The relationship between the body and cinema here appears unambiguously positive, if not utopian. Cinema promises a sort of erotic liberation. It both reflects and clarifies Tsiolkas's experience of himself. It is precisely the moment at which the personal finds a form of public validation. Elsewhere in Tsiolkas's work, however, the connotations around forms of visual media are much murkier and much more compromising. As we will see, this is especially true in regard to pornography, which is a recurring trope in Tsiolkas's work. In contrast to the utopian potential of cinema, it points to a thoroughly instrumentalized media space in which the body is at the mercy of consumer culture and the technologies of the market: "It is in the buying, watching and selling of porn that the reality of living in a consumer culture is made clear to me. Capitalism repackages my pleasures."[12] The relationship between pleasure and its mediation is clearly very variable, and depends on the particular media form at stake. What Tsiolkas seems to insist on, however, is that the body is neither simply a natural entity existing outside of culture, nor entirely mediated or constructed by culture. If this approximates a theoretical position, it is probably something similar to Elizabeth Grosz's account of the constitutive incompleteness of our bodies. In her 1994 *Volatile Bodies*, Grosz insists that a capacity for cultural incorporation is central to our constitution: "As an essential internal condition of human bodies, a consequence of perhaps their organic openness to cultural completion, bodies must take the social order as their productive nucleus. Part of their own 'nature' is an organic or ontological 'incompleteness' or lack of finality, an amenability to social completion, social ordering and organization."[13]

In this book I want to argue that the sharp edge of Tsiolkas's political orientation consists partly in his scrutinization of how the amenability of our bodies to "social completion, social ordering and organization" can both facilitate and impede the formation of emancipatory collective experience. In the difference between Schepisi's film and the sort of pornography that Tsiolkas readily identifies with the culture industry, we encounter, at least implicitly, an argument about how different cultural forms and different processes of social completion might involve very different kinds of political potential. Tsiolkas insists that different cultural forms frame experience in qualitatively different ways. Hence his resistance to what he calls "a deliberately anti-elitist yet moronic populism" associated with the notion of film as escapist entertainment. Precisely in their lack of aesthetic and epistemic rigor, such manifestations of the culture industry, Tsiolkas suggests, serve a directly ideological purpose: "To make cultural illiteracy and historical amnesia a goal is ludicrous and, I would suggest, the real elitism."[14] But how would one go about measuring the emancipatory potential of other forms of cultural production? The very phrase "emancipatory potential" is really a kind of shorthand for processes that, in late capitalism, have become very difficult to specify. As Slavoj Žižek put it in a 2011 speech delivered at Liberty Plaza, the epicenter of New York's Occupy Wall Street movement, "it's easy to imagine the end of the world. An asteroid destroying all life and so on. But you cannot imagine the end of capitalism."[15] The statement indicates the difficulties of forming or imagining the sort of collective entities that might be able to displace hegemonic processes and institutions. In the context of Liberty Plaza, it also suggests that an awareness of these difficulties might itself be the first step in the formation of a counter-hegemonic perspective. Awareness of the processes that block or disorganize counter-hegemonic social experience, in other words, is a crucial part of the content of that experience.

Even a cursory glance at Tsiolkas's work suggests that such counter-hegemonic identities are central to his thinking and writing. In his essay on *The Devil's Playground*, he touches on a range of cultural forms and institutional contexts that have impacted his relationship to collective experience. The Australianness of Schepisi's films, he writes, "assisted me in resisting the Yankee colonisation of my imagination." A few years later, however, his undergraduate education at the University of Melbourne alienated him from his "familial and cultural roots."[16] Later in the essay, he glimpses something in American culture that is antithetical to the formation of working-class experience: "the crucial relevance of working-class experience in my coming to an understanding of the world—crucial in the sense that it was never simply academic for me but real, lived, constant and something that won't go away—is not something that Americans seem adequate at understanding."[17] These comments may be insular, but they also clearly register the tensions between cultural mediation and the maintenance of the sort of social experiences that Tsiolkas sees as important to his own life and, no doubt, important to his developing sense of political commitment. This is not to say that immigrant or working-class experiences, on their own, simply produce a progressive politics. We know perfectly well that they do not. Yet because they embody perspectives that are central to contemporary relations of production, but marginal to hegemonic ways of knowing the world, they nevertheless contain the potential, or the promise, of a collective experience capable of displacing dominant ideological forms. This promise or potential might be thought of as the horizon against which Tsiolkas's often bitter explorations of alienation take place. If we imagine *Jump Cuts*, with its experimentally dialogical form and its deliberate referencing of cinematic technique, as an attempt to consolidate a kind of collective experience that galvanizes queer, immigrant and working-class elements, then we might imagine the plights of Tsiolkas's early fictional protagonists (Ari in *Loaded*, Tommy in *The Jesus Man* or Isaac in *Dead Europe*) as embodying a range of emotional and corporeal responses (arousal, anger, hatred, shame) that register their distance from this admittedly hypothetical horizon.

This returns me to my opening claim about the autobiographical dimensions of Tsiolkas's fiction. Those early novels especially seem to register the anguish of the body trapped in a series of cultural processes—processes of "social completion, social ordering and organization," as Grosz puts it—that impede the formation of collective experience or register its impossibility. It is as if Tsiolkas's characters are masks through which he can articulate his own sense of the difficulty of moving from atomized forms of personal experience—mediated by consumer culture, suburbia, the stigmatization of queer sexuality or the alienating effects of middlebrow Anglophone culture—toward some sense of social reconciliation. Tsiolkas's fictional universe is one in which personal and public experiences are mutually sustaining: they form and deform each other. The expressivity of his early writing, with its compulsive gravitation toward the obscene, could be thought of as recording the ensuing feeling of alienation. His representations of the body, of sexuality and of sexual exploitation conditioned by forms of mass media and consumerism are frequently permeated by a sort of gestural violence that at the very least invites us to imagine a compositional process in which authorship is itself defined by the anguish and anxiety it registers. Hence the sense that in reading Tsiolkas's early novels we are encountering a kind of laying bare, a form of self-exposure that is constantly encountering the limits of literary and, more broadly, public discourse. The controversy, and the sense of risk, generated by his work—around questions like pornography, misogyny and anti-Semitism, for instance—stem from this sense of exposure. Tsiolkas creates an unmistakable sense of trying to rend away the veil of convention (to demolish, we could say, a certain kind of literariness) in a way that allows his work to become a human document registering the manifold social matrices that write and rewrite the body.

In this sense what Roberto Esposito says of Pier Paolo Pasolini might, with some qualification, also be applied to Tsiolkas, at least in the early part of his career:

Moving in the opposite direction from the diminishing role of the author (displaced by the automatic function of writing as theorized by late twentieth-century structuralist criticism), rather than disappearing behind the autonomy of his work, Pasolini made his art a sort of living appendix of himself. Not only did he refuse to shield his texts from the emotions, sensations, and excitements that he felt, he literally filled them up with his feelings, sucking his writings into his overflowing, subjective experience.[18]

Pasolini, Esposito goes on to say, tried to "contaminate" literature by implicating it in his own private "maelstrom." He rejected the idea of poetry as an "immunitary body—both protected from and protective of the violent life by which he, instead, was relentlessly interpellated, seduced, and violated."[19] Robert Gordon gets at something very similar when he writes that Pasolini's work is driven by the "almost mythical aspiration to being-in-the-text, to textual transubstantiation [...] It represents a recourse to the essential signifier of an 'authentic' body as a public locus of discourse, in response to the exclusion from discourse and from normative sexual ideologies."[20] It is important that the term "authentic" is framed by scare quotes here. The body implied by Pasolini's work, Gordon suggests, is not some simple, self-sufficient entity that is able to manifest itself in text or image, even though Pasolini's work is often informed by what sometimes seems like a fairly naïve, visceral enthusiasm for pre-industrial cultures and sexualities. With this in mind, "violent life" becomes an intensely ambiguous embodiment of something that is both internal and external to the social order. If it cannot offer the possibility of liberation or return to a pre-social essence, it can still mark an intensification of the process of social incorporation to the point at which that process becomes intolerable. To put this another way, and in terms that clarify my engagement with Tsiolkas, the body formed and deformed, figured and disfigured by discursive practices exterior to it, the body that both completes and mutilates itself through a process of social incorporation, can still *appear* to be an eruption into the space of culture. And presenting this body as a new locus of discourse can still evoke the aura of radicality even as we are forced to acknowledge the ways in which discourse constructs or completes the body. The excitement over the figure of Ari in *Loaded*—and around grunge fiction more generally—probably reflects that semblance of the radical, while Tsiolkas's gradual move away from this mode may well reflect a growing awareness of the paradox it contains.

Of course my coupling of Tsiolkas and Pasolini is not an arbitrary one. For much of his career and in much of his work, Tsiolkas has oriented himself— sometimes implicitly, sometimes explicitly—toward Pasolini, and his writing can often be read as a channeling or a recontextualization of aspects of Pasolini's oeuvre. Our sense of the Pasolini text as an ongoing experiment in volatile forms of queer and subaltern affect that increasingly register Pasolini's own pessimism about the difficulties impeding the formation of counter-hegemonic collective experience offers a context that, I will argue, can illuminate many of the foundational concerns of Tsiolkas's work. The 2005 play *Non Parlo di Salò*, which Tsiolkas co-wrote with Spiro Economopoulos after the Australian re-banning of Pasolini's *Salò, or the 120 Days of Sodom* in 1998, makes the relationship between the two perfectly clear.[21] But it is the early poem "Pasolini's Ashes," a version of which was published in *Jump Cuts* in 1996, that reveals the gravity and insistence of these identifications:

The gauntlet has been thrown,
dare I pick it up,
follow your ghost along the paths of semen?
Easier to betray you.
Now that our bodies have succumbed,
now that your spirit
is extinguished, I am no longer human.
Gorging shit from polystyrene boxes,
hitting up on video sex,
consumption has made a junkie out of me.
There is no longer a proletariat, Pier Paolo,
not one that you would recognise.
Your legacy is a cruel dare, easy to denounce
now that Marxism has been shattered.

Air, fire, water, earth, I roam this planet searching
for the authentic me and find instead
Narcissus gazing in and out of my reflection:
The violence of labour marks my body
(I am not an actor);
The violence of displacement traps inside my skull
(I can't articulate);
The violence of benevolence
wraps tight around my heart
(I cannot feel)

There is no escape, no eluding history.
But if I turn away, who should I follow?
Should I pay for my pleasures
in the sanctioned confines of leather rooms
and red-velveted sex clubs?
For me, Pier Paolo,
there is no Franco Citti,
no handsome Nino. They too now pay
top dollars to enter the club, for in there,
there is no danger.

It is easy to denounce you,
but I prefer the treacherous paths you have revealed.
If this means a life surrounded
by a chorus of derision and contempt,

I will be it. It is preferable. For I was born
peasant,
the last child of the proletariat.
This is madness, this is insanity, I know,
but I refuse to die bourgeois.[22]

The text has a callowness about it, or the appearance of a callowness, that partly reflects the ways in which our own moment has made the idealism of its proletarian identifications seem naïve. That said, anyone familiar with literary publishing in Australia today will no doubt be stunned that a text like this was supported by a major publisher. Part confession, part polemic, it is a compelling index of the ways in which Tsiolkas's work grasps the processes of history and politics as seemingly interior experiences turned outward to the public as a form of exposure. At the same time it grasps the mediated character of subjectivity. Part of the anguish of the poem stems from the insistence with which the speaker finds his desire appropriated by or solicited through the compromising logics of the culture industry. The body has succumbed to consumerism. It is mired in the shit of capitalism. It is no longer human. The search for authenticity has become a bewildered journey through a hall of mirrors. With history over and the proletariat vanquished, the speaker is left to clutch at a potentially quixotic gesture of refusal: "I refuse to die bourgeois." In this context the legacy and memory of Pasolini are a challenge, a "cruel dare" in which the symbiosis of sex and politics promises at least the semblance—the ghost—of an alternative. At the moment that a proletarian politics has become impossible, an experience of sexuality apparently unconditioned by consumerist norms might at least mark the possibility of a utopian alternative to the present. Following Pasolini's ghost along the "paths of semen" presumably offers the promise of existing at a remove from the degrading and addictive realm of consumerism, although Pasolini himself would lose faith with the idea of Eros as a defense against the homogenizing forces of consumer capitalism. Elsewhere in *Jump Cuts*, as we have seen, the objectification of desire in pornography is one of the most obvious ways in which capitalism intrudes into the space of the subject and compromises its integrity. Later in the text the same idea extends to prostitution.[23] Both are prominent topoi in the poem. But if the problem posed by "Pasolini's Ashes" is the capture and mediation of desire, in what sense can Pasolini, himself a public image as much as a persistent intellectual presence, offer a viable alternative? When the speaker describes himself searching for authenticity and finding instead "Narcissus gazing in and out of my reflection," are we supposed to understand the relationship between Pasolini and the speaker as compromisingly specular?

That Tsiolkas is called by the figure of Pasolini suggests the impossibility of identifying with a contemporary context defined by the triumphs of capitalism, the absence of a genuinely working-class culture in its midst, and the commodification of sexual dissidence. All these themes loom large in the diatribes collected in *Scritti corsari*, Pasolini's last collection of essays. Indeed the final stanza of Pasolini's career is one of unrelenting pessimism. If there is a discernible arc to his career, it resides in the realization that the subaltern body of the Friulian peasant—"a-temporal and a-rational," as Wallace Sillanpoa puts it[24]—and of Rome's dispossessed sub-proletariat had, by the early 1970s, been incorporated into the latently fascist circuits of consumer capitalism. At this point, Pasolini believed that the homogenizing effects of capitalism had become so total that they had left almost nothing of the West untouched. As Esposito explains, Pasolini grasped the ways in which "neocapitalist power" had passed from a logic of exclusion to a logic of inclusion: "Far from opposing the desire of the 'masses' for enjoyment—of any kind—the new biopolitical regime coopts it, stimulating this desire, or even prescribing it as a sort of new categorical imperative."[25] The vitalistic possibility of bodies, cultures and intimacies existing outside the sphere of social mediation, in other words, had all but ceased. This is clear in Pasolini's 1975 "Repudiation of the Trilogy of Life." He had made the trilogy of films—*The Decameron*, *The Canterbury Tales* and *The Arabian Nights*—between 1971 and 1974, believing that "the 'innocent' bodies, with the archaic, dark, vital violence of their sexual organs, seemed to be the last bulwark of reality."[26] Now, as he was working on *Salò*, he believed that the "progressive struggle for the democratization of self-expression and for sexual liberation has been brutally surpassed and thwarted by the decision of the consumerist establishment to concede a vast (but false) tolerance."[27] His corresponding repudiation of the body was related to his sense that the youth of the Roman sub-proletariat had become thoroughly, and compulsorily, assimilated into the heterosexual hedonism of consumer society, and that "the masses have ceased to exist anthropologically."[28] Being summoned by Pasolini, being dared to follow his ghost, Tsiolkas cannot avoid a confrontation with this moment that calls into question the political quality of corporeal experience. The cruelty of the summons partly depends on the futility of the undertaking, on the sense that Pasolini's career already embodies an impasse, and the realization that, as he writes in the "Repudiation," "Life is a pile of insignificant and ironic ruins."[29]

In this respect it is telling that the title of Tsiolkas's text harkens back not to the end of Pasolini's career, but to one of its key moments of political awakening. Pasolini's poem "Le ceneri di Gramsci" ("Gramsci's Ashes") was composed in 1954 and published in a collection with the same title three years later. As Maurizio Viano writes, it "signals the end of the hermetic self-absorption that had characterized Pasolini's previous poetry. Here his confrontation with history starts—a confrontation between the private and the public, which will valorize the personal as political, deviancy as a pre-rational, pre-ideological way of antagonism."[30] This comment gets at the tension driving the poem. Pasolini's elegiac encounter with Gramsci also highlights an ambiguous kind of distance in which the body, its pleasures and its drives pull against the imperatives of political rationality and critique. The moment of political awakening, in other words, also affirms a corporeality in excess of what Gramsci seems to represent. Pasolini writes of the "scandal of contradicting myself, of being/with you and against you; with you in my heart,/in light, but against you in the dark viscera."[31] Even though the poem concludes with an anticipation of the pessimism that would later engulf Pasolini, it is still evocative of a moment prior to his late-career repudiation of the body and of the body of the people.

Tsiolkas's return to Pasolini might well model the pessimism of the "Repudiation," but its most noticeable point of reference is a text that holds out the possibility of an embodied, subaltern experience that is still capable of resisting consumer capitalism. The effect of Tsiolkas's poem, like that of much of his work, emerges through this paradox: we know that the body cannot offer any simple, unmediated alternative to the forces that figure and disfigure it, and yet the "dark viscera" of Pasolini's text continues to evoke the possibility of a pleasure that will never manage to disassociate itself from the alienation of capitalism. To follow Pasolini to the end is to encounter the collapse of an idealism centered on the body as a locus of both sexual and political freedom; if "Pasolini's Ashes" marks a beginning for Tsiolkas, then it is a beginning that already contains this end.

The idea of being summoned, or interpellated, by a ghost activates one the West's most powerful and foundational narratives of commitment. It is a narrative in which the call of the dead promises to actualize possibilities that are not empirically present in the here and now. It is also a narrative in which that call is morally and politically irresistible precisely because it is otherworldly. It seizes the subject with the promise of an eventfulness that is imminent to a situation that seems to exclude it. For Jacques Derrida, this idea of the ghost is central to a renewed sense of the political: a responsibility "beyond all living present," one that "disjoins" the present. "Without this *non-contemporaneity with itself of the living present*," he writes, "without that which secretly unhinges it, without this responsibility and this respect for justice concerning those who *are not there*, of those who are no longer or who are not yet *present and living*, what sense would there be to ask the question 'where?' 'where tomorrow?' 'whither?'"[32] That Pasolini's ghost stands at or near the beginning of Tsiolkas's career marks the moment that Derrida touches upon; the moment at which the present is not enough, the moment at which it figures something beyond itself in order to motivate a kind of speech that is out of joint with it. And while the content of this summons is a paradoxical combination of hope and despair, its orientation to Pasolini also points to the possibility of the left-wing or queer artist as an adversarial celebrity: a public intellectual. In this sense it is not unreasonable to see Tsiolkas's vision of Pasolini as a media image that begins to organize alternatives to the culture of the living present, and to anticipate some of the ways in which Tsiolkas himself will become incorporated into the circuits of the culture industry.

The ambiguous confluence of sexuality and politics that we find in Pasolini's work establishes a background against which many of Tsiolkas's texts take on a broader topicality than their immediate, often Australian, context of reception might indicate. Of particular interest here is the power that *Salò* has in Tsiolkas's oeuvre. In the context of Pasolini's "Repudiation," *Salò* looms as a final, apocalyptic statement about sexuality as a form of sovereign violence. The arc that links *Loaded*, *The Jesus Man* and *Dead Europe* (texts that Tsiolkas himself has referred to several times as a trilogy) is in many ways informed by the compromising proximity of sexuality and politics that we find in *Salò*. In a way all three novels explore the impossibility of extricating the libidinal from its integration into the forms of life defined by the atomized, hedonistic subjectivity of consumer capitalism. That Tsiolkas sees his own voice as implicated in this problem is clear from another moment in *Jump Cuts* that seems to anticipate a possible terminus to the "paths of semen" that Tsiolkas proposes to follow in "Pasolini's Ashes." The passage in question recounts a moment of early adolescent sexual awakening centered on the contact between Tsiolkas (eleven or twelve at the time) and his uncle on a hot summer's day on the Mornington Peninsula, but it quickly conjures a metaphorical space, a secluded room, to evoke and contain the fantasies of sexual abandon that are subsequently aroused. It was while looking at his uncle's penis as he rubbed oil into his chest, Tsiolkas tells us, that he entered this room for the first time. At this point he can "no longer vouch for the safety of truth."[33] The room is the space of fantasy, first and foremost, but it is also a space in which abjection becomes the expression of a sort of political rage that quickly becomes a will to power, a form of sovereign violence in which the body of the other is a pure, political element in the theater of authoritarianism. The sense of "laying bare" at work here makes it hard to read this passage as ironic or self-mocking.

> I have no secrets. I will not lie. I have brought pubescent children and animals to this room [...] We have raped, we have tortured, we have humiliated the angels and the demons in this room. I keep slaves in this room, and yes, I have made the black man slave again in here. The

fascist is a slave here too. This room is called Hell. Everyone, anyone who has lived, who has died, who has been imagined, has submitted to my will in this room. Uncle Kosta was the first man who made a hole into this room, and since then I have turned all humanity into a massive fuck.[34]

The space of private fantasy is also a prison cell, a torture chamber. The expression of sexual desire as absolutist violence reminds us of *Salò*'s grafting of Italian fascism onto the horrors of Sade's Château de Silling. It is the extreme articulation of what will drive much of Tsiolkas's early work: in the absence of community, in the absence of an ameliorative political idiom, in the absence, as the passage from *Jump Cuts* concludes, of love, sexuality itself becomes dangerously coupled with forms of violence that anticipate a Sadean vision of annihilation. What emerges here is not simply the laying bare of latently sadistic impulses: it is the deployment of sexuality and a sexualized subject to evoke the processes of sovereignty inherent in late capitalism. One might also interrogate the conception of fantasy at work in the passage. If, as Negt and Kluge argue, fantasy embodies an "unconscious practical critique of alienation," it also, at least here, seems to reproduce the very worst of the social forces that might call it into being in the first place.[35] We might consider fantasy a communal medium, but Tsiolkas takes us to something that has been emptied of all utopian content, a sadism in which fantasy seems compulsively egocentric and ultimately far worse than our alienated reality. The libidinal component here, we will see, is supposed to be continuous with the violence of capitalism. One of the problems that Tsiolkas encounters in *Loaded, The Jesus Man* and *Dead Europe* is that fantasy is always compromised by the material reality it seeks to escape.

The seemingly abrupt shift from *Dead Europe*, which is implicated in the space of this compromised fantasy structure, to the more controlled, observational voice of *The Slap* indicates an acknowledgement of this problem. What we glimpse here is Tsiolkas stepping back from the moment at which the coupling of politics and obscenity threatens to overwhelm his writing with the perverse logic of a subject structured by the violent excesses of pornographic fantasy. Instead, in *The Slap* we have a range of characters, each with his or her own capacity for fantasy, rather than a text dominated, if not consumed by, the fantasy of its central character. The point at which Pasolini's "dark viscera" meets its end in the compulsive hedonism of permissive consumerism has receded. So too has the sense in which Tsiolkas's fiction has an adversarial relationship to its broader habitus. In fact, with the publication of *The Slap* and then *Barracuda*, Tsiolkas became a best-selling author whose work cannot easily be separated from the other media forms that underpin and inform it.

Whatever sense of radicality we might want to attribute to Tsiolkas has to be understood in relationship to the forms of public circulation and commercial recognition that increasingly define the career of a figure whose work often seems to anticipate its movement from print to screen.

Tsiolkas, of course, remains first and foremost a novelist, despite the range of media with which he is involved. In a recent *Meanjin* interview he is very clear about that and talks about the importance of secluding himself "from the white noise, the din of public scrutiny."[36] Still, it would be naïve to think that the circulation of his work is untouched by its migration into other media forms or his prominence as an object of media attention. It would also be naïve to think that the way in which he now writes fiction is not in some way influenced by these other media forms. Part of the success of *The Slap*, I will argue, hinged on the fact that it mimics a mass media orientation to the "incident" or the "event" that grounds its topicality. The novel's ability to structure a debate around the empty signifier (the slap) is exactly what made it so amenable to the reading group format. *Barracuda*, with its explicit orientation to the mass sporting spectacle (specifically the Sydney Olympics) and its organization around a vision of mediatization, also has to be understood in relationship to non-literary forms of cultural production. Both novels owe something to the forms of tabloid culture they seek to displace. As print culture and especially literary fiction continues to lose traction in an increasingly diverse media environment, it is clear that relationships and synergies between different media and different forms of discourse within specific media fields are of considerable commercial value. More than any other contemporary Australian writer, Tsiolkas's public profile and his commercial prospects are tied to this broader cultural landscape. While it is important to assess his writing independently of these relationships, the politics of his work also has to be linked to questions of reception, readership and audience in which a diversified media landscape plays a vital role. This is all the more important when one considers the centrality of film, television, commercial music and photography to the novels themselves. If Tsiolkas's sense of the writer as a heretical figure compelled to "speak the unspeakable, the unpopular, the uncompromising, the dangerous and the seditious"[37] rests on the assumption of literature's distance from other forms of cultural and economic production (and the regimes of value they assume), the fact that his most recent novels are fairly seamlessly integrated into a broader media landscape forces us to rethink the relationship between the political and the postulation of aesthetic autonomy.

Let me be clear: I am not raising these issues in order to frame an argument about capitulating to the culture industry, although I do think articulating what is lost once literature obviates its resistance to other media is worthwhile. By stressing the interconnectedness of different media, however, we are probably much better placed to argue for literature's political efficacy. How, after all, is a politics possible without a public? How do mass media forms shape that public and force us to rethink what we might mean by the term politics? These issues are raised with a bracing kind of clarity in John Hartley's discussion of what he calls a "postmodern public sphere." Quickly displacing the myth of the classical public sphere linked to print culture and enlightened opinion formation, Hartley instead stresses the role of popular media in the shaping of identities, attitudes and affects; in "producing and distributing knowledge, visualizing and teaching public issues in the midst of private consumption, writing the truth of our time on the bodies of those image-saturated 'telebrities' whose cultural function is to embody, circulate, dramatize and teach certain public virtues within a suburban cultural context."[38]

It would be misleading to describe Tsiolkas as a "telebrity" in the sense that Hartley intends, yet the ways in which public meanings are linked to his work and his life might also constitute an interesting case study of the postmodern public sphere. A great deal has already been written about Tsiolkas (and more is being written all the time). A lot of it is entertainment journalism that integrates biographical anecdote, often with a vaguely confessional aspect, into accounts of how Tsiolkas himself circulates as a media image or entity; so literary awards, sales figures and television adaptations are the obvious cues. This is not how anyone wants to imagine his or her political efficacy playing out, but the fact remains that Tsiolkas's prominence in the realm of entertainment journalism has been extremely important in the circulation of a value set linked to difference, multiculturalism and a sort of critical introspection that cuts against the grain of national pride and complacency. To date, a lot of the academic criticism on Tsiolkas has tended to reflect what the mass media has already accomplished (although the criticism written about *Dead Europe* is notable for its ability to draw the discourse of theory into the field of Australian literary studies, sometimes in interesting, but sometimes in very formulaic ways). In pointing out that Tsiolkas's work marks the appearance of the multicultural and the queer in the field of literary representation, there is a sort of belatedness that stems in part from the fact that other media can circulate these forms of difference and identity much more rapidly and much more broadly than academic criticism.

There is a strong sense, I think, in which Tsiolkas's relationship to other forms of media (a relationship I am glossing with the term "celebrity") draws on the presence of obscenity in his work and reinforces our sense of him as a political writer. At the same time, though, this circuit might work as a form of containment, a way of recoding the critical edge of novels that are often squarely directed against neoliberalism, late capitalism, globalization and their relationship to a postmodern public sphere. For me, and I suspect for many others, what makes Tsiolkas's work so compelling is the feeling that it is always on the verge of displacing the very forms of experience that it establishes. There is something inherently volatile about the writing. Every time Tsiolkas's work seems to settle into an affective, gestural or political groove, it also threatens to explode the very space it has carved out for itself. This might be its most enduring quality, and its clearest comment on its social and political situation.

The chapters that follow orient principally to Tsiolkas's five novels, yet in them I have tried to capture the range and diversity of Tsiolkas's productivity, especially his work as an essayist and playwright. I have found it difficult, however, to segregate the novels from each other, and as a result my chapters, with the exception of the first, are organized around the point at which one novel overlaps or intersects with the novel that follows it chronologically. The first chapter discusses *Loaded* as an anti-*Bildungsroman* that deploys what Lee Edelman calls the negativity of queerness to distance itself from neoliberal narratives of social integration. But Tsiolkas is not simply or unproblematically invested in this notion of negativity. In fact as the novel unfolds, we see that it also symptomatizes the condition of political atomization at the heart of late capitalism. The paradox here is that the evocation of a libidinal element outside the circuits of capital and biopower also supplies the basis of one's integration into those circuits. I read this paradox against the pessimism of the late Pasolini and argue that it anticipates the more apocalyptic versions of libidinal negativity that Tsiolkas will explore in some of his subsequent novels. The second chapter refocuses on *Loaded* in order to introduce Tsiolkas's orientation to non-literary forms of media, here popular music experienced through the Walkman. The novel's interest in mediated forms of experience offers a counterpoint to the more frightening and extreme vision of media experience set out in *The Jesus Man*, which, I argue, develops Tsiolkas's critique of neoliberal alienation by insisting on the ways in which sexual desire is inseparable from forms of mass consumerism and social incorporation. The pornographic orientation of Tsiolkas's second novel does not offer an alternative to an alienating social order, but an intensification of its logic. If part of the appeal of *Loaded* is its embrace of what McKenzie Wark calls a media aesthetic, *The Jesus Man* explores this aesthetic as a fundamental expression of late capitalism and of the body's submission to market technologies. Tabloid television and pornographic video constitute the vector in which this relationship becomes apparent. Like *The Jesus Man, Dead Europe* is a text that develops a pornographic sensibility. Chapter 3 explores the ways in which Tsiolkas's third novel reframes the pornographic as one of the defining logics of globalization. I situate the novel's interest in the obscene in relationship to some recent discussions of cosmopolitanism, and argue that its focus on the underground sex industry in post-communist Prague crystallizes its position on what James Clifford calls "discrepant cosmopolitanism." By placing *Dead Europe* alongside *Non Parlo di Salò*, I also refer it to Tsiolkas's ongoing engagement with Pasolini's exploration of the relationship between sexuality, sovereignty and capitalism.

These first three chapters really constitute a sequential movement through the early part of Tsiolkas's career, which I see as embodying a fairly coherent exploration of the relationship between sexual transgression and capitalist incorporation. Chapter 4, however, articulates what I see as a marked shift in Tsiolkas's trajectory. With the publication of *The Slap*, a lot changed for Tsiolkas. He was suddenly commercially successful and internationally visible, and much more obviously integrated into a broader media landscape linked to notions of intellectual celebrity. My discussion of *The Slap* returns to *Dead Europe* in order to think about the formal and political shifts in Tsiolkas's work, and to begin to ask what is at stake when literary texts distance themselves from the claims to aesthetic autonomy that have historically defined their normative component. But I also argue that the relationship between *Dead Europe* and *The Slap* reveals the clarity with which Tsiolkas engages with what Pascale Casanova has called "world literary space." *The Slap*'s success, I suggest, hinges on its refusal of conventional, Eurocentric visions of the metropolitan as a locus of symbolic capital, and its corresponding evocation of a decentered world in which the suburbs reappear freed from the stigma that had hitherto defined their place in the Australian imaginary. The novel's multiculturalism is, of course, central to this process, but it also enters into an uneasy relationship with the much more strategic way in which the novel clears a space for its own reception, one that depends on allegorical evocations of ethnicity that enable it to enact its own eventfulness. If *The Slap* orients to the multicultural suburb as the actuality of contemporary Australia, it is also haunted by the suspicion that suburbia is still the same mundane, aspirational space it has always been. The success of the novel as a positive reevaluation of everyday Australian experience depends on the ways in which it displaces these reservations and foregrounds instead the anachronisms of an Anglo-Celtic sensibility that looks decidedly out of step with the present. Its strategic negotiation of world literary space, in other words, also compels it to modulate the force of its critical relationship to the world it depicts.

The final chapter brings to light what has always been implicit in Tsiolkas's work: its orientation to media aesthetics and media experience. With the publication of *Barracuda*, I argue, there can be no doubt about the ways in which Tsiolkas's work has integrated itself into the media landscape. Like *The Slap*, *Barracuda* is critical of popular media forms, but it is also emphatically oriented to them. In fact it is very difficult to discuss either novel independently of the commercial media spectacles to which they refer. This orientation to other media forms indicates a new sense of realism in Tsiolkas's most recent work. It also correlates political efficacy with commercial success. Precisely by attenuating the autonomy of the literary, Tsiolkas has also been able to expand his readership and maximize his reach as a social and political commentator. His position today as a literary celebrity capable of talking authoritatively about a wide range of issues originates in the increasingly middlebrow quality of his work. This is not a criticism. In fact the middlebrow itself is a chronically under-theorized category. As Brigid Rooney has shown us in her discussion of Tim Winton, it involves a complex negotiation of residual conceptions of aesthetic autonomy and emergent notions of popular accessibility.[39] This negotiation reflects a heightened sense of political urgency in the face of the New Right, the war on terror, and the debates about border security and national identity that have defined public discourse in Australia over the last decade. But the idea of the middlebrow does also raise questions about how we imagine the relationship between the aesthetic and the political, and about the degree to which we should be instrumentalizing literature in the interests of politics. *Barracuda* is also very clearly a *Bildungsroman*, a form that Tsiolkas seemed to reject at the outset of his career. That the phrasing of a mature, communally oriented experience, in opposition to the experience of alienation, depends on this conventional nineteenth-century form suggests the crucial role that a residual conception of the literary might play as a consciousness-raising medium in competition with other, more corrosive media productions.

Today, the ways in which Tsiolkas's vision and his work have been integrated into the political and commercial structures of the Australian public sphere are fairly clear. This is not the terminus of "Pasolini's Ashes." In a way Tsiolkas's development seems to constitute its own kind of *Bildungsroman*, a narrative of maturation and integration that involves both renunciation and reconciliation. That the career of Australia's most controversial contemporary novelist is increasingly accompanied by this framework no doubt says something fairly decisive about Australian literary culture, but that might also be beside the point. In a conclusion to this book I reflect on the promise and the perils of embracing the forms of integration that Tsiolkas, at other moments in his career, has been so eager to refuse in the interests of a heretical, illiberal tolerance that, in our current moment, seems increasingly difficult to sustain.

Chapter 1

THE DOWN-CURVE OF CAPITAL: *LOADED*

The morning is ending and I've just opened my eyes. I stare across the cluttered room I'm in. I yawn. I scratch at my groin. I feel my cock and start a slow masturbation. When I'm finished, and it doesn't take long, I get up with a leap, wrap a towel around my naked body and make a slow journey downstairs.

I hear noises from throughout the house. A robotic voice is squealing over a bass-beat on the CD. The very narrow stairs stretch down before me. I walk past cobwebs, stains on the carpet, a biro on one step, a cigarette butt on another. In the lounge I grab a packet of cigarettes and light one. On the mantelpiece I notice an old family photo. I've forgotten this photo. My brother in a red shirt and black shorts has one arm around the old man and another around my mum. She looks like Elizabeth Taylor, or at least is trying to, and Dad is wearing a grey suit with a narrow black tie. He's trying to look like Mastroianni, or like Delon. The tie belongs to me now. I'm in the picture too. Sitting cross-legged on the grass, in a blue shirt, aiming a plastic gun at the camera. The colours in the photo are rich, bright. Colour photos don't do that any more. Technology makes things look too real. I turn away from the photograph and look at last night's mess strewn across the lounge room. It's not my place.[1]

The opening of *Loaded*—the beginning, in fact, of Tsiolkas's career—has a certain artlessness about it that might also be described as immediacy: first-person voice, present tense, a consciousness that roves over the banal, empirical detail of what is simply at hand. There is little ability or willingness to determine which of these details has weight and which does not. If this produces a sort of reality-effect, it also runs the risk of reproducing for the reader the tedium of everyday objects and observations. In fact, before two pages have elapsed, Ari, the novel's narrator, declares that he is "already bored" (3). The feeling we get from these opening pages is that the proliferation of everyday detail is crowding out the conventions of narrative, if not the possibility of narrative itself. The "once upon a time" of storytelling, the moment at which plot is inaugurated, cannot quite release itself from a world that verges on the inexpressive and the formless. Ari's experience is, at least initially, at the mercy of the world that surrounds him, and it is not clear that this can provide the catalyst for a legible narrative.

Of course there is an element of scene-setting here: cobwebs, stains, a cigarette butt. And the family photograph that grabs Ari's attention no doubt foreshadows the novel's interest in the friction between the structures of heterosexual reproductivity and a dislocated, deterritorialized, emphatically queer consciousness that becomes more evident the further we read. But to try to explain the novel's opening in this way is to miss the significance of its meandering, disoriented tone. *Loaded* is, after all, a novel that spends an enormous amount of its time trapped in and overwhelmed by the details of the everyday. It is also a novel that explores the reactive forms of affect—boredom, anger, hatred, arousal, ecstasy—that accompany this sense of entrapment. If there is a central tension in *Loaded*, it does not really involve the obvious oppositions that are often used by critics to contextualize Tsiolkas's work: Greek-Australian/Anglo-Australian, queer/straight, or working-class/bourgeois. All of these oppositions play important roles in the novel, of course, and they are absolutely central to the way in which it entered public discourse. But they are secondary to a much more fundamental opposition between the formlessness of the everyday and the possibility of a conceptual rubric that might allow Ari—or the reader, for that matter—to fashion a viable narrative out of the rubble of his fragmented, quotidian experience.

On the face of it, this might be thought of as a formal problem. The immediacy of what has been called "grunge fiction," which is often bound up with its autobiographical ambience, requires a departure from what now appears to be the artifice of structure and craft. But even by the standards of other grunge texts, *Loaded*'s opening feels denuded. Unlike some of the works with which *Loaded* was initially compared—Andrew McGahan's *Praise* and Justine Ettler's *The River Ophelia*, for instance—there is not a central sexual relationship that can guide the narrative. And unlike the short stories in Edward Berridge's *The Lives of the Saints*, there is not the structural economy of the anti-epiphany to impose formal unity. Instead *Loaded* seems to subtract the conventions of narrative coherence in order to confront us with the very thing that narrative tries to obviate: the formlessness of the material world, the stuff, the detritus of the everyday that threatens meaning, or our ability to make meaning. The novel is ostensibly set over the course of a single day, but this does not enable it to coordinate complex relationships between characters or to impose much of a narrative structure. In fact *Loaded*'s increasingly frequent introspective and retrospective digressions render this temporal framework largely irrelevant. There is almost no sense in which the episodes Tsiolkas recounts need to be read sequentially. That a day breaks down into interchangeable fragments of time, or moments of affect, is itself indicative of the novel's attempt to step outside of conventional narrative logics.

Nevertheless, the world Ari inhabits is, at least implicitly, organized around narratives: narratives that attach to work, marriage, reproduction, upward mobility, suburban normality and aspirational consumerism. Every time someone asks Ari whether he has a job, we get a glimpse of this world of tediously insistent narratives that threaten to subsume him. Ari's friend Joe, for instance, "has it all worked out": "He's got a job, got a girlfriend, got a car. Soon he wants to get married" (10). The story set out here—and the novel is very clear that it is a story, a work of fiction—is utterly alien to Ari. He encounters it from the outside, as a piece of the material world, not as a framework that he can use to process and order that world. It is as if the stories that enable characters to achieve their social integration have no more validity than the products they consume and the waste they leave behind. In fact the novel's insistence on apparently unfiltered observation correlates to Ari's aggressive refusal of the narratives with which he is confronted. This relationship comes into such sharp focus because Tsiolkas has also refused the sort of conventional structures that we usually associate with fiction: plot, character development, conflict and resolution. Ari's first-person voice presents the issue of narrative integration not as one simply bound up with the novel's formal organization, but as one embedded in his experience of his world—a world in which the narratives we have at our disposal are also tethered to the material or ideological reproduction of society. The problem of making meaning or producing coherence through narrative is thus a central part of the novel's content, and an important indication of its engagement with its historical context. It also marks the vexed relationship between the specificity of Tsiolkas's own background and what *Loaded* posits as the false universality of an aspirational, middle-class worldview—the worldview that was in fact fundamental to the development of narrative fiction in the late eighteenth century and then throughout the nineteenth century.

In this respect *Loaded* clearly presents itself as a sort of anti-*Bildungsroman*, in which conventional narratives of social integration and maturation are visible precisely because of the clarity with which Ari refuses them. This refusal can, in part at least, be explained by Tsiolkas's sense that he was formed by experiences that are largely antithetical to the processes of normalization associated with the *Bildungsroman* form. In a terrific conceptual history of the concept of *Bildung*, Pheng Cheah shows us how this notion of cultural education has historically implied the development of "natural dispositions or capacities" toward a reconciliation with a collective social or political body.

It has thus functioned as a mode of maturation that forms the basis of a "collective existence," and this also gives it a regulative function.[2] The term designates the "inner-directed formation of an individual in the image of a personality prescribed by moral norms."[3] This also means that, as Cheah's discussions of Fichte and Hegel demonstrate, it enables the possibility of ethical action in a world that is exterior to the individual: civil society, the nation, an "existing articulated whole."

> *Bildung* teaches the youth to renounce his revolutionary enthusiasm and submit to the existing world by recognizing its actual rationality, its existence as the substrate of his rational activity and not its obstacle [...] *Bildung* in this optimal sense is the individual's immersion and participation in objective spirit, that is, the shared customs and values, the ethical substance that enables meaningful reciprocal action in a collective setting.[4]

It is for this reason, of course, that the form of the *Bildungsroman* was imagined as so central to literature's world-building capacity, but it is also unsurprising that the genre would become problematic in circumstances where difference disrupts or fragments the assumption of a consensually mediated "collective setting."

It is thus no surprise that both modernist and postcolonial fiction often registers a refusal of stable national and social identifications in what Jed Esty calls an "antidevelopmental temporality" that suspends or interrupts narratives of maturation.[5] If, as Esty argues, the ultimate horizon of the *Bildungsroman* is a nationalism "based on an ideal of organic culture whose temporality and harmony could be reflected in the developing personality," then it also follows that the experience of "colonial modernity" would disrupt "cherished continuities between a people and its language, territory, and polity."[6] In a specifically Australian context, the melding of immigrant, working-class and queer experience in a novel like *Loaded* effects a similar kind of disruption: national allegories that orient to the transition from adolescence to adulthood are disabled by experiences that resist social integration into what now reveals itself to be a false collectivity.

Tsiolkas, we know, is very precise when he talks about his political and cultural formation and the ways in which it alienated him from a putatively dominant Australian reality. Both of his parents were Greek immigrants to Australia and both were factory workers for much of their lives. Tsiolkas describes them as "peasants" partly in order to indicate their marginality to educational structures in the strife-torn Greece that they had left behind. In Australia they were both "trade-union people." This immigrant, working-class background was crucial to Tsiolkas's developing worldview, but it also meant that he experienced his own passage through higher education as entailing at least a degree of estrangement, both from his family and the society he was now approaching:

> I think going to university, and coming from a working-class background, made me very conscious of entering a really bourgeois world; I was suddenly wrenched out of my particular class and found myself entering another class—this was a seismic experience. I became *déclassé*—an experience both empowering because it opened up opportunities for me, and also alienating as it separated me from the class I was born into.[7]

Whatever the reality of Tsiolkas's own process of social integration, this sense of being "*déclassé*," of being marginal to prevailing narratives of identity, plays an enormous role in *Loaded*, in which Ari is continually confronted with forms of life that demand a surrender, or a declaration of identification that he is constitutively unable to give. But being Greek, gay or working-class does not provide the basis of an alternative identity either, though Ari's background does enable him to recognize aspirational bourgeois experience as a form of alienation. At the moment of the novel's publication in 1995, these concerns would have been especially topical. In the state of Victoria, Jeff Kennett's Liberal Party had been in power since 1992. As state premier, Kennett had delivered Melbourne in particular over to a narrative of cultural and economic renewal linked to privatization, the ongoing disorganization of the labor movement, gambling and public projects that combined monumentalism and featurist kitsch. Ari's non-involvement in narratives of social integration and mobility has to be understood against this broader context in which Kennett's brand of neoliberalism was materially transforming the character of lived experience with sometimes startling speed and visibility.

But it is not just that Ari refuses a dominant mode of narrative linked to residual notions of *Bildung*. He refuses narrative itself and any sense of character development that evolves through time. Without the possibility of a counter-narrative, what is one left with? How does critique manifest itself? In *Loaded*, critique appears to be inseparable from forms of affect—anger, boredom and arousal—that register Ari's relationship to the fragmented materiality of the everyday. In fact we might even say that in *Loaded* critique is a form of affect; a gestural, highly emotive idiom that reverberates through Ari's voice. This might seem like a stretch: critique and affect are usually seen as very different registers. But their proximity, if not their simultaneity, in Tsiolkas's novel is, I want to suggest, an important index of how *Loaded* encounters its political situation. The fact that Ari's friend Joe has his "world worked out," means, of course, that he understands almost nothing about the social constitution of his own experience. Ari can clarify this, but not for Joe exactly. His mode of critique enters the text as part of an enclosed, reactive interiority:

> We all have to sell ourselves. But you don't have to get married, you don't have to sell all of yourself. There is a small part of myself, deep inside of me, which I let no one touch. If I let it out, let someone have a look at it, brush their hands across that part of my soul, then they would want to have it, buy it, steal it, own it. Joe's put that part of himself up for the market and he would be the first to say it's because he can't put up with the demands. Parents, friends, bosses, girlfriends, girlfriends' parents, cousins, aunts, uncles, even the fucking neighbours. They all want to sell, buy, invest in the future. (10–11)

The negativity of this critical mode is not, for the most part, a way of communicating with other characters in the novel. It is a monologue, a rant, a particular form of commentary that derives its efficacy precisely from the ways in which it holds itself back from full-blown, public enunciation. If we can call this critique, there is also something petulant about the passage that forces us to qualify the term. It is clear in its refusal of an aspirational middle-class world, but it is also bound up with an adolescent rebelliousness that oscillates between the solipsistic and the nihilistic. The explicitly political component of this moment is evident enough to distinguish it from the other gestural idioms that fill the novel, yet only barely. If there is an expectation that critique at least implies a relationship to organizational or activist structures that belong to the realm of public, political life, then the more subjective, affect-laden version of it that we often encounter in *Loaded* confronts us with the shards of the political: the fragments, or after-effects, of a conceptual universe that no longer seems properly operative or readily available. Ari cannot integrate himself into a broader social horizon partly because that horizon itself does not exist in a way that can actualize a meaningful, critically engaged existence. The novel's refusal to release itself from the immaturity of its main character embodies this sense of a cognitive crisis. *Loaded*, I believe, is an important novel because it manages to inhabit the affective, gestural rubble of a world that seems to have sublimated the political into the multiple, private universes of its atomized subjects. In this respect the novel reflects the neoliberal disorganization of public, political life in which narratives of prosperity are channeled through a relentlessly individualized model of subjectivity bound up with private pleasure, wealth and security. In this sense *Bildung* already seems like a fiction. It is as if the passage from an immediate experience of the everyday to something that might count as collective historical or political experience has been blocked in accordance with a broader thesis about the neoliberal abandonment of history. Tsiolkas touches on this in his 2008 essay "On the Concept of Tolerance": "History—that sphere of knowledge most important to the left because in presenting it not as the linear and progressive triumph of great men (and now, occasionally, a few great women), it offers, instead, history as eruptive, disruptive, as a challenge to liberalism's suppression of the silences, violences and human misery on which this triumphalism is based—history has been abandoned."[8]

The disorganization of collective historical experience, however, is not encountered simply as alienation in *Loaded*. Readers of the novel, in fact, routinely celebrate the hedonistic ethos at its core: its often delirious immersion in drugs, music and a furtive, transgressive sexuality. The unflinching and uncensored way in which *Loaded* describes casual sexual encounters is integral to its refusal of heterosexual reproduction, family life and suburban conformity. This could be construed as the "progressive" element of the novel, the moment at which it contributes to an emerging sense of difference at odds with the putatively "normal" circuits of bourgeois society. *Loaded*, however, also propagates an apocalyptic sensibility that couples even its most apparently normative moments with abjection. In this respect, at least, it seems to conform very exactly to what Lee Edelman has described as a negativity— closely associated with the death drive—that refuses the biopolitical obsessions of what he calls "reproductive futurism." What Edelman sets out here is a thoroughgoing refusal of the "terms that impose an ideological limit on political discourse as such, preserving in the process the absolute privilege of heteronormativity by rendering unthinkable, by casting outside the political domain, the possibility of a queer resistance to this organizing principle of communal relations."[9] The work of queerness, he insists, is to step outside of this apparently normative framework and to embrace its negation; the stigma of abjection. Tellingly, Edelman links the "structuring optimism of politics" with narrative. Queerness's refusal of this link is anti-social in a very literal sense:

> Truth, like queerness, irreducibly linked to the "aberrant or atypical," to what chafes against "normalization," finds its value not in a good susceptible to generalization, but only in the stubborn particularity that voids every notion of the general good. The embrace of queer negativity, then, can have no justification if justification requires it to reinforce some positive social value; its value, instead, resides in its challenge to value as defined by the social, and thus in its radical challenge to the very value of the social itself.[10]

What Edelman sets out here is a steadfast refusal to put queerness into contact with processes of *Bildung*. Instead he frames the possibility of constituencies outside of the integrative social horizon it summons. If, as Cheah's more recent work suggests, *Bildung* is also central to the formation of human capital as an object of biopolitical management, then the sort of refusal Edelman sets out has a broad topicality precisely because it points to a space outside of and potentially immune to what Cheah calls the "subjectifying or humanizing aspect of biopower."[11] For much of *Loaded* this refusal might well describe Ari. Indeed the novel takes us a long way down this path. But not all the way. If the novel grasps narrative integration as a form of fantasy, it also cannot escape the suspicion that the sort of negativity Edelman explores is crucially implicated in the compulsively privatized orientation of neoliberal subjectivity. The novel, in other words, offers a sort of utopian negativity as the basis of its pleasure, but because it cannot completely let go of its investment in the apparently lost possibility of working-class life and consciousness, this pleasure is also compromised by the specter of the forms of political existence destroyed by late capitalism. That Tsiolkas can end up complicating, if not displacing, notions of queer negativity is a recognition of the degree to which "the particular" plays a part in the ideological production of late capitalism—the degree to which the affect of critique contained in the production of negativity also symptomatizes the waning of a left-identified politics in which Tsiolkas remains deeply invested. For this reason the novel also begins to alienate itself from the identifications that offer Ari a form of solace and a means of escaping from, or numbing himself to, the alienation of the everyday. *Loaded*'s negativity is finally central to its sense of ruin. It is as much a symptom of, as it is a solution to, the crisis it sets out.

* * * * *

Loaded's refusal of the dominant, ideological narratives of middle-class life is most obvious in the way in which it approaches the issue of geography. If the temporality of narrative fails to offer it a viable structuring device, the cartography of the city turns out to be much more promising. Spatiality here has much more primacy than temporality. It becomes a medium in its own right, one that finally enables Ari to grasp a sense of working-class displacement. It is as if the material spaces of the city carry within them a form of cultural-political memory, although at times this is admittedly very vague. The novel is set in Melbourne, and its four sections each orient to a different point of the compass such that Ari is able to take the reader on a virtual tour of the city reconceived as an imaginative space: from the inner-city suburb of Richmond to the outer suburban wastes of the East and back to the immigrant communities of the North, and then to the South, where the suburb of St. Kilda appears as a refuge about to be eclipsed by its rapid gentrification, to conclude with a brief glimpse of the working-class West as a place where the myths of class solidarity seem to collapse once and for all. This sense of urban geography is impressionistic and very uneven, but it does enable the novel to develop an acute sense of correspondence between physical space and the various narratives that Ari refuses. At the same time, Ari's perspective is one of dislocation and itinerancy; a sort of existential homelessness at odds with the ethos of suburbanization that constitutes one of the novel's clearest objects of critique. The physical space of the city provides the novel with its only really viable organizational framework, aside from its first-person voice. This puts *Loaded* into fairly direct dialogue with the competing discourses around urban and suburban space that have always played an important role in discussions of Anglo-Australian culture. On the one hand, the novel belongs to a long tradition of anti-suburban writing that stretches back to the late nineteenth century but finds its most obvious manifestations in texts written after World War II. Patrick White's Sarsaparilla novels, with their horrifying visions of spiritual vacuity and malevolence, come to mind. So too does George Johnston's ultimately hysterical antipathy to the sterile desolation of his fictional Beverly Grove in *My Brother Jack*. One might also think of Germaine Greer's *The Female Eunuch*, Robin Boyd's *The Australian Ugliness* and Barry Humphries's Dame Edna Everage as belonging to this anti-suburban tradition. On the other hand, *Loaded*'s mapping of the city and its default reliance on a dichotomy between inner and outer suburban spaces intersects with the conflicted forms of journalism that have threatened to turn the Australian press into an arm of the real estate industry. Anyone who has glanced at Melbourne's *Age* or the *Sydney Morning Herald* over the last couple of decades will know what I mean. Both have managed to tie a sense of culture, cultural capital and even cultural celebrity to inner-city living built on the traces of older working-class and immigrant communities in what have become "blue chip" locations. These publications routinely draw attention to the infrastructural challenges of suburban sprawl, but at the same time they remain tethered to the selling of suburban real estate in some of the most over-inflated markets on the planet. While *Loaded*'s adversarial relationship to suburbia is perfectly clear, the way in which its subversive ethos would become assimilated into and recolonized by forms of media tightly integrated into these markets (often through the dubious journalistic category of "lifestyle") would become more pressing as Tsiolkas moved from the margins to the center of the Australian literary scene.

    Loaded's first glimpse of the East takes us to a vision of suburbia that is of a piece with the anti-suburban tradition on which I have just touched.

But as the novel points to the emptiness of middle-class aspirations, what it highlights most decisively is a kind of formlessness that refuses legibility. The suburbs might supply an aspirational class with an aspirational narrative linked to the cultural and economic profile of particular places, but Ari's initial evocation of the East stresses an unreadability that derives from an apparent absence of difference. The suburb, in other words, embodies the history of class stratification, but it also extinguishes the traces of that history in the production of a standardized suburban geography:

> every street around here looks like every other street, every stranger you meet walking along looks like the same stranger you passed blocks ago. The blocks are huge. Big brick buildings, one after another. This could be Balwyn, could be Burwood, could be Vermont. Could be Mitcham. Maybe if you grew up around here all the space might mean something to you. East, west, south, north, the city of Melbourne blurs into itself. Concrete on concrete, brick veneer on brick veneer, weatherboard on weatherboard. Walking through the suburbs, I feel like I'm in the ugliest place on the planet. (37–38)

This sense of blurring clearly puts pressure on the way in which the novel evokes urban geography. It also shifts from being an apparently specific feature of the eastern suburbs to a universal feature of the entire city. Balwyn, Burwood, Vermont and Mitcham are all proximate to each other, but if "east, west, south, north, the city of Melbourne blurs into itself," then the spatial organization of the novel runs the risk of obsolescence. It is for this reason that *Loaded* also has to work against the idea of illegibility and redraw the boundaries and distinctions without which Ari's movement through the city would fail to produce a conceptual or cognitive map. But the way in which this happens cannot obviate the fact that what is really at issue here is not an accurate account of class- and ethnicity-based demographics, but the ability to draw a much more basic distinction between a world that has eradicated the layers and sediments of its own history, and a world in which those traces are still discernible, or even part of a lived experience. Hence Ari's sense of the suburbs blurring into a ubiquitous, standardized accumulation of non-places produces a sense of rage that equates white Australia with the Americanization of space, and juxtaposes this to an inner-city with an overtly industrial ambience:

> I detest the East. The whole fucking mass of it: the highways, the suburbs, the hills, the rich cunts, the smacked-out bored cunts. The whitest part of my city, where you'll see the authentic white Australian, is in the

eastern suburbs. A backdrop of Seven Elevens, shopping malls, gigantic parking lots. I was picked up by a guy once, he lived in this shithole suburb somewhere, Burwood or Balwyn or Bentleigh or Boronia, and I woke up in this strange man's bed, got up and made myself a coffee, went into the front yard, looked down the street and thought oh-my-fucking-god-is-this-America? I didn't feel sane again until I reached the corrosive stenches of the city. Lead and carbon dioxide in my lungs to make me forget the Disneyland I had woken up to. (41)

The vision of Americanization evident here is one of the mainstays of an earlier tradition of anti-suburban writing. And in keeping with that tradition, this passage works hard to draw distinctions between suburb and city, but it can also barely conceal its nostalgia for the idea of a world in which class-based distinctions are still legible. If the "flatlands of suburban hell" erode difference in the creation of a homogenized, atomized landscape of consumerist pleasures and television screens, the city's "corrosive stenches" suggest the immediate prehistory of late capitalism: an industrial landscape in which pollution evokes both working-class and immigrant communities. The relief Ari feels at reconnecting with this world has a strong autobiographical resonance. At the same time this sense of relief has a lot to do with the novel's longing for a political idiom that, it soon becomes clear, is no longer possible. The "stenches" of the city cannot attach to class difference any more than the factories and warehouses that, even in the mid-1990s, were already being converted into up-market apartments, restaurants or performance spaces.

Passages like the one I have just quoted produce critique as a form of affect: their explicitly political content cannot be separated out from loathing or rage, and they subsume the traces of a left-oriented position into highly individualized forms of expression that cannot be reconciled with the public language of politics even though we immediately recognize that they are political in orientation. For this reason they also run the risk of becoming ephemeral in the scheme of the novel. Hence a few pages later the sense of a racially demarcated East is drastically revised in a way that, once again, simultaneously obliterates and redraws distinctions. Ethnicity capitulates to the homogenization of consumer capitalism, which in turn insists on its own form of exclusivity: "Ethnicity is a scam, a bullshit, a piece of crock. The fortresses of the rich wogs on the hill are not there to keep the *Australezo* out, but to refuse entry to the uneducated-long-haired-bleached-blonde-no-money wog." As one form of exclusivity morphs into another, Ari's encounter with the East produces a kind of hysteria that comes from not knowing, exactly, what it is he is trying to oppose. Critique in thrall to affect is pushed to a vanishing point beyond which all that really remains is a rage at not being able to stabilize the concepts and categories that can produce a politically legible geography. One of Tsiolkas's most characteristic modes, at least at this point in his career, is to produce this rage in a purely negative will to violence: "No matter what the roots of the rich wogs, Greek, Italian, Chinese, Vietnamese, Lebanese, Arab, whatever, I'd like to get a gun and shoot them all. Bang bang. The East is hell. Designed by Americans" (43). The impossibility of directing rebelliousness through the process of *Bildung* produces a sense of blockage that threatens to consume Ari's voice altogether.

This sort of dynamic raises the problem that Fredric Jameson has discussed in his work on postmodernism as the cultural logic of late capitalism. I have already evoked the idea of "cognitive mapping" to suggest the problem Ari has with stabilizing a conceptual awareness of his material environment. The phrase, of course, is Jameson's. He uses it to describe a hypothetical cultural-political work that might be adequate to the challenges of postmodernism. One of the problems of postmodernism for Jameson is that it makes it almost impossible for individuals to locate themselves spatially, historically and politically. It produces a disjunction between the individual and her material environment that results in "the incapacity of our minds, at least at the present, to map the great global multinational and decentered communicational network in which we find ourselves caught as individual subjects."[12] By contrast the "aesthetic of cognitive mapping" is linked to a "political art" capable of overcoming the particularity of the individual and of reimagining a form of political praxis in circumstances from which "traditional production" and "social classes of the classical type" have largely disappeared.[13] How these dynamics manifest in the actual experience of physical space is a much broader and more complex issue, but suffice to say that Jameson's sense of being physically lost in postmodernity corresponds to a rich body of work on the poverty of contemporary non-places in which a crushing kind of homogeneity effects a literal dismantling of residual cultural and political identifications.[14]

That *Loaded* is based around notions of cartography and navigation suggests its interest in these issues, as much as its embrace of negativity suggests its interest in the particular. The difficulty of stabilizing a viable cognitive map and the novel's gravitation to the negativity of the particular are, of course, intimately related. *Loaded*'s refusal of future-oriented discourses stems partly from the fact that it cannot produce a sense of temporality that does not involve alienation and atomization. Temporality either leads back into the conservatism of aspirational narratives linked to accumulation and exclusivity, or it founders in the inexpressive materiality of the everyday, which comes to include a mediated, televised sense of world history as a constant flow of catastrophes that are barely distinguishable from each other. The impossibility of locating oneself, of imagining a meaningful way of engaging with the material world, again produces the simultaneity of critique and affect as the vanishing point of the political.

> Pol Pot was right to destroy, he was wrong not to work it out that you go all the way. You don't kill one class, one religion, one party. You kill everyone because we are all diseased, there is no way out of this shithole planet. War, disease, murder, AIDS, genocide, holocaust, famine. I can give ten dollars to an appeal if I want to, I can write a letter to the government. But the world is now too fucked up for small solutions. That's why I like the idea of it all ending in a nuclear holocaust. If I had access to the button, I'd push it. (64)

That the impossibility of a future-oriented political discourse evokes an apocalyptic sensibility is, at this point in the novel, predictable enough. Less predictable is the fact that it is also tethered to sexual arousal: "As we got to Princes Bridge station I was imagining the apocalypse. I was getting so excited it was making my dick hard" (64). This unlikely confluence brings us to what made *Loaded* so compelling for many of its readers. The passage I have just quoted thematizes, albeit in an improbably exaggerated manner, the fundamental link between the novel's deployment of sexuality and its refusal of the forms of political amelioration associated with liberal democracy. It is through a radically deterritorialized sexuality that Ari seems able to counter the illegibility of his environment.

The more intensely this vision is linked to abjection, the more pronounced the cognitive distress of the novel becomes. When Tsiolkas's focus shifts from the East to the North, this trajectory becomes clear. The North, according to Ari, is a series of immigrant ghettos, a dumping ground: "The North isn't Melbourne, it isn't Australia. It is a little village in the mountains of the Mediterranean transported to the bottom of the southern hemisphere [...] The North is a growing, pulsating sore on the map of my city, the part of the city in which I, my family, my friends are meant to buy a house, grow a garden, shop, watch TV and be buried in. The North is where the wog is supposed to end up. And therefore I hate the North, I view it with as much contempt as possible" (81–82). At the same time, however, the immigrant communities of the North facilitate the itinerant forms of sexuality that are increasingly at the center of Ari's self-conception. If he loathes the cultural conservatism of "old ways, old cultures, old rituals" (82), he is also drawn to the "ovals and parks and river banks" where he can find "fat Arab men and chain-smoking Greek men who stand with their dicks out at urinals, cigarette in their mouths, waiting for you" (83). It is in this world that Ari finds a way of resisting the narratives of what Edelman calls reproductive futurism.

It is the North where I search for the body, the smile, the skin that will ease the strain on my groin, that will take away the burning compulsion and terror of my desire. In the North I find myself, find shadows that recall my shadow. I roam the North so I can come face to face with the future that is being prepared for me. On my knees, with hate written on my face, I spit out bile, semen, saliva, phlegm, I spit it all out. I spit out the future that has been prepared for me. (83–84)

The sense of abjection that occurs at this moment is also a sense of introjection: taking in ("on my knees") and spiting out. Ari embraces his identity as a kind of queer outlaw, which also cuts him off from the future-oriented discourse of social and biological reproduction. It is not clear that we can see any of the utopian hopefulness that José Esteban Muñoz finds in cruising at this moment, although a subsequent essay by Tsiolkas, "Into the Liquid Ether" (2008), suggests the pleasure of casual sexual encounters in a way that feels more recuperative than anything we get in *Loaded*.[15] That Ari directly places himself in the realm of the abject is the novel's clearest expression of its negativity. This comes into focus as the novel's attention shifts to the South, where he imagines a population of outcasts with which he can identify:

To the South are the wogs who have been shunted out of their communities. Artists and junkies and faggots and whores, the sons and daughters no longer talked about, no longer admitted into the arms of family. In the South, in the flats and apartments smelling of mildew and mice, are all the wog rejects from the North, the East, the West. Flushed out towards the sea. When you look straight across the ocean you look into the face of your dreams [...] The constraints placed on me by my family can only be destroyed by a debasement that allows me to run along dark paths and silent alleyways forbidden to most of my clan and my peers. To be free, for me as a Greek, is to be a whore. To resist the path of marriage and convention, of tradition and obedience, I must make myself an object of derision and contempt. Only then am I able to move outside the suffocating obligations of family and loyalty. (132)

We can see here not only the world of the outlaw, but related to it a lumpen, sub-proletarian world of "whores and faggots and junkies" (133) that, paradoxically, reinscribes Ari's sense of being Greek by embracing an abjection that seems to be internal to it. But this does not form anything like a conventional class linked to a conventional ameliorative narrative. In fact, what we get here is exactly the opposite—not the promise of futurity, but a terminal sort of refusal in which both temporality and spatiality are closed down: "The sea breeze of the southern ocean, the breeze that comes up from the end of the world, makes some strong, draws me to the whores and faggots and junkies. I am a sailor and a whore. I will be till the end of the world" (133).

If this is a moment of negativity, there is no doubt that it is also the novel's most affirmative moment. It was for this reason, one assumes, that the cinematic adaptation of the novel concluded with it. In Ana Kokkinos's 1998 *Head On* we see Ari, played by Alex Dimitriades, embracing his dislocation in what looks like Melbourne's docklands. As Sneja Gunew writes, this moment also reinscribes the ethnic identifications that Ari has seemingly renounced earlier: "The film ends with Ari having […] questioned and violently rejected all the ethnic (and several other) categories of identity formation, none the less executing a Greek dance on the beach—repeating the movements he had performed for his father."[16] Still, it is important that the novel does not finish with the South. Ari's gravitation to the whores and junkies at the end of the world has to be redescribed as the end of a certain conception of class politics. Negativity and the failure of narrative are reframed as symptoms of the way in which other activist frameworks—frameworks deeply rooted in Tsiolkas's class background—have become impossible. *Loaded*'s shortest and most discursive section thus takes us to the West and the apparent end of those grand narratives of progress and amelioration that had class solidarity as their point of orientation.

> In the working-class suburbs of the West where communal solidarity is meant to flourish, the skip sticks with the skip, the wog with the wog, the gook with the gook, and the abo with the abo. Solidarity, like love, is a crock of shit. The rich don't fear the unionised worker, they don't fear the militant. They fear the crim, the murderer, the basher. Crime doesn't pay but it is the only form rebellion open to us. And to survive the thief must eschew solidarity. (142–43)

Not class, but crime. Not solidarity, but the solitude of the criminal. If the West evokes an industrial city, it is also on the verge of falling out of time, of losing its class-based specificity and its ability to mark older narratives of working-class amelioration that Ari sees as a facet of a vanished childhood. "The noise of the factory was the soundtrack to our childhood," he tells us. All of that belongs to the past: "The factories are being pulled down, the skies are emptying of smoke, and the flat, dry ground of this city is now home to thousands and thousands of petite boxes where people who used to be workers live" (143). In this post-industrial city, community is also impossible, a fossil-concept from a period that has passed: "Community. Don't comprehend the word. The mania of our culture is the desire to accumulate and accumulate, to become richer, to become classier, to become more secure, wealthier. It is impossible to feel camaraderie if the dominant wish is to get enough money, enough possessions to rise above the community you are in" (143).

This moment, which is oddly essayistic, clarifies a great deal of what we have read over the preceding 140 odd pages. As the global West, not just Melbourne's West, becomes post-industrial, the concepts and categories that had hitherto provided the left with a way of understanding and narrativizing its own plight have become impossible. In *Loaded* Ari is the symptom of this loss of clarity and identity. As Ian Syson puts it in a landmark discussion of grunge literature, "*Loaded* is a working-class novel written in an age when it is not possible to write one. The narrative is crying out for the comfort of an old-fashioned ('Street Fighting Man') literary politics of class conflict in which Ari's alienation can be explained, soothed and channelled into class action."[17] This possibility is, of course, long gone. In the absence of community, in the absence of a class, Ari is thrown back on himself, on his own body, on his own capacity to experience and generate a pleasure that is in excess of the functionalized narratives of heterosexual normalcy and suburbanization that have settled over an older, now vanished city. But outside the fold of power or hegemonic identification, he is also abject, redundant, obsolete:

> There is no future available to the refo and the wog any more. Nowhere to run, like the song. They don't need factories any more, they have elegantly-sculptured machines powered by microchips. They don't need labour any more. Not now, now that they have the internet. Nowhere to run, like the song. The sewers keep filling up, they are fucking overflowing and the refuse is choking up the atmosphere. From Singapore to Beijing, from Rio to Johannesburg [...] I am surfing on the down-curve of capital. The generations after this are not going to build on the peasants' landholdings. There's no jobs, no work, no factories, no wage packet, no half-acre block. There is no more land. I am sliding towards the sewer. I'm not even struggling against the flow. I can smell the pungent aroma of shit, but I'm still breathing. (144)

That the abjection of the sewer is directly tied to the loss of traditional forms of class-based identity is the novel's most powerful and important implication. Ari, finally, is nothing but his own capacity for pleasure: "I'm not Australian, I'm not Greek, I'm not anything. I'm not a worker, I'm not a student, I'm not an artist, I'm not a junkie, I'm not a conversationalist [sic], I'm not an Australian, not a wog, not anything" (149). The novel's concluding moments replay its opening: vacancy, the formlessness of the everyday, the complete absence of any sort of integrative horizon in which innate capacities might develop and realize themselves in the objectivity of the social. As Syson puts it, "the end of the novel finds Ari in a depressing stasis, staring at the ceiling and unwittingly waiting for the great leap forward."[18]

Loaded's movement from the South to the West, from an embrace of debasement to a stark statement of the impossibility of community, embodies a contradiction that is integral to the novel's vitality. Tsiolkas's interest in Pasolini is one way of coming at this contradiction. While I do not want simply to graft one onto the other, the similarities in orientation are extremely instructive. Pasolini's melding of Marxism and homosexuality was, for a large part of his career, fixated on a sub-proletarian milieu that had been produced by the transition from agrarianism to capitalism, and related migrations from the country to the city, but not properly integrated into the order implied by the confluence of capitalism and urbanism. As Fabio Vighi writes, for Pasolini "the anti-social condition of non-participation which, for example, typified the Roman sub-proletariat of the 1950s was a proper status to be upheld and promoted insofar as it implied a radical opposition to the codified, institutionalized order of Italian bourgeois society." His protest, Vighi continues, was based on his identification with "social groups that had not yet been co-opted into the specific socio-symbolic order defined politically by the liberal-democratic ideology, and economically by capitalism."[19] What is at stake here is not a conventionally imagined class. It is the world of fickle, floating relationships that we see depicted in *Ragazzi di vita*, or in a film like *Accattone*. It also reminds us of the confluence of queerness and itinerancy in Jean Genet's *The Thief's Journal* and John Rechy's *City of Night*, two important influences on Tsiolkas's early work. The absence of identities that can be fixed and comprehended as expressions of capitalism, liberal democracy or socialism, puts this milieu outside of the conceptual matrices of post-war modernity. Its criminality was an indication of its deterritorialization, and it was partly for this reason that Pasolini also saw it as a space of unmediated sexuality. The absence of a political framework linked to visions of futurity, in other words, also enabled the expression of those forms of life stifled by visions of both bourgeois and proletarian "progress." As what Pasolini called the "cultural and anthropological crisis" of the late 1960s became more obvious—a crisis that for Pasolini was linked to the mass media—"the 'innocent' bodies, with the archaic, dark, vital violence of their sexual organs, seemed to be the last bulwark of reality." Eros, he believed, was still a physical presence lodged in a "human environment barely surpassed by history."[20]

The relationship between the sexual and the political that I have just sketched constitutes one of the zones in which queer identity is most obviously articulable. For Pasolini, however, it was a zone that would also be eventually co-opted into the logics of consumerism. As we have seen, by the time he wrote "Repudiation of the Trilogy of Life," Pasolini was sickened by the hedonism that he saw as an expression of, not a bulwark against, capitalism: "the progressive struggle for the democratization of self-expression and for sexual liberation has been brutally surpassed and thwarted by the decision of the consumerist establishment to concede a vast (but false) tolerance."[21] The forms of sexual freedom propagated by the consumerist establishment had also, Pasolini believed, produced "physical degradation." The result was the collapse of the measured optimism with which he had once approached the issue of Eros and sexual liberation:

> The youth and boys of the Roman subproletariat—the ones I have projected into the old and resistant Naples, and later in the poor countries of the Third World—*if now* they are human garbage it means that potentially they were such also *then*; they were, therefore, imbeciles compelled to be adorable, squalid criminals compelled to be likeable rascals, vile good-for-nothings compelled to be saintly innocents, etc. The collapse of the present implies the collapse of the past. Life is a pile of insignificant and ironic ruins.[22]

There is an enormous amount to be said about this passage, but perhaps two things stand out above all. Firstly, we get the sense that the sub-proletariat was always prone to political or ideological appropriation. The way in which Pasolini's final film *Salò* will reposition the male body in the ranks of fascist foot-soldiers feels like a revision of his previous orientation. Secondly, the sense of ruin with which the passage concludes powerfully suggests the impossibility of a normative dimension that can withstand the onslaught of capitalist modernity. The bulwarks have been demolished. What we have instead is the debris of the hopefulness that Pasolini once invested in the idea of Eros, which now seems to exist entirely within the domain of human capital and neoliberal biopower.

Pasolini's late essays, especially those collected in *Scritti corsari*, repeatedly make this point by connecting the false tolerance of consumerism with fascism. Consumerism is "nothing but a new totalitarian form, something entirely totalizing and alienating which approaches the extreme limits of anthropological degradation or genocide (Marx)—consequently, its permissiveness is false: it is the mask of the worst repression ever exercised by power upon the masses of citizens."[23] The reference to genocide gestures at the vision of fascism, structured around the relationship between sexuality and sovereignty, that is at the center of *Salò*. For now, however, all I want to point out is the way in which Pasolini finally came to see the sub-proletariat as the raw material of a political catastrophe: fodder for both consumerism and totalitarianism. The subtext here is very similar to what we see in Marx's famous analysis of the *Lumpenproletariat* in *The Eighteenth Brumaire of Louis Bonaparte*. Precisely because the *Lumpenproletariat* is not a class or a community but simply an accumulation of individuals, it lends itself to almost instant appropriation. It sells out to whatever regime can best cater to its inherently atomized, hedonistic impulses.

Braced by the pessimism of this perspective, we can return to the concluding moments of *Loaded*. Tsiolkas's exploration of the West correlates the absence of community with the atomizing forces of late or global capitalism. This has a lot to do with the passing away of older industrial landscapes and of a historical narrative organized around conventional class-based identities. What we are left with in the wake of community is the individual as a locus of both pleasure and abjection. At moments this ambiguous vision of the individual feels like the assertion of a freedom, of something resistant to the alienating structures of late capitalism. At others, this sense of a liberated subjectivity is almost entirely mediated (by music and narcotics). As compelling as Tsiolkas's vision of queer sexuality is in this novel, there is almost no sense in which it can produce tangible or durable communal identifications or structures. In fact, the way in which Ari's sexuality is also a form of aggression suggests the opposite. That pleasure and abjection are constantly shadowing each other emphasizes this negativity. It is as if the novel's most concerted attempt to think deterritorialized subjectivity cannot ever let go of the feeling that Ari always remains a symptom of the greater vision of collapse the novel's concluding section sets out. The body politic has vanished, leaving only the body in its wake. From this perspective what Lee Edelman sets out as the negativity of the particular is also indicative of a perspective limited by its historical circumstances. While the novel's negativity is a part of its appeal and is bound up with its apparently liberating refusal of all narratives of social reproduction and utility, that refusal can also be construed as a fantasy structure that reproduces the very forms of atomization that are so central to capitalism. Tsiolkas himself is very clear about the ways in which nihilism emerges from the "collapse of socialist ethics," but he also insists, in what seems like a rereading of *Loaded*, that dreams should not entirely detach themselves from the communal: "Dreams are important, but they have to be tempered by an understanding that you have to share those dreams and illusions with a community, with people around you, they can't be constantly only focused on the ego and the self."[24] This reorientation to the social and to what Cheah describes as the process of *Bildung* will be, as we will see, an important part of Tsiolkas's more recent work.

The way in which Tsiolkas sees himself as working through these issues is in fact very close to the position of Pasolini's late prose. In a 2013 interview with Heather Taylor Johnson, Tsiolkas explains his initial desire to "reconcile Marxism with the liberationist politics of feminism, sexual politics and what I guess is post-colonial politics." He sees himself failing in this, "in that feminism and queer are underpinned by bourgeois understandings of selfhood and identity." As a result he cannot simply give himself over to the "liberationist idea that the transformation of the individual can resolve these tensions and contradictions."[25] Later in the interview this repudiation of bourgeois selfhood becomes more emphatic, and rhetorically charged: "the entitled, narcissistic bourgeois subject at the heart of the neo-liberal globalised world is an infection, a virus. It is a subject and a politics that wants to force everyone to become a mirror of itself, to force everyone to be the 'same,' to desire the 'same,' to live the 'same,' to believe the 'same.'"[26] For both Pasolini and Tsiolkas, however, the sense of homogenization associated with consumer culture barely touches on the dire, dystopian potential of capitalist modernity. As we will see in the following chapters, the individual liberated into the excess of his own desire also reproduces the forms of sovereign violence associated with the worst atrocities of the twentieth century. Pasolini's rejection of his *Trilogy of Life* will lead to *Salò*; Tsiolkas's exploration of the violence inherent in the particular will lead to *The Jesus Man* and *Dead Europe*. If the first of these novels almost ended his career, at least in so far as its failure forced him to contemplate giving up writing, the second undoubtedly saved it. While both these novels developed, Tsiolkas was also becoming involved with the Melbourne Workers Theatre, a company and forum in which questions around the efficacy and agency of working-class identity were being thought out and worked through by politically committed artists and directors. As we will see in the next chapter, the way in which the Melbourne Workers Theatre framed the crisis of class politics in the era of neoliberalism will be an important context for, and counterpoint to, Tsiolkas's increasingly pessimistic fiction.

Chapter 2

INSIDE THE MACHINE: FROM *LOADED* TO *THE JESUS MAN*

In the last chapter I suggested that *Loaded*'s orientation to the negativity of the particular symptomatizes the waning of more traditional forms of political discourse linked to notions of class, or to forms of communal solidarity at odds with the atomizing forces of capitalism. The novel's implicit longing for a working-class or communal politics means that it also ends up distancing itself from Ari's nihilistic, hedonistic self-absorption. At the same time, the constant confusion of affect and critique—or the production of critique as a form of affect—allows us to argue that Ari's negativity is something like the afterlife of a politics, the spectral remainder of a worldview that is no longer capable of anchoring the sort of cognitive map for which the novel's cartographic orientation cries out. Of the numerous critical responses to the novel, few have stressed its working-class orientation or grappled with this sense that its most euphoric moments are bound up with a negativity that it ultimately seems to disavow. Ian Syson's discussion of *Loaded*, which I touched on in the last chapter, stands out in this respect. So too does Ivan Cañadas's discussion of the relationship between *Loaded* and *Head On*, which I will get to in a moment. As we will see later in this chapter, Tsiolkas's involvement in the Melbourne Workers Theatre leaves no doubt that these issues weigh upon him and inform a commitment to diverse genres and media forms that reflect his interest in counter-hegemonic cultural spaces.

For the most part, however, critical discourse about *Loaded* has tended to endorse Ari's position and tried hard to extract a politics from it. For Anja Schwarz, the novel maps a "new set of spatial as well as linguistic strategies" that put it at odds with "hegemonic readings of identity and space."[1] She relates this directly to debates about immigration, implying that *Loaded* allegorizes a broader tension between difference and the fiction of a homogenized, Anglo-Celtic Australian nation. Elizabeth McMahon suggests something similar when she writes that "Ari's walking knowledge of Melbourne produces an alternative map of the city according to ethnicity, particularly the map of second-generation Greeks; and of sexuality, specifically male homosexuals."[2] Both essays orient to difference—ethnic and sexual—and both anchor their political topicality in it. Rather than lingering on the politics of class or of underlying relations of production, which as the novel itself suggests are no longer really intelligible, they assume a politics that turns ultimately on liberal conceptions of tolerance and recognition.

There is no doubt that this orientation to difference is a crucial aspect of the novel. *Loaded* clearly confronted and quickly unsettled the sort of Anglo-Celtic, heteronormative moorings that define so much Australian cultural production. As the New Right gained ground with the rise of One Nation, the ascendency of John Howard's Liberal Party and the institution of a regressive immigration policy, this orientation would only become more urgent and topical.[3] The version of Ari's journey offered by Schwarz and McMahon, however, does slide rather easily into the forms of entertainment or lifestyle journalism that integrate the literary text, or the literary author, into a broader set of value-generating discourses. In this respect it is no coincidence that McMahon's essay evokes notions of *flânerie* to describe Ari's movement through the city. She draws on Michel de Certeau and his distinction between "space" and "place" to describe the ways in which Ari's itinerancy is framed by different spatial registers. Put simply, the terms refer to two different ways of being in the world, or "two sorts of determinations in stories." "Place" is related to the fixity of the empirical or the material, "the *being-there* of something dead, the law of the 'place,'" as de Certeau puts it. "Space," by contrast, emerges through "the action of historical *subjects*."[4] Elsewhere de Certeau is terrifically evocative on what he calls the "long poem of walking," which "manipulates spatial organization" and "creates shadows and ambiguities within them."[5] McMahon's account of Ari's *flânerie* is conducted in a similar spirit. For Walter Benjamin, however, the figure of the *flâneur*, while not without its poetry or a relationship to the radicality of avant-garde practice, already indicates assimilation into a commercial print-culture and the textual forms that reflect this: ethnographical or physiological journalism that would increasingly orient to the difference lurking in the folds of urban life. According to Benjamin, this sort of city writing was initially about mapping locations and social types, partly in order to appease middle-class anxieties about the new experience of anonymity in rapidly growing urban centers. The market's need for novelty, however, quickly forced this sort of journalism away from the task of normalizing the unfamiliar, and instead towards defamiliarizing the everyday. Hence the city became the site of a heterogeneity linked to deviance, abnormality and a refusal of the social order for a voyeuristic middle-class reader safely insulated from any real sense of threat.[6] If *Loaded* is a textual embodiment of the ruins of proletarian lifeworlds, those ruins also lend themselves to a range of recuperative political and commercial idioms that, the novel demands, we should read against this fundamental form of loss.

It was difference, of course, that would partly secure *Loaded*'s currency. Especially for urban, educated, middle-class audiences, difference is a particularly talismanic concept. Its relationship to the more rarefied climes of poststructuralism aside, it functions in a wide variety of public discourses, all of which seem to overlap with each other. In the sphere of the political, it evokes notions of rights and recognition that are hard-wired into modern conceptions of the state. In the sphere of the economic it evokes notions of consumer choice. In the sphere of the cultural it evokes fragmentation and independence from a putatively hegemonic representational framework or from instrumentalized forms of governmentality. It is the rubric that brings the state and the market together; the point at which their potentially volatile relationship produces a shared set of values.

Ana Kokkinos's cinematic adaptation of *Loaded* would consolidate this sense of the novel being primarily about spaces of freedom, linked to sexual and ethnic difference, that are mapped out against the tyranny of traditional Greek patriarchy and a broader, heteronormative Australia. The film's currency depended in some way on its relationship to the cultural capital of the literary. At the same time the circulation of the novel was greatly expanded by its relationship to the more popular media form. As Ivan Cañadas has argued, Kokkinos's adaption of the novel involves a specific recasting, or recalibration, of its political emphasis. If, in *Loaded*, Ari's rejection of community is "implicitly founded on a learned respect for the values of class solidarity," *Head On* stresses ethnicity and sexuality in a way that divorces them "from their basis in class-consciousness." This has the effect, Cañadas suggests, of reducing Ari to "an immature teenage cynic."[7] At the same time the film is much more squarely focused on the tension between queer identity and the conservative, patriarchal structures of the Greek community. Cañadas concludes by claiming that "perhaps the cultural and political climate in the late twentieth and early twenty-first centuries—even in the medium of *alternative* cinema—makes *class*, rather than sexuality, a new sin 'that dares not speak its name.'"[8] What the essay gets at is the way in which media forms, and the public sphere organized by them, structure an experience of the political in a very specific manner. *Head On* is an exhilaratingly visceral experience and a landmark piece of queer Australian cinema, but I do not think it is contentious to say that the film pushes *Loaded*'s interest in waning forms of working-class politics well into its background, partly because the novel's orientation to urban cartography is almost entirely absent. In *Loaded*, Tsiolkas's sense of a ruined, entropic landscape marks a shift between different conceptions of the political. In *Head On*, at least as Cañadas reads it, the traces of that shift have been significantly attenuated, and a politics of sexual and ethnic difference anchors personal and historical narratives more to what Ben Authers calls "rights-based liberalism" than to notions of proletarian experience.[9] In this framework the first-world city is the scene of both multicultural and queer becoming (though not in the sense of uncompromising negativity intended by Lee Edelman). Difference, in other words, secures a sense of the political oriented to tolerance and freedom, but operates within a framework that leaves relations of production untouched. This is in fact something that Tsiolkas himself has discussed very directly. Recalling his attendance at a 1983 meeting of EPNA (Greek-Australian Progressive Youth), he foregrounds the tension between sexual identity and class politics, a tension he is able to negotiate retrospectively despite his personal investments. When the discussion in the meeting stressed the complicity between gay liberation movements and "the commercial realities of First World capitalist states," Tsiolkas felt deflated: "I was a homosexual from a working-class background. They didn't deny this, but observed that as a communist, class politics should come first, not my sexuality." It is a position that Tsiolkas found confronting but that he ultimately seems to affirm: "The commercial gay world I came out to as an adolescent had no interest in dismantling the state or undermining the inequities of capital."[10] As Authers has argued, *Loaded*'s conflicted relationship with the forms of Greek-Australian identification that are most obviously available to Ari also registers the ways in which these forms of identification reproduce the aspirational narratives of middle Australia.[11] Authers sees the novel's solution to this in the "recognition of difference" that is "more intensely personal, more fluid, and also potentially more engaged" than what he calls "official manifestations" of multiculturalism.[12]

It is tempting to read the novel in this way and to celebrate its gravitation to a reanimated form of difference that interrupts the "unified plurality" of the multicultural nation.[13] But the line between this interruptive version of difference and the plurality of state- or market-driven versions of multiculturalism is a fine and constantly shifting one. It is hard to see how this sense of a departure from the hegemonic distinguishes itself from consumerist fantasies about cosmopolitan urban space that emerge out of lifestyle, real estate and entertainment journalism. By the time *Head On* had been released, Tsiolkas himself was becoming a marker of difference in these broadsheet discourses. Mass media forms do not produce much consistency in this respect. Rather, they assemble a diverse range of overlapping opinions and postures. While *Loaded*'s initial impact was linked to a range of other so-called grunge texts that seemed to share its interest in early adult hedonism, boredom and nihilism, the novel quickly detached itself from what would prove to be an ephemeral category compromisingly linked to commercial logics. As Paul Dawson put it, "grunge is not so much a literary movement as a market category. It has been used to fuel the myth, beloved of the Australian media and book publishing industry, of a conflict between generational cultures."[14] Tsiolkas was clearly more complex than what, in Philippa Hawker's words, that "neat and tidy marketing package" could suggest.[15] At the same time his integration into broadsheet entertainment journalism had a lot to do with the vaguely confessional tone of interviews and biographical anecdotes that understandably had a "coming out" feel to them. It also drew on the fact that Tsiolkas's own public comments—in regard to Australia Day, the Melbourne Writers Festival or the literary scene in general—were often caustic and confrontational. These views conveyed a complexity that the media could take or leave as its need for concision dictated: "If you want to read about, say, what it's like to be young, Greek and gay, Christos Tsiolkas will tell you," Jane Sullivan wrote in the *Age*.[16]

Tsiolkas's insertion into this sort of media universe was, of course, an inevitable part of *Loaded*'s marketing and largely beyond his control. But *Loaded*, like other examples of grunge fiction, is notable for the insistence with which it assimilates other media forms into its own textuality. For McKenzie Wark, this media orientation was central to the impact of grunge fiction in the 1990s.

> Grunge writers were just a particular kind of young writer who used the repertoire of images that they had in common with others who pay attention to media aesthetics. That these books sold well is less a tribute to the marketing genius of publishers, and more to the simple fact that readers recognized in grunge writing a common world of media experience.[17]

For Wark, *Loaded* stands out in this respect, partly for the clarity with which it explores the possibilities created within what he calls "media vectors." That Ari's fantasy life is stimulated by listening to music with headphones illustrates this.[18] Both McMahon and Schwarz also stress the role of popular music in *Loaded*'s circulation of difference. Dwelling on this for a moment opens up a crucial dimension of Tsiolkas's conception of fiction—its receptiveness to non-literary media. Ari moves through the city to a soundtrack composed of the music he has on his Walkman or the tracks he hears at the various venues through which he passes. His interiority owes a lot to the pleasure of sound, which he links to a feeling of ecstasy. The Jackson Five's "I Want You Back," for instance, creates for Ari "a magic world of harmony and joy, a truly ecstatic joy, where the aching longing to be somewhere else, out of this city, out of this country, out of this body and out of this life, is kept at bay."[19] For Schwarz, the act of listening to music helps Ari articulate a break from "the rigid disciplining map of Melbourne."[20] For McMahon, music is "a powerful agent of motility and speed" and central to a reading of the novel that stresses the ability of dance to solicit "the pleasure of ritual trance and the bodily experience of union and connection." As McMahon clearly understands, the fact that in *Loaded* "the *flâneur* is given momentum and musical accompaniment" points to the novel's "inherent cinematic qualities."[21] For Wark, the importance of this attention to non-literary media is also a bit broader. Tsiolkas's work dramatizes the mobility of media images and sounds, that is their ability to create meaning independently of their origin. This makes Tsiolkas indicative not just of a generational shift, but of a disciplinary shift that grasps the fugitive potential of popular media forms. In contrast, what Wark calls the "Burbler" aesthetic, by which he means the aesthetic norms of suburban baby-boomers, closes down "the virtual play of meaning in the everyday that freeing images from origins creates."[22] It goes without saying that this also disparages popular cultural forms and their manifold possibilities. Looked at in this way, *Loaded* reimagines the literary for an environment dominated by popular media. It imagines its own pleasure, if not the possibility of its completion, in relationship to technologies that extend well beyond the limits of print.

Stressing the centrality of the Walkman to the novel is also a way of elucidating its autobiographical underpinnings. In a fascinating 2006 essay entitled "Mix-Tape: The Technology of a Passion," Tsiolkas returns to the relationship between subjectivity and technology that, we have seen, is at the center of his book on *The Devil's Playground*. In fact, the original title of *Loaded*, we learn, was *Novel with Soundtrack*. It comes as no surprise to find that Ari's negativity is fairly close to the way in which Tsiolkas recalls the collision of music and suburbia, interior and exterior spaces, in his own life:

> compilation tapes were not only love letters. Sometimes they were manifestos, screams of rage against a world going to shit. There was no better feeling than sitting on a tram, the suburban world consuming all around you. While you sat there thinking of how much you wanted to blow the whole fucking place to kingdom come.[23]

Elsewhere in the essay, this sense of atomized subjectivity is bound up with a kind of aesthetic pleasure not dissimilar to what Herbert Marcuse set out in his famous account of "affirmative culture": "the assertion of a universally obligatory, eternally better and more valuable world that must be unconditionally affirmed: a world essentially different from the factual world of the daily struggle for existence, yet realizable by every individual 'from within,' without any transformation of the state of fact."[24] Tsiolkas's account of listening to music recreates something very similar to this.

The Walkman propelled me into the world, gave an urgency to my step, allowed me to feel euphoria anywhere I was. Yes, it shut out the world but it fills your head and mind and body, the beats pump through your body, it fills you up with music, it makes you drunk on music, it is an intoxication […] The music was the real world and the shapes and colours and shadows that flitted past my eyes were what was not real […] I live inside the machine. The turntable, the cassette player, the Walkman and now the MP3 player. Inside the machine I can still fantasise that I am both the singer and the song, that I can move a crowd to exhilaration, that I can change the world. That I can move the world. That I have a voice.[25]

While this passage brilliantly distills the pleasure of listening, the point at which music and cityscape meet is also a moment of fantasy in which experience seems radically transformed and removed from a merely empirical sense of the everyday. The intensity of these moments, however, should not distract us from their conventionality, or even their banality. Tsiolkas describes a thoroughly ordinary, consumerist experience as if it involved some sort of resistance to the world it in fact helps to structure. That's not to disparage popular music. Life for many of us would be intolerable without it. And perhaps we can talk about genuine forms of resistance at these moments; the resistance of a sort of Situationist *derivé* of urban space that momentarily reconstructs the everyday around desires latent within it. Elsewhere in the essay Tsiolkas describes music's ability to organize relationships, forge intimacies and evoke memories. But his intense investment in this media, his willingness to be "inside the machine," might be compared to his similarly intense antipathy to television, a medium that he sees as central to suburban alienation.

We can already glimpse this in *Loaded*, where television generates a sense of visual disassociation that powerfully evokes the absence of a viable cognitive map and the bewildered immersion in a spectacle that has dissolved distinctions between moments of significance and moments of utter triviality.

On the television monitor I watch flickering images: a woman in a miniskirt, a man in leather, a beachscape, the bombing of Baghdad, a burial in Sarajevo, mushroom clouds, desert, a couple kissing, guns, the Virgin Mary, the red crescent, the hammer and sickle, silence = death, the US flag, tits, bums, crotch shots, guns, another mushroom cloud. Young black guys pointing fat fingers towards me, white guys spitting at my face; women licking their lips shoving their arses towards me. I forget the cigarette in my hand and it burns my finger.[26]

Ari is, admittedly, "coming down" in this passage, but his near-comatose condition finds its corollary in the meaningless profusion of images on the monitor. This is similar to what Hans Magnus Enzensberger describes as the "zero medium," by which he means the point at which content is so marginalized from the materiality of media forms that it is entirely coincidental and the viewer is essentially liberated from the burden of meaning.[27] There is no possibility of a postmodern public sphere here. Television is like a drug, but then, let's not forget, so is music. What begins to emerge here is a fairly deliberate sifting of different media that seems to draw distinctions around active appropriation and passive consumption. As Tsiolkas himself was beginning to become part of the media spectacle, albeit in the form of a fashionably quotable author, his work was developing a position about mediaticity that would highlight the variable ways in which media forms and subjectivity interact.

If *Loaded* is a novel with a soundtrack, *The Jesus Man* is a novel of channel surfing and pornographic videos. The shift from relatively benign (and sometimes uplifting) to clearly destructive media forms involves a marked raising of the stakes around questions of interiority, fantasy and escapism. If *Loaded*'s working through of these issues is fine enough to evoke a range of critical opinions around the problem of Ari's mediated subjectivity, *The Jesus Man* leaves no room for doubt: the media landscape evoked in the novel is pathological, and a central component of a violently alienated world that can only resolve itself through self-annihilation. The outer-directed violence that Ari imagines inflicting on suburbia becomes an inner-directed death drive. Like *Loaded*, *The Jesus Man* has an unmistakably autobiographical tone. Its key themes match up fairly directly with the way in which Tsiolkas talks about his own adolescence: the move from Richmond to Blackburn, a brief flirtation with Christian orthodoxy, a guilt-racked relationship to his own body and so on, most of which is set out explicitly in the essay on *The Devil's Playground* and in *Jump Cuts*. The novel's use of the autobiographical, however, does not produce much formal cohesion. Rather it seems to manifest in an anxiousness about closure and completion that, I will argue, indicates the deeply fraught character of its libidinal investments, and the sense of Tsiolkas himself struggling to extricate the novel from these in order to secure a normative position protected from a pathology that threatens to become all-consuming.

The novel purports to be a saga organized around three brothers of Greek-Italian heritage: Dominic, Tommy and Louie Stefano. In fact it lays its stress in a much more particular way. Dominic will end up being marginal while Louie, the novel's framing narrator, is a bit innocuous. His role is really to tell us about his brother Tommy, the real focus of the novel, and the aftermath of his suicide. Tommy is introduced as someone who is "happiest watching

TV." In the novel's opening moments he already appears alienated from his parents and siblings, "sitting close to the screen, the rest of the family behind him, not in view."[28] Louie, by contrast, has a more diverse set of interests that foreground a disquiet about the mass media that drives so much of the novel: "Of course, I remember the television as well, that it was always on. But some of my earliest memories—very early memories, those memories that reach back beyond when time became concrete, before time became clocked— are of being a small child and listening to the adults tell stories, their words competing with the TV" (6). Here storytelling and oral culture are opposed to television; Tsiolkas opens the novel by insisting on the possibility of narrative forms that pre-exist and offer an alternative to what will be an increasingly addictive medium. The novel's opening scene—a vision of crows on a beach devouring the organs of what we assume were livestock—also points to the role of myth as the framework Louie wants to evoke in order to tell a story that is ostensibly about his family, but primarily about his brother's fatal immersion in the toxicity of late capitalism, which will itself become the stuff of media mythology. "Myth," Louie stresses dismissively, aware of the ways in which myths impose their own fictions: "But in wishing to describe a family it would be ludicrous to deny it its myths. Memory and myth, like fiction, tend towards the cataclysm, the catharsis, the tragic and the painful" (7).

These comments, which have an almost metafictional quality, come to us in a preface. When the family history begins in earnest, the narrative voice switches to the third-person, with only occasional first-person interjections. It is 1975 and Gough Whitlam has just been sacked. The importance of the moment, itself the stuff of myth, to the novel's subsequent vision of alienation cannot be overstated. The dismissal of Whitlam's Labor government by the governor-general (the Queen's representative in Australia), after the opposition blocked its budget, is the pivotal moment in narratives that announce the end of the socialist orientation of the Australian Labor Party. A subsequent federal election gave power to the Liberal-National coalition. By the time the ALP was back in power, under Bob Hawke and Paul Keating, it was committed to privatization, deregulation and the rapid instrumentalization of higher education (which under Whitlam became entirely free, enabling a massive democratization of the tertiary sector). By the time Tsiolkas was working on the novel in the late 1990s, reactionary Liberal governments held office both federally and in his home state of Victoria. It was a time when the hopefulness of the early 1970s had been almost entirely eclipsed by a neoliberal hegemony. The fact that Louie's mother responds to the dismissal of Whitlam by calling for a revolution reminds us of the resigned manner in which Australian parliamentary democracy did in fact manage this moment of crisis: "There has to be war, thundered his mother. A revolution. She was excited, beneath the tears there was an excitement. This is a coup, this is another junta" (17). The ambience of working-class, immigrant militancy and of Richmond as a working-class neighborhood—"Across the street the factory was all banging and whirring of machines" (19)—takes us into the world threatened with extinction by suburban relocation and inner-city gentrification. Tsiolkas evokes the intensity of the moment: demonstrations, strikes and the sense of rage simmering over the asphalt surfaces of the city.

When the novel switches its focus to Tommy, the television is on and he is watching an Americanized version of the Christmas story. We already have a sense of his religious fixations (as a child he has an icon above his bed), but now we begin to sense the way in which the media will structure his inner life around a spectacularized but impoverished corporeality:

> Mary was blonde, an LA nymph. Joseph was soap-opera handsome, young and smooth.
> Tommy was thinking, sipping at his beer, how cheap Mary looked, what a cheap American slag. There was dancing in Jerusalem, the young Mary had just spotted the pretty Joseph. The camera cut back and forth, back and forth, to the blonde Mary with the silicon breasts, to the bearded Joseph with the sculptured chest. Their eyes met. Commercial break. (39)

That television, suburbia and visions of prosthetic femininity are tightly linked in this novel is clear when Tsiolkas takes us back to the family's relocation away from the inner-city, two years after Whitlam's sacking. Tommy sees *The Stepford Wives*, in which Katherine Ross is transformed into a "soft-porn goddess"—"Her eyes are dead. They are the only part of the flesh that remains of the real woman and they are lifeless" (48). The morbidity of the inorganic world represented by the movie offers Tommy the basis of a sexual fantasy, but also a numbed remoteness from the pain of his own dislocation:

> In the suburbs, where no-one walked at nights and where every home had a garden. The television was a connection with a previous life and he immersed himself in it. His old friendships were now a bus and a train ride away. So they stopped. The kids in the new school were strange. Only a very few had mothers who spoke with an accent. A sea of blondes, and he had become a foreigner in his own country. When Tommy saw *The Stepford Wives*, he was mesmerised. Because, scared of the sudden smashing of his world, he had only one desire. To not be hurt, picked on, accused. Tommy had decided to become a zombie. (48)

This complex, which clearly echoes a moment in Tsiolkas's own life, is at the center of Tommy's increasingly mediated identity. In a compulsively atomized existence, television offers a form of escape that might initially parallel the realm of private sexual fantasy. Their steady interpenetration, however, comes to structure a perversely mediated form of sexual empowerment related to Tommy's alienation and his sense of social redundancy. Like Ari, he is surfing the downward curve of capital. He works at a printing house that is on the verge of being restructured and rendered obsolete by digitalization. But unlike Ari, his response to his situation does not carry anything that a reader might be able to retrieve or to understand as positive or pleasurable. It is almost as if Tommy is being offered as a rereading or redescription of Ari that reveals not a sexual politics, but perversity as the point at which postmodern subjectivity confronts its disempowerment. Outside the processes of *Bildung*, there is no possibility of a meaningful interruption or a resistant negativity. What we are left with is the pathology of atomization.

Like *Loaded*, *The Jesus Man* is also a novel mired in the everyday: entropic urban and suburban landscapes, the tedium of public transport, the monotony of clock-time and media forms strung between banality and increasingly sexualized forms of violence. When Tommy reads the newspaper, he might as well be channel surfing: "A guy had murdered five children, blasted about thirty more, a place called Stockton in California. They seemed to be getting crazier over there. Another article on the Madonna and Sean Penn divorce. And a good picture of Gabriela Sabatini. Tommy loved the tennis. The legs, the photo had caught her legs" (53). It is already clear that the interface between suburbia and the media landscape structures a particular kind of need in Tommy: the alienation of work and the fleeting, though addictive pleasures of objectified, inorganic bodies form a vector that will be filled out and defined by pornography. Part of what makes the novel so confronting is the way in which Tsiolkas's prose recreates the violence of this space. As we enter into passages that are precariously suspended between interior monologue and a more conventional omniscience, the language of obscenity takes on its own kind of facticity. It evokes Tommy's perspective, but it also manages to break free of its moorings in the private life of a character to become the prism through which the reader is forced to see Tommy's interior drama. We get an early example of this when Tommy goes into an adult video store. The language Tsiolkas uses to describe the video packaging avoids any sense of euphemism. Instead it is crudely, and unapologetically, objectifying:

He moved slowly across the shelves. A black girl was being fucked by a black cock, sucking on a white cock. The white guy was old, grey and with a gut. The black guy was young and thick. The black girl had a shaved cunt. Thirty-nine dollars and ninety-five cents.

Piss, on the back of one slick, a white girl was getting pissed on. Another frame. She was squatting. Pissing.

A young bloke, dark-haired, entered the shop. He moved over to the back wall, the faggot wall. Tommy looked over. The faggot wall had a large poster of a man with a tremendous cock, a cock that fell to his knees. Tommy wondered what the cock would feel like to hold. To wank with, to use two hands to come.

He picked up another video, *Thai Sex Excursions*. He massaged his crotch. (57)

The emphasis on race in this passage, and some obvious lexical choices, do not simply describe the scene of pornography as Tommy encounters it, they create it on the page in a way that repeats its logic. It is as if both character and reader are trapped within a pornographic gaze that violently anatomizes the bodies in its field of vision. There is no attempt to insulate the writing from its ability to offend. Tsiolkas's prose, in other words, becomes a product, or a symptom, of the world it describes. But it also works as a clarification, or a distillation, of that world; an attempt to render explicit what remains implicit on television, or in a newspaper, or in the furtive glances that encounter anonymous bodies caught in their deadening routines. Pornography, and the violence of its objectification, seem to be latent in the everyday experience of late capitalism.

Tsiolkas's descriptions of Tommy watching pornography or immersed in his own imagination are difficult reading. What aggravates this is Tommy's propensity to seize on tabloid crime as the basis of his own fantasies. When he watches a news story about a missing schoolgirl, he wonders how he would go about abducting a child and what he would do: "he would blindfold her and just keep her in a room, just for a few days. He would just get her to suck him off, slap her if she refused, he'd just fuck her, a few times. Just to see what it was like. A girl's cunt, hairless, smooth, tight" (60). Later, when he hears a newscast reporting the discovery of the abducted girl's body, a voyeuristic interest in the horror of the crime produces both arousal and shamed disavowal: "her tortures were referred to obliquely and therefore seemed even more tantalising. Was her corpse sodomised? The torture is unimaginable, thought Tommy. His eyes were moist, her suffering was tragic. But it was also perverse. His eyes were moist, he was conscious of his cock" (80). This moment is quickly subsumed into the informational flow of the zero medium, in which virtually everything else becomes the inconsequential backdrop of Tommy's somatic reactions: "The story ended. Christopher Skase to buy United Artists. Oliver North on trial. Eleven million gallons of oil in Prince William Sound, somewhere off the Alaskan coast. Football and the prediction of rain, rain throughout the weekend" (80–81). The problem here is a familiar one in Tsiolkas's fiction. Aside from his own physical reactions to things, Tommy cannot locate himself in regard to the world beyond himself. Having dispensed with the idea of cartography and navigation that at least gave Ari the semblance of a cognitive project, *The Jesus Man* fixates on the interior conflict between Tommy's violent, misogynistic form of sexual empowerment and his sense of shame at his own abjection.

In this respect, Tommy embodies at least one version of the interior life of late capitalism. It is a disturbed, exclusively male version, to be sure, but the novel is clear in its sense of Tommy as somehow representative, even if it isn't quite clear on the implications of the sort of symptomatic representation it develops. Tommy is the fodder of late capitalism, the redundant material of a downsizing industrial system. When he loses his job as a result of restructuring and his inability to adapt to new technologies, the novel intensifies his, and its, rage around an unnerving collision of race and sexuality. It is Tommy's alienation that produces forms of fetishization that almost instantaneously generate objects of resentment and violence. In the white noise of the media an Aboriginal man on death row in the United States—for the rape and murder of a "blonde woman"—becomes an ambiguous point of identification through which Tommy can imagine a sexualised revenge on the institutions that have made him obsolete. He wanders through a city that "screamed his exile" until he ends up with a prostitute in a scene—played out largely in Tommy's imagination that makes these identifications clear. The sentence "The Aboriginal man rapes and kills a blonde woman" cues the scenario and stresses its emblematic qualities.

> He closed his eyes and drifted far into the fantasy, imagining himself black and violent, the woman on her knees before him someone he could kill. It would be so easy, she was so young, so soft. Slowly his torso jerked forward, forward to his fantasy, rapid thrusts into the prostitute's mouth. He imagined the Aboriginal man above the bleeding body of the blonde, her face bruised, her lips fat, her cunt raw, shitting herself. Fucking her from behind. Fucking her so hard she was bleeding. (126)

The passage reproduces the objectifying, racializing logic we have already seen at work in Tsiolkas's prose. That Tommy identifies with an Indigenous Australian implies its own fraught processing of Australia's colonial history.[29] The implications here are as predictable as they are problematic. If Tommy's rage appropriates images of frontier violence mired deep in the colonial imaginary, it also reanimates a racism that imagines sexual violation as an act defined by the color line; black men avenging themselves on white women. As confronting as the above passage is, it isn't yet the climax of a scene that identifies penetration with murder. Nor is it the point at which Tsiolkas's language is at its most violent and dehumanizing. As the passage continues, it becomes almost intolerable for the reader, but also for the novel itself, which implicitly acknowledges that there is no way out for Tommy, no way back from the pathology of this moment.

The sense of psychic distress that drives Tommy's story intensifies when he meets an obese evangelical Christian distributing leaflets on the street. The man, Neil, reflects his own negative body image. He also shares Tommy's addiction to pornography and, it turns out, his longing for the cataclysm: annihilation as the only possibility of redemption. But that is not all the two share. When Tommy discovers Neil performing oral sex on his younger brother, he is returned to a traumatic moment in his own childhood in which, in a moment of experimentation, he has his younger brother—Louie, the framing narrator—perform oral sex on him. These details do not come to light until later in the novel, but even their intimation in Tommy's encounter with Neil is enough to establish guilt in transgression not only as the bond they share, but as the basis for a kind of doubling, or mirroring effect. Neil, it seems, wants Tommy to kill him. He understands that his death is the only escape from the obscenity of his body. Tommy's hatred of Neil is, in turn, a hatred of himself. As he nears his impending implosion his world is dominated by the "shuddering light" of the television, which is always on, and the mirrors which taunt him with the sight of his own body. When he masturbates to pornography the icon on the top of the television set is there to castigate him, but it is primarily through the abjection of Neil's existence that Tommy recognizes himself. Neil's prayer room has semen stains encrusted on its walls. When Tommy discovers sadistic child pornography and newspaper clippings about the abductions and murder that have appeared earlier in the novel, it is clear that he can see some possibility of absolution in the idea of killing Neil. Tommy's story ends in a mire of religious rhetoric and psychotic delusion. He murders Neil and then, with a shard of glass from a smashed mirror, castrates himself. Suicide is redemption, a casting off of his diseased, obscene flesh.[30] At the point of his death the smiling eyes of the virgin forgive him. That Neil will turn out to be Indigenous returns us to the vague sense that Tommy's self-loathing is channeled through his (dis)identification with racialized notions of violence and abjection.

Everything that comes after Tommy's suicide feels anti-climactic. The novel continues for another 170 pages, struggling to complete itself. When we return to Louie's first-person voice, Tommy's death has become fodder for an exploitative tabloid media, and the Stefano family is forced to experience itself through the lens of mass media sensationalism. At the same time Louie's voice meanders through familiar territory: his enthusiasm for music, the low-key moments of political engagement that evoke a fairly tepid undergraduate milieu, the confessional loneliness, and excitement, of homosexuality. Aside from the revelation that Tommy and Louie had had oral sex with each other, there is little in the way of plot development to hold the reader's attention, although Louie's formulaic attention to Indigenous issues and politics— "there's got to be compensation for what the Europeans did to the black man" (336)—seems to underline the sense in which Tommy's inner life has been mediated through a largely racialized imaginary in which colonial history and immigrant identities are problematically linked. But without the pathology of Tommy Stefano, the novel quickly becomes both impressionistic and essayistic, especially when Louie gets to explain his thesis project. It speaks volumes for a publisher's confidence in Tsiolkas that he was able to publish so much, so early in his career, that works in this way. At moments Louie's voice reminds us of the wandering dialogues in *Jump Cuts*, which received mixed reviews a few years before.[31] His thesis on the media clearly draws on his own experience of his brother's death. It is as if Tsiolkas, after taking his readers through one of the most harrowing and confrontational ordeals in recent Australian writing, is eager to provide a sort of conceptual debrief. "I hate the media," Louie tells us: "They have made their image my last memory of my brother [...] The most astounding thing I discovered in those first few hallucinatory months was how the story being communicated in the news is so removed from your everyday experience" (314).

Tsiolkas's attempt to take us beyond Tommy's story is palpable. It is as if the novel, having descended into the abyss of pathology, in which it becomes thoroughly compromised by the violence it represents, has to secure a form of discourse, or critical reflection, that allows it to rejoin the world of public political-cultural dialogue. Tsiolkas seems to know that he has to lead the reader away from the moment of Tommy's death, that he has to work through it toward a form of narrative closure, if not reconciliation. And yet he cannot seem to produce anything capable of nullifying that moment of trauma. The result is a startling lack of formal cohesion. The implicitly autobiographical dimension of Tommy's story makes this all the more urgent. By the time the novel was released, most dedicated readers of Tsiolkas's work would have known enough about him to relate Tommy's story to aspects of his own life. The material in *Jump Cuts*, the book on *The Devil's Playground*, and the recently published interviews in John Vasilakakos's *Christos Tsiolkas: The Untold Story*, can leave no doubt about this. *Jump Cuts* tells us that Tsiolkas had been "seduced into the world of evangelical thought" in his early puberty. We also learn that at the age of fifteen he set up a baptismal icon and a shrine of flowers in his bedroom.[32] When his family moved to the outer suburbs, his life looked very similar to Tommy's:

> For two years I was insomniac when my parents moved from inner-city Richmond to suburban Box Hill. At first I thought my sleeplessness was caused by the silence of the streets and the darkness of a suburban night. But it was the battle with the Devil that made sleep impossible. I resisted masturbation for as long as I could, often reading till four or five in the morning, or getting up to watch late-night television. But finally the moment came when I would flick off the screen or put down the paperback and my body would go crazy. My head would fill with fantasies of boys and men, my cock would stiffen and my hands would grab. I tried everything to deny wanking, prayers scratched at my body until I bled.[33]

These moments seem to resonate with the way in which Tsiolkas describes the character of Turner, in *The Devil's Playground*, as a reflection of his own anxieties about his sexuality. Turner's interest in mortification leads Tsiolkas to describe his desire to "eliminate homosexuality": "ripping my skin, to get at the disease, to flush it out [...] I don't want to make light of how overwhelming the desire to kill my instincts was at the time."[34]

While these details create an unmistakable autobiographical resonance, what is more striking than incidental similarities between character and author is the fact that so much of Tsiolkas's non-fiction is confessional in orientation. He couches it with a particular emphasis on truthfulness, as if the urge to confess is almost an involuntary one. The self-lacerating style of his autobiographical revelations is reflected in the unflinching way in which he reveals the inner workings of his characters. The style of his autobiography is, in other words, the same style that we get in his fiction. Hence the moment in *Jump Cuts* at which he takes us to the private hell of his perverse sexual-political fantasies involving pedophilia, bestiality and racism: "I have no secrets. I will not lie [...] We have raped, we have tortured, we have humiliated the angels and the demons in this room."[35] Is there any doubt that the extremes of Tommy's sexual fantasies, or the abjection of Neil's prayer room, at least figure this confessional space that Tsiolkas claims (on behalf of us all) as his own? In an extremely revealing comment to John Vasilakakos, Tsiolkas says that he wrote *Loaded* almost in a state of "euphoria"—as an outpouring of fury.[36] The impression one has reading Tommy's narrative in *The Jesus Man* might not suggest the euphoria of authorship, but it does conjure a vision of writing as the compulsive recording of fantasies not yet inoculated against traces of racism and misogyny. The impact of *The Jesus Man* has a lot to do with this sense of the author unable to keep himself off the page, unable to escape the relay between corporeality and textuality. That Tsiolkas felt compelled to keep the novel going well beyond the moment of Tommy's death, however, feels like an anxious attempt to displace, by way of contextualization or misdirection, a traumatic *jouissance* that simply cannot be contained by the discourses that are ostensibly about it. *The Jesus Man*, in other words, cannot live down its own moment of rupture, the cut in the text that is the endpoint of Tommy's narrative.

If *Loaded* and then *Head On* had made Tsiolkas the sign of a difference that was readily assimilable into public discourse, *The Jesus Man* intensified that difference into a perversity that was in excess of what could be made publicly intelligible, at least to a mainstream audience. The novel implies a model of authorship at odds with the one increasingly mandated by commercial publishing, in which an orientation to the marketplace implies a form of self-discipline that apparently underwrites the formal quality or craftsmanship of the textual commodity. Moments in *The Jesus Man* feel much more spontaneous than this. It is as if they had been written in a state of uncontrollable hatred or arousal, as if authorship were, as Friedrich Kittler says of modernism, either a "simulacrum of madness" or the expression of a nervous condition.[37] The novel's destructive ethos vastly exceeded *Loaded*, even if the seeds of Tommy Stefano were already present in Ari's negativity. Whether it was the youth-oriented notion of grunge, a more durable sense of the multicultural, or finally an emerging notion of queer negativity, *Loaded* had qualities that enabled it to work within the bounds of public discourse, and potentially to reshape them. *The Jesus Man*, by contrast, reshapes difference into an absolute and uncompromising kind of alterity linked to obscenity and an illiberal, sexualized rage. And yet the novel insists that illiberality is also implicit in the everyday experience of late capitalism. It is central to the culture we inhabit, and to the fantasies that culture circulates.

This notion of illiberality also plays a role in Tsiolkas's first excursion into the world of the theater. Tsiolkas became involved with the Melbourne Workers Theatre through Andrew Bovell, who had already worked on *Head On*. Together with Bovell, Patricia Cornelius, Melissa Reeves and the composer Irina Vela, he wrote *Who's Afraid of the Working Class?*, which was first performed in May 1998 in the Victorian Trades Hall. The work consists of four interspersed scripts that collectively conjure a disconcerting vision of the working class in a state of crisis that, as the play's director Julian Meyrick puts it, emblematized the "vast betrayal the Kennett Government had perpetrated on all Victorians."[38] Meyrick's writing on the play and its production history evokes the traces of a working-class identity—the fragments of a population that has not quite vanished into the demoralizing homogeneity of late capitalism, but is just about to. In 1997, he tells us, "the writers and composers went to a pub in West Melbourne famous for its vibrant, resistive, blue-collar atmosphere. What they found was a commercial shell, rattling with cable TV and pokies."[39] The moment seemed to confirm the collapse of a politicized, proletarian culture. As Meyrick went on to write, the loss of a certain idealism, or hopefulness, around working-class agency informed the pessimistic mood of the play: "The notion that working-class struggle was the conduit to general emancipation was on the slide, and what was replacing it was something altogether more fragmented, frightened and confused. Marxism talks a lot about 'contradictions' but the reality of lives pulled apart by opposing forces is anything but a philosophical conundrum."[40] This sense of a re- or disorganization of working-class life is also evident in the history of the Melbourne Workers Theatre itself, which had moved from a company initially housed in the Jolimont railyards (on the eastern edge of the city center) and dedicated to bringing politicized theater to the workers themselves, to a company that had had its identity "substantially renegotiated," as Alan Filewood and David Watt put it, partly because of the way its relationship to union politics had changed. The company moved away from "shop-floor performance" and started to lose its specific focus on a "trade union model of working-class experience," replacing it with "a larger, functional 'working experience' model."[41]

For Tsiolkas the crisis of proletarian experience and politics seems to have been pronounced as he began working with Bovell, Cornelius, Reeves and Vela. This was also the period of Pauline Hanson and One Nation. Marginalized, working-class Australians seemed to be flocking to a facile racism that channeled their insecurities into an identification with a demagogue. The short story "Civil War," initially published in 1995 and republished in *Merciless Gods*, directly raises these dynamics in its frightening vision of white, working-class Australians organizing for a race-war against Australia's Indigenous population.[42] Talking about the political underpinnings of *The Jesus Man*, Tsiolkas is very clear about this: "The working class, by Louie's time, is the Hansonite class."[43] This idea is evident in the ease with which Tommy Stefano's resentment drifts into violent racial and misogynistic fantasy. Similar themes are evident in Tsiolkas's contribution to *Who's Afraid of the Working Class?* In both works this sense of the working class becoming "Hansonite" should not be taken in a literal sense, even if that is how Tsiolkas intended the comment. Rather it suggests the way in which working-class marginalization, disenfranchisement and disorganization have funnelled people into a set of identifications that are in fact antithetical to their interests. We can see this idea played out in the infamous "Kennett Boy Monologue" that opens the play. Here working-class alienation produces both a sexual and a political identification with Jeff Kennett. The Kennett Boy sees his working-class parents as losers; the "brain dead" remnants of a class that has lost its relevance. By contrast he is awed by Kennett's ruthlessness, power and ability to inflict his will on the body politic. Kennett seems to revivify the sort of patriarchal authority absent in this own father:

> Kennett doesn't give a shit about anyone, does whatever he likes. He even stands up to that ugly piece of shit, Howard. And that's the leader of his fucking party! Kennett is a legend. Bet my old man wouldn't mind being like that, instead of following orders all his fucking life. Weak cunt! Just a day, just one day, I'd like to see my father be like Kennett. Just fucking once.[44]

For the Kennett Boy, this authority is also sexually attractive. Kennett becomes a prop in a fantasy scenario that allows sexual obsession to evoke (and displace) other forms of identification. He wants to "go down" on Kennett. He masturbates over the thought of being covered in Kennett's semen. He wants to fuck Kennett. The mania of these identifications does not seem ironic. That is not Tsiolkas's style. If the monologue is excessive and the Kennett Boy an implausible, even absurd creation, its point is impossible to miss. In the absence of a viable narrative of working-class agency capable of engaging with or displacing a dominant conservatism, class-based resentment seems to turn against itself. The Kennett Boy, unable to reconcile his queerness and his class background and unable to extract a viable politics from his father's generation, ends up wallowing in his rage, which produces a negativity that neoliberalism effortlessly coopts into its vision of aspirational individuality. If *Loaded* had implicitly rejected the idea of *Bildung* and the form of the *Bildungsroman* as a model of regulative social integration, what Tsiolkas offers now is barbarity as the basis of a violently competitive society.

The monologue is clear about the ways in which its identifications are founded on the apparent impossibility of reconciling desire with a recognizable working-class politics, which now seems characterized by its lack of agency and efficacy. When the Kennett Boy recalls going to an anti-Kennett rally with his parents, the thrill of being empowered by the collective generates an irrational enthusiasm vastly in excess of what the occasion can encompass. The Kennett Boy's rage spills over the limits of the political forms available to it and becomes, in the absence of anything else that can accommodate it, sociopathic.

I loved being there in all that mass. I thought we could do anything, fucking pull apart this shithole of a city if we wanted. I wanted it to get angrier, I wanted it to get bloody, like it happens on the news overseas. The cops were there, waiting. I wanted it to get bloody, so I could bash some cunt cop right in the middle of his fat, ugly face. I wanted to kill a cop, then go right off and torch fucking Chinatown. That would have been a fucking winner, man. Kill a cop and kill a gook. But it wasn't that kind of rally. It was [*contemptuously, in an effeminate accent*] political.[15]

Resentment becomes racism, a will to violence with no sense of the sort of solidarity that might in fact foster a viable political opposition. A little later the Kennett Boy recalls seeing Jeff Kennett himself looking out from Parliament House, unmoved and unperturbed, and at that moment Kennett becomes a way of imagining his repressed queerness and a way out of the quietism he sees embodied in his parents. This is what I think Tsiolkas means with the comment that the working class has become the Hansonite class: it is resentful, disorganized and hence ready to have its discontent directed out through a residual set of prejudices that work against its interests.

Elsewhere in the play Tsiolkas gives us a different version of this idea, one that resonates uncomfortably with *The Jesus Man*. In scene one of "Suit," he shows us an encounter between an Aboriginal insurance salesman (Jamie) and a prostitute (Claire). Here the racial tensions (and anxieties) of Australian society, foregrounded in a subsequent scene, seem manifest in a recursive misogyny that has Jamie systematically humiliate Claire, even as she role plays a kind of bigotry that seems essential to his moment of climax. To make sense of this, we can only assume that Jamie's sexuality has been woven into a sort of sadomasochism that, on the one hand, plays out a fantasy of dominating and humiliating white women, and, on the other hand, simultaneously confirms his identification with colonial visions of Aboriginality. That the collision of political history and sexual desire produces a profound mystification of Jamie's experience, and an avoidance of the fairly obvious fact that he and Claire are both marginalized figures, seems to be the point. As in the "Kennett Boy Monologue" we are trapped in the pathology of a character whose inability to locate himself in a viable political narrative manifests in a sort of sexualized hatred both of Claire and of himself. This is also, of course, Tommy Stefano's story. In fact, Tsiolkas's contribution to *Who's Afraid of the Working Class?* feels as if it is in a fairly close dialogue with *The Jesus Man*, right down to the spurious religious epiphany with which it concludes. Here Jamie encounters Gina De Stanzos. She is the wife of Sammy De Stanzos, the father of the Kennett Boy in the opening monologue. Gina is on the street, mourning her dead son. In what is a deliberate attempt to alienate an Anglophone audience, she speaks her native language throughout the piece: "Italian or Greek, depending on the actor," so the stage directions tell us. One can only imagine the surreal (non)conversation that ensues between two people who must seem to be communicating through gesture and intonation, rather than a shared language. Gina tells Jamie about her dead son. Jamie tells her he has been retrenched. As the radio news reports on a "work for the dole" scheme, the discovery of a body in Dandenong (possibly the body of Gina's son) and a Hamas attack in Jerusalem, Gina's prayers get louder. Finally she strips and walks into a white light. This is a moment of ascension. She has joined the God that both she and Jamie believe to be white. What are we to make of this? The moment of redemption contrasts strongly with the hate-filled hopelessness of the "Kennett Boy Monologue," and yet one suspects that, as solutions to the political and economic structures foregrounded in the play as a whole, religion (a white god) and Jeff Kennett are similarly delusional.

What is not delusional is the materiality of the kind of political drama practiced by the Melbourne Workers Theatre. Here was a space largely free of the media forms that play such a malevolent role in Tsiolkas's novels. *Who's Afraid of the Working Class?* might not be a call to arms, but it at least coordinates a view of disenfranchisement and alienation in a way that gestures at the potential forms of solidarity eroded by neoliberalism. Tsiolkas's involvement with the company would be ongoing. He co-wrote *Fever* (2002) with Bovell, Cornelius, Reeves and Vela, and *Non Parlo di Salò* (2005) with Spiro Economopoulos, both of which were performed by the company. The political content of these plays may well be less important than their contribution to a media form uncompromised by the homogenizing, alienating effects of the culture industry. One of the starkest paradoxes of Tsiolkas's career is that while many of his characters seem lost to the violence of their own alienation, Tsiolkas himself has been able to work in contexts that assume the collaborative, democratizing structures absent in his novels. Tommy Stefano, Jamie and the Kennett Boy are all victims of economic rationalization, subsumed by the machine, and doomed to a negativity that devours the communal structures Tsiolkas ultimately wants to summon. The ways in which their experiences are disorganized and pitted against their own interests emerge with a clarity that suggests Tsiolkas's commitment to excavating the context of mystification in which proletarian life has become largely disabled as a meaningful political force. The anger of his characters and of his writing should be read as deliberately ill-tempered testimony to this vanishing horizon and the sense of impotence its absence engenders.

Chapter 3

THE PORNOGRAPHIC LOGIC OF GLOBAL CAPITALISM: *DEAD EUROPE*

That pornography exemplifies the processes of commodification is a truism. What distinguishes it from other manifestations of commodity culture is that it also stands at the outer edge of what our society is prepared to accept in the name of the commodity. For this reason it is internal to the liberal-capitalist order but also appears as a limit case that tests the boundaries of its tolerance. It is the "obscene underside" of the economic relations most of us take for granted. In *The Metastases of Enjoyment*, Slavoj Žižek uses this phrase, "obscene underside," in a wide-ranging discussion of the paradoxes of communal identity. He argues that, via the conduit of what he calls "solidarity-in-guilt," the foundation of community consists in practices that transgress the (moral) law that also regulates community.[1] Žižek finds this process in the carnivalesque inversions of traditional patriarchal societies. As the "public Law" casts off its "patriarchal dress" and assumes a "neutral-egalitarian" character, however, inversion becomes bound up with the rehearsal of an apparently disavowed authoritarianism. "What now erupts in the carnivalesque suspension of the 'egalitarian' public Law," he writes, "is precisely the authoritarian-patriarchal logic that continues to determine our attitudes, although its direct public expression is no longer permitted. 'Carnival' thus becomes the outlet for the repressed social *jouissance*: Jew-baiting riots, gang-rapes ...".[2] The use of a word like "erupts" in this context seems to localize these expressions of "repressed social *jouissance*"; it gives them the character of occasions or events (riots, rapes) that punctuate the everyday, but do not really belong to it. In a consumer society increasingly mediated by constant access to the Internet, this sense of eruption belies the ways in which repressed *jouissance* secretes through very banal, and seemingly perpetual, acts of consumption. The fact that violent pornography is only a screen or a mouse click away for most consumers in the West effectively normalizes it, rendering it entirely unexceptional, without attenuating the sense in which it violates communal notions of propriety. It is as if the contradictions of the social order have been regularized and genuinely democratized. In capitalist societies, where economic processes are underwritten by forms of objectification, coercion and violence that are often at odds with a professed liberalism, the everyday consumption of objectified bodies brings the imaginative life of the consumer into constant contact with an authoritarianism that makes him (the gendering of the pronoun seems unavoidable) the bearer of the process Žižek describes.

Even in situations where the production and consumption of pornography has little to do with exploitative and dangerous work practices, representations of violence or violence itself, this point still holds. We do not have to believe that representations are equivalent to acts—that, as Parveen Adams puts it, "pornography and rape," "a fantasy and a crime," are one and the same, although they may well be—in order to understand that pornography occupies a threshold.[3] Even in its most mundane forms, pornography embodies the logic of objectification; it infringes on a version of the human in a manner that is understandably disconcerting, at least from the perspective of a liberal public sphere that has always relied on the fiction of a disembodied subject freed from its economic and biological determinants. The myths of intimacy that have defined Western culture since the early nineteenth century— and that are almost exactly coterminous with the shift from an explicitly patriarchal to a "neutral-egalitarian" sense of the law—have no place for an erotics of objectification that, throughout the nineteenth century, would lose its associations with older notions of libertinage and become increasingly associated with abnormality.

It is clear that the connotations around pornography change radically depending on the media that produce it. This is not the place to rehearse a history of pornographic media, but it is worth pointing out that before the popularization of the Internet, at a time when pornographic material was still predominantly sold in bookshops or shown in cinemas, its political connotations could be very different from what we might imagine today. As recent work on post-war publishing has shown, presses like Grove in New York and Olympia in Paris were able to integrate pornographic material into a broader conception of aesthetic and political radicalism precisely because of the sense in which obscene material presented a challenge to the norms of bourgeois intimacy that were mired in the conservatism of the 1950s and a cold-war consensus. As Loren Glass has shown us, the Grove list managed to conflate very different figures and ideologies into a syncretic sense of nonconformity that had a lot to do with battling censorship and publishing hitherto banned or demonized writers. Grove articulated a relationship between experimental literature and the forms of sexual experimentation that informed what Glass calls the "popular politics of sexuality in the 1960s."[4] D.H. Lawrence, Henry Miller, William Burroughs and Jean Genet all became Grove bestsellers, but Grove also published the Marquis de Sade and did a thriving trade in Victorian pornography.

The identity of the press hinged on eliding the differences between these versions of "obscene" writing.[5]

For those of us born in the late 1960s, and no doubt for an earlier generation of baby boomers, these connections between political, aesthetic and sexual experimentation had an institutional solidity that is probably absent today. They were rehearsed in the logic of literary and academic publishing and in classrooms that, for a while at least, tried to become sites of a kind of avant-garde intellectual life. Today, it is difficult to believe that a text like Georges Bataille's *Story of the Eye* was standard undergraduate reading in the mid-1980s. In many ways Tsiolkas and Soldatow's *Jump Cuts* is an echo of this moment. It reminds us that Tsiolkas's life and career in fact spans the period in which pornography has migrated from the realm of print-culture to the digital and has thus largely lost a sense in which it might have been understood in relationship to other forms of "transgressive" cultural expression and to the debates around them. I am dwelling on this because it is important to understand that Tsiolkas's early novels (up until *Dead Europe*, say) contain the sedimented traces of this recent past in which something like a pornographic sensibility might have signified a broader critique of bourgeois society.

I will argue later that Tsiolkas's uneasy passage into the mainstream of Australian (if not global) literary culture has a lot to do with managing what seems to be a residual interest in pornography and the discourses around it. But I want to dwell on the relationship between pornography and experimental writing a little longer because I think it is important to understanding the aesthetic context of Tsiolkas's work and its ability to generate its own sort of formal density, which is partly what enables it to assert its distance from other forms of social and economic production. In the immediate wake of 1968, J.G. Ballard, William Burroughs and Pierre Guyotat—to take three quite different figures—produced highly experimental texts that seem to depend at least partly on their incorporation of obscene or pornographic elements. In the work of these writers, explicitness about sex and the body not only overshoots the demands of narrative and characterization but dissolves these altogether in the constitution of a new sort of writing that assaults the pieties and practices of conventional literary fiction as well as the apparently self-evident assimilation of the aesthetic into the marketplace that Fredric Jameson identifies as a crucial aspect of late capitalism. According to Jameson, postmodernism—"the cultural logic of late capitalism"—is typified by the fact that aesthetic production, once at least apparently autonomous in regard to the market, "has become integrated into commodity production generally."[6] In these circumstances, literary uses of pornography can have a critical function that goes beyond a fairly predictable, and sometimes disingenuous, rejection of bourgeois taste and behavioral norms (often with Reichian overtones). While literary uses of pornography position texts in terms of both a specific market niche and a broader vision of the market as a desiring machine that diffuses the pornographic impulse through more mundane forms of commodity culture, the textual production of a world saturated by obscenity can also reconstitute an autonomous space that disassociates itself from immediately recognizable, quotidian forms of cultural consumption precisely because of the extreme and uncompromising manner in which it appropriates their logic. Texts that work like this also tend to alienate the readers they attract, as if they are deliberately trying to complicate the possibility of their own consumability. They offer the stage on which the subject of a profane consumer culture comes into view via a sort of *Verfremdungseffekt* bound up with the "shock" of the obscene. In this respect, the literary appropriation of pornography may well be a specific instance of commodity culture, but it also pushes the logic of commodification to an extreme that reveals its inherently inhuman character. It is as if we are reading texts ravaged by the *jouissance* that Žižek describes. For this reason the pornographic also seems to symptomatize a general sense of disintegration, or even traumatization, that is latent in the fabric of modern life, yet so self-evident in these texts that it no longer needs to be referred to anything in particular, beyond a general and nebulous sense of the damage caused by political and economic forces. What emerges here is the potential for catastrophe lurking in capitalism's contradictions. We are reading the literature of a not-too-distant future, which is also the literature of a disavowed present.

In *The Atrocity Exhibition*, for example, Ballard's "mimeticization" of atrocity in the psychogeographies of suburbia has a clear political subtext that is evident in its ironization of the role played by images of the Vietnam war in the mediascape of the late 1960s. But this subtext only really emerges through the novel's interest in a perverse, prosthetic sexuality formed at the intersection of media technologies (obsessed with global catastrophe and conflict) and mundane, quotidian spaces. Ballard's subsequent novel, *Crash*, which he described later as the "first pornographic novel based on technology," set itself the task of exploring the "brutal, erotic and overlit realm that beckons more and more persuasively to us from the margins of the technological landscape." Pornography, for Ballard, "is the most political form of fiction" because it deals with "how we use and exploit each other, in the most urgent and ruthless way."[7] Both texts distill the logic of the everyday into an account of the violence and perversity encoded in its surfaces. In a very different, though no less experimental manner, the pornographic extremes of Burroughs's *The Wild Boys* turn on images of guerrilla warfare, pitted against the obscenities of power, that were central to the radical internationalism of the period. In France, around the same time, Pierre Guyotat produced his controversial text *Eden Eden Eden*, a sort of anti-novel set in the apocalyptic rubble of the Algerian war. Emily Apter describes it as a "revolutionary novel of 1968" in which "personhood is exploded into an expansive multiple: at once sexualized and textualized."[8] In the cases of all three writers, pornography evokes a terminally pathological social space and reconfigures our sense of the subject and the language appropriate to it. The result is a volatile textuality that summons the disfiguring logic of capitalist modernity.

In an Australian context, the extreme experimental element I am evoking here has never really existed, at least not as a consistent feature of the literary landscape. Novels like *The Jesus Man* and *Dead Europe*, however, owe a lot to it, in that they approach pornography as a way of opening up a broader engagement with the logic of capitalism and its capacity to generate catastrophe. The difficulty that contemporary critics and reviewers have in discussing Tsiolkas's work after *Loaded* (which has been comfortably assimilated into critical discourse via the relatively safe category of "grunge fiction") and before *The Slap* (which was almost immediately treated as an emblematic work of modern Australian fiction) has a lot to do with the broader difficulties in processing forms of fiction that explore the obscene. In Tsiolkas's case, a commitment to radical political critique *and* to the exploration of violent pornographic impulses and subcultures, has left critics floundering with the banalities of their own discomfort. A certain level of critical unease did not really hinder *Dead Europe*'s ability to win awards and the mainstream respectability they bring. It won the *Age* novel of the year and the Melbourne Prize for literature (though one suspects its failure to win the Miles Franklin Award reflected some degree of trepidation). Nevertheless one gets the sense that the novel's acceptance also required the persistence of incomplete or blinkered readings that foreground issues like multiculturalism, the immigrant experience, and old world-new world relations, not issues like sex tourism, prostitution and the violent libidinal impulses tethered to predatory forms of globalization. Indeed Tsiolkas himself has suggested that the reception of *Dead Europe* has tended to mainstream the work in a way that renders its deliberate exploration of pornography as a violent, exploitative process bound up with the "sphere of capital" questionable or contentious.[9] At the same time the novel has come to play an important role in academic discourse largely as a result of its ability to organize theoretically driven discussions that orient to topical issues like cosmopolitanism, spectrality, trauma, memory, governmentality and bare life.[10]

The much more polarized reception of *The Jesus Man* indicated just how difficult it is to engage with these issues within the insular space of mainstream reviewing. While the novel did receive a good deal of tepid praise for its courage and audacity, very few reviewers seemed to grasp the extent of its political engagement. It took Anthony Macris, author of the experimental novel *Capital, Volume One*, to explain the ways in which Tsiolkas explores the "media complex" and its ability both to transform and deform its subjects.[11] Probably more typical of the novel's reception was Cameron Woodhead's dismissal of it as "inexpertly drawn filth."[12] The divergence of opinion here turns, needless to say, on the question of the novel's relationship to pornography, but it also indicates just what a precarious undertaking it is to work so insistently at the limits of public acceptability. Fiction about the obscene always risks being infected by the discourses and representational practices it explores. Part of the controversy around novels like *The Jesus Man* and *Dead Europe* stems from the fact that they occupy this space and dramatize its tensions.

That *Dead Europe* returns to the pornographic sensibility of *The Jesus Man* indicates the urgency of the issues the earlier novel raises, but also a sense of Tsiolkas being personally implicated in them, or at least feeling as if he still has to think through their implications. Tsiolkas is very articulate about the political stakes of this: "from a young age I've been attracted to certain styles of writing and certain styles of art and communication, and the pornographic imagination has been part of that […] What pornography lays bare for me is the contradiction of desire and sexuality and this libertarian impulse that I have in me about sex and desire, and then the cruel commerce of the marketplace."[13] The sense of having to work through this contradiction gives both novels a large part of their narrative urgency, but we would do well to recall just how problematic *The Jesus Man* has been in Tsiolkas's conceptualization of his own career, which might explain the sense of wanting to return to the preoccupations of a novel that was largely misunderstood. In a 2013 *Meanjin* interview Tsiolkas says that the "commercial failure and mixed critical reception" of the novel engendered "a very dark period" in which he considered giving up writing. As he set to work on what would become *Dead Europe*, he also realized that this sense of failure was an inevitable part of the writer's vocation, one that could not in any way attenuate the compulsion informing his commitment to fiction: "what I discovered was that through the very process of writing I was exorcising my demons and my ghosts."[14]

This sense of exorcising demons points directly to the Gothic preoccupations of *Dead Europe*, but it also suggests the ways in which that novel is still caught up in, or perhaps haunted by, the libertarian impulse that cannot be easily (if at all) immunized against the cruelty of the marketplace in which it inevitably participates. One way of understanding the relationship between these two texts might lie in the literalization of monstrosity that drives *Dead Europe*. In *The Jesus Man*, Tommy cannot disentangle himself from the guilt-inducing, mediatized circulation of repressed social *jouissance*. He does not simply experience moments at which the public law is suspended. He embodies the indistinction between public law and its obscene underside. Since this indistinction is an expression of an underlying social logic, there is really no way of resolving the impasse that defines him. The fact that the novel struggles to find any convincing form of closure—other than Tommy's death and the protracted working-through it generates—indicates as much. It is as if the rigor of the novel's vision has hindered its ability to fashion the sort of cathartic narrative that one imagines readers of literary fiction would want. Literalizing the impasse of Tommy's character in a kind of monstrosity that seems to infect, possess or haunt changes the possibilities considerably. The Gothicism of *Dead Europe* localizes the predatory dimension of capitalism in a kind of monstrosity marked by a hunger that straddles the line between the literal and the figurative and that can ultimately be purged or expunged as a way of effecting closure. In this manner *Dead Europe* creates at least the formal illusion of a return to the human.

While this might involve a diminution of *Dead Europe*'s critical force, or at least its open-endedness, the transnational orientation of the novel also enables it to present a clearer account of the larger historical processes underpinning the condition Tommy embodies. In fact *Dead Europe*'s use of the vampire suggests the prescience of its engagement with the relationship between cosmopolitanism and global capitalism. It is precisely in the novel's foregrounding of the vampire as an avatar of the inhuman (or the abhuman) that it is able to displace a naïve, utopian sense of the cosmopolitan that is inevitably bound up with a fiction of human becoming. What *Dead Europe* confronts us with most emphatically is the radically heterogeneous quality of cosmopolitan experience and the forms of exploitation that account for this. This is what James Clifford calls "discrepant cosmopolitanism." When Clifford coined the phrase, he had in mind the "cultures of displacement and transplantation [that] are inseparable from specific, often violent, histories of economic, political, and cultural interaction."[15] Because these histories of interaction are frequently the same ones that, at least indirectly, underpin the cosmopolitan freedom and prosperity of affluent metropolitan centers, the study of discrepant cosmopolitanism often involves an understanding of how different sites in the global economy are related to each other. As Michael Davidson puts it—a bit more bluntly than Clifford—"the cosmopolitanism produced through globalization yokes together the elite and the abject, the globe-trotting business man or wealthy tourist, as well as the migrant laborer, sex worker, and political exile."[16] The ligatures of the transnational, in other words, are relationships of inequality that derive their legibility from the fact that they place mobile, de-nationalized populations in situations where they are not afforded the legal protections of citizenship. This is also the territory that Tsiolkas approaches in *Dead Europe*, in which exploitative relationships appear in the form of a sort of carnal capitalism with the literal consumption of bodies as a potential outcome. In this respect the novel belongs to a broader body of recent literature and cultural theory that has tried to dispel the neoliberal embrace of a global ethos in which the urge to move beyond the limits of the national is celebrated as an unconditional good.

Recent scholarship on the relationship between literature and globalization has shown us that the novel has never really been securely bound by narrow conceptions of national or regional space. With that in mind it makes little sense to evoke terms like "cosmopolitan," "global" or "transnational" as indexes of a break with an older conception of literary culture. Still, the way in which the field of literary studies uses these terms often assumes that they have a normative dimension that has only recently become apparent. What is at stake here are forms of textual practice that, in Shameem Black's words, "foster ethically resonant identifications with others" and thus revise residual forms of representation that hinge on various kinds of objectification.[17] This impulse is deeply humanist, and humanizing. And yet such inclusive conceptions of the human also underwrite the processes of colonialism and neo-colonialism in a way that constantly limits or qualifies notions of the human. As Pheng Cheah has argued, a universal notion of the human and the forces that threaten it—embodiments, in other words, of the inhuman—are the products of the same set of material relations. The inhuman, Cheah explains, suggests the "finite limit of man, a defective feature of human existence that is not *proper* to the true end of man but that we have thus far failed to control."[18] Hence "commodification, technology, totalitarian domination, and the like" are related to animals, ghosts, death and the subhuman, all of which have to be transcended in order to realize the freedom assumed as an ideal by cosmopolitanism.[19] But what Cheah emphasizes is that the human/inhuman dyad is part of a fantasy of cosmopolitan becoming that obviates the ways in which global capitalism can produce the human and inhuman simultaneously, precisely because the forms of production and accumulation it assumes are "based on inequality and the hierarchical division of means and ends."[20] Nowhere is this more evident than in fantasies of the global city as a site of cosmopolitan or multicultural identity. This wish-image often obscures its economic underpinnings; that is, its participation in what Saskia Sassen calls a "transterritorial marketplace" concentrating systems of financial control into a handful of metropolitan centers.[21] What emerges here is the inseparability of cultural cosmopolitanism and the institutions underwriting neoliberal economics on the one hand and, as Cheah points out, the parochial tendency to understand globalization's human effect in terms of the movement of people to specific, highly industrialized centers on the other. "This ruse," Cheah writes, "equates the power of transcendence with travel, mobility, and migration and tacitly establishes the metropolitan scene of multicultural recognition as the model for cosmopolitan freedom as such." The freedom associated with the metropolis, he goes on to say, "is not only inaccessible to the majority of the world's population [...] it is also severely undermined by the fact that the efficacy of these new cosmopolitanisms is generated by, and structurally dependent on, the active exploitation and impoverishment of the peripheral majorities."[22] What the "metropolitan scene of multicultural recognition" screens out are precisely those spaces that constitute the material substance of the transterritorial marketplace: its sites of industrial production, its zones of rapid and often violent deregulation, its processes of pauperization, and its networks of immigration, all of which create a vulnerable and often dislocated labor force without proper access to the public structures that might elsewhere guarantee the rights of citizenship that are supposedly enhanced by liberalized markets.

The sort of cosmopolitan fantasy Cheah dispels proliferates like a virus through forms of lifestyle, travel and entertainment journalism that readers of Australian newspapers know all too well. This is the privileged—the elite— side of a discrepant cosmopolitanism in which business travel and tourism are taken for granted and in which the everyday pleasures of cities like Melbourne and Sydney are partly bound up with their echoes (in restaurants, cafes and retail culture more generally) of European or North American cities. The familiarity of this scenario for Australian readers—the cosmopolitan city as a place where discernment and good taste run amok—is a crucial part of *Dead Europe*'s background. Tsiolkas ironizes or displaces metropolitan norms of taste and judgment by focusing our attention on a vision of the metropole that dramatizes the fissures and inequalities inherent within notions of cosmopolitan freedom. This sense of displacement or ironization develops through an examination of the inhuman potential that emerges at the very moment that older, national or regional formations are loosened by processes of economic liberalization. In this sense *Dead Europe* is, quite literally, a horror story of globalization in which discrepancies in rights, wealth and security generate populations that seem permanently exposed to violence and exploitation.

The novel tells the story of Isaac Raftis, a Greek-Australian photographer who goes to Europe, where he finds his sexual hunger morphing into a more literal form of hunger. This transformation turns out to be, in part at least, a reflection of his environment. Everyone, it seems, is preying on everyone else. Europe after the fall of the wall is a Hobbesian space—a war of all against all—in which commodification and exploitation are unhindered by the law. But Isaac's story is also a genealogy, a story about cultural and ethnic inheritance, and this works in concert with its exploration of cosmopolitan mobility to create a powerful vision of the nonsynchronicity at the heart of the contemporary. The split-frame organization of the novel creates a sense of Isaac's ancestry and his dislocated actuality moving inexorably towards each other. On the one hand, Isaac's family comes from a remote Greek village mired in archaic superstitions and violent prejudices. During the German occupation, Isaac's grandparents—Michaelis and Lucia Panagis—agree to hide a Jewish boy. They are paid in gold and jewels for this, and yet the boy's shelter amounts to little more than a form of imprisonment. He is hidden in the crypt of an old church, where he virtually starves in his own filth. Unable to conceive with Michaelis, Lucia has sex with the boy (it is a predictably abject encounter), falls pregnant as a result, and then urges her husband to murder him. This murder releases a curse in the form of a demon that lingers lovingly over Lucia and her son but destroys in turn the other infants of the village. The racial implications of this moment remain ambiguous, perhaps even a bit confused. The curse is the index of a crime, but it also embodies a vision of the Jew as malevolent, parasitic and ultimately vampiric. Isaac's vampiric tendencies result from this curse and thus have their origin (however vaguely conceived) in the prejudices of the European peasantry. They reference extreme xenophobia, a vanished, premodern world of superstition and the difficulty of adapting to modernity. But the vampire is, in some sense, also a projection of that world of prejudice, at least in so far as the novel raises the suspicion that the curse manifests the spirit of the murdered Jew. Other aspects of the novel—the obese and thoroughly venal Jewish "pimp" Syd, for instance—underline the presence of a residual anti-Semitism, even though Tsiolkas's desire to displace this seems just as emphatic.[23] Suffice it to say that the history of Isaac's family is mired in the inhuman world of blood, soil, ghosts and curses that cosmopolitanism is supposed to transcend. Isaac's visit to his mother's village seems to revive the family curse. The demon attaches itself to him, infects him and gradually manifests itself through him.

On the other hand, however, Isaac goes to Europe partly as a sex tourist. He pays for sex with a young Russian boy in Athens, and by the time he gets to Prague finds himself in a world that preys upon the discrepancies of Eastern Europe's rapid fall into the free market. In other words his position as a tourist and consumer also carries within it the traces of the vampire. We move between Isaac's present and the family history that has formed him until we understand the ways in which the vampire is the point at which these frameworks overlap or slip into each other. The vampire suggests a traditional, superstitious world anxious about its survival and a hedonistic, highly individualized subjectivity that has detached itself from land and people. It is as if Isaac is colonized both by the atavistic curse that lurks within him and by the libidinal, morally unaccountable forces driving the world of casinos, prostitution and strip-joints that he moves through as a consumer hungry for more extreme experiences. Graham Huggan captures this ambivalence precisely when, discussing Tsiolkas, he links the "vampire's traditional function as a folkloric embodiment of atavistic drives and instincts to its modern-day appearance as a destructive world citizen in which it is the 'folk,' in turn, who are preyed upon by a freewheeling but deeply alienated cosmopolitan elite."[24] Modern vampire phobias, he goes on to say, are "first and foremost, anxieties surrounding global circulation," a point that Ken Gelder and Paul Salzman make, though in a different register, when they read Isaac's journey as a latter-day iteration of the "Byronic Grand Tour" (which via John Polidori represents a tentative origin for Anglophone vampire literature).[25]

The logic of the novel begins to become clear in a section entitled "The Brothel of Prague," in which Isaac encounters an old friend from Melbourne, the photographer Sal Mineo. The reference to the actor Salvatore Mineo Jr., who appeared in *Rebel Without a Cause* and openly embraced his homosexuality in the late 1960s, gestures at Tsiolkas's interest in the relationship between queer identity and cinema. Tsiolkas's Sal, it turns out, has traded the aesthetic and the ethical dimension of high culture for the commercial payback of pornographic photography. At this point Isaac too begins to realize that the idealism of art that he had once associated with the city might be contingent on certain forms of metropolitan privilege. His naïve longing for the cultural grandeur and history of the European metropolis confronts the necrotic reality of a continent both mired in its past and suffocating in its present. The Prague Isaac once imagined has succumbed to the world of American fast food, urban alienation, prostitution and pornography. Its assimilation of consumer culture has created both banality and depravity. Against this background, Isaac's idealism looks anachronistic. "Do you know what contempt these blokes have for you, with your headstart in capitalism," Sal tells him in Prague. "Beauty and art and fucking politics. They'd sell their fucking children for a buck. And you want to talk about fucking aesthetics and ethics."[26] This part of the novel presents Prague as a city of sexualized consumerism: it is a network of pornographers, brothels and sex clubs. It also has a clear political subtext involving the creation of victim populations with limited rights before the law. In the midst of this, Isaac's sexual fantasies are inseparable from the violence that appears to be latent in his environment. When he masturbates over one of Sal's models, an adolescent called Milos, the vampiric dimension of his sexuality becomes clear: "When I closed my eyes I saw myself ripping into his taut, sweet buttocks, jamming into him […] I closed my eyes and now I was fucking him harder, he was bleeding. And as I imagined blood I felt waves of excitement and my thrashings became delirious as I imagined his face, bloodied and bruised. I could lick the blood, taste the blood, eat the blood, and as I imagined this, I roared out my orgasm" (192). This scenario anticipates a piece of pornographic theater that Isaac witnesses in a club designed to make well-dressed, cashed-up Europeans feel like libertines. Amidst a surfeit of decadent kitsch, including candlelight, Puccini arias sung by Maria Callas and half-naked waiters decked out in black trousers and suspenders, a female performer assumes the voice of an eleven-year old boy and narrates, with "smoky inflections" and the odd "operatic shriek," the moment of his "deflowering" (224–25). While this is happening her narrative is acted out onstage and the audience takes on an orgiastic character that culminates in a mess of hard currency and semen. But the violence of penetration is real, and though Isaac is excited, he also realizes that he is in hell. At this moment, he glimpses the demon that has followed him from his mother's village superimposed on the staged scenario.

> From where I stood, I could see the boy's face. His eyes were screwed shut, and every time Pano bucked into his frail body I could hear tight, pained grunts. His pain excited me. The boy's thin body shuddered and as I looked down at him it seemed that his skin had fallen away and his very bones were visible; and when I searched his face it had darkened, his hair was now black, not fair, and the gaunt face that leered up at me was looking straight into my eyes and his eyes were shining, they were laughing, and I knew those eyes, had always known those eyes. (226)

The image of the predator lurking within Isaac appears in the body of the victim. But the demon also carries a trace of the other victims (Jewish victims) that haunt the novel. This confluence of victim and predator (or the Jew as both victim and the source of a curse) generates the central ambiguity in the novel's treatment of Judaism.

This highly stylized scenario and its use of the narrative voice-over is also loaded with intertextual meaning that helps us to articulate its politics. It evokes the story-telling procuresses who provide verbal incitements to libertine violence in *The 120 Days of Sodom* and Pasolini's cinematic adaptation of it, *Salò*. It is an important allusion. In 2005 the play *Non Parlo di Salò*, which Tsiolkas co-wrote with Spiro Economopoulos, was performed by the Melbourne Workers Theatre. The play responds to the Australian banning of Pasolini's film, but it also brings to light the key role that Pasolini's exploration of power and sexuality plays in Tsiolkas's work. We have already seen how important Pasolini is to Tsiolkas's sense of radical cultural production. It would not be exaggerating to say that *Loaded*, *The Jesus Man* and *Dead Europe* are all written in the shadow of Pasolini. Tsiolkas, at least in retrospect, imagined the novels as a trilogy about the "failure of reconciling liberation and the body, of reconciling the individual and class" in the wake of communism's collapse.[27] We might think of this sort of statement as an echo of Pasolini's "Repudiation of the Trilogy of Life" in the midst of consumer capitalism's false tolerance.

What is important to grasp here is that Pasolini's *Salò*—the most controversial production of his career and the one that clearly resonated most strongly with Tsiolkas—is also a kind of renunciation. Hitherto Pasolini had been invested in the ambiguous relationship between sexual expression and the political potential of populations outside of or marginal to capitalist modernity; the rural populations of Southern Italy or the Roman sub-proletariat, for instance. His repudiation of the optimistic sensuality expressed in his trilogy responds to his mounting pessimism at the totalizing character of capitalism and its integration of the body into "the hedonistic ideology of consumerism and consequently of the American type of modernist tolerance," which he saw operating through "the production of superfluous goods, the imposition of consumer frenzy, through fashion, through the media (above all, through the imposing presence of television)."[28] The result was that the confluence of political idealism and sexual longing vested in the populations of "rural and paleoindustrial Italy" had disintegrated, precisely because these cultures had themselves been sublimated into and instrumentalized by capitalism. At his most vehement, Pasolini described this form of instrumentalization as so total that it amounted to a new kind of fascism. He saw its effects most obviously in the illusion of a sexual freedom that merely replicated the false freedom of capitalism's market technologies:

Today the sexual freedom of the majority is, in reality, a convention, an obligation, a social duty, a social anxiety, characteristic of the quality of the consumer's life that cannot be renounced. Therefore, the false liberalization of affluence has created a situation as much and perhaps more insane than that at the time of pauperism. In fact, first: the result of sexual freedom "bequeathed" by the power is a veritable and appropriate wide-spread neurosis. Ease has created an obsession, because it is an ease that has been "propagated" and imposed from above. This is due to the establishment power's tolerance which is directed solely at the sexual demands expressed by a conformist majority. It protects only the couple (not only, naturally, the conjugal one), and the couple has thus become a paroxistic condition instead of a sign of freedom and happiness (as it was in democratic hopes). Second: all that is sexually "diverse" is ignored or rejected with a violence equal only to that practiced by the Nazis of the *Lager* (no one even remembers that the sexually unorthodox ended up there).[29]

At least at this moment Pasolini can understand his own queerness as marginalized and victimized by the new, false tolerance of a fascistic consumerism. But he also believed that consumerism "approaches the extreme limit of anthropological degradation or genocide" because it has abolished older forms of morality that maintained the "sacredness" of others, of life itself. The continuity between fascism and consumer capitalism, it would seem, consists in a biopolitical materialism: "the lack of a sense of sacredness in the lives of others, and the end of every sentiment of sacredness in themselves."[30]

Salò allegorizes the integration of sexuality into these totalitarian structures. Its literal exploration of fascist excess is also supposed to evoke a much broader sense of the body becoming a form of "merchandise," a profane object, rather than a life invested with the sacred. In an interview conducted during filming, Pasolini described this sense of objectification as one of the central insights of Marxism: "Marx defines power as the force that merchandises the human being. The exploitation of one man by another is a sadistic relationship. It is not different if the wielder of it is a factory owner or a despot of another sort."[31] That Pasolini's use of male prostitutes has to linger in the background of these comments suggests the extent to which his own sexuality is also implicated in the structures he explores. Hence the force of his "repudiation" of "bodies" and "sexual organs" violated by the "consumerist establishment" also seems like a form of self critique. What he might once have imagined as a space of alterity has become another way of turning bodies into merchandise. From this perspective sexuality unmediated by power seems all but impossible. This is the world of *Salò* and of Sade's *The 120 Days of Sodom*. It is a world in which the body is the foundation of a sexual experience that merely extends (and intensifies) other forms of control and violence. As Giorgio Agamben puts it, discussing Sade's *The 120 Days of Sodom*, "the very physiological life of bodies appears, through sexuality, as the pure political element."[32] Like Pasolini, Agamben also sees the continuities between sadomasochism, fascism, and the broader organization of political life around the usability and disposability of bodies—what he refers to as bare life:

> Sade is as contemporary as he is because of his incomparable presentation of the absolutely political (that is, "biopolitical") meaning of sexuality and physiological life itself. Like the concentration camps of our century, the totalitarian character of the organization of life in Silling's castle—with its meticulous regulations that do not spare any aspect of physiological life (not even the digestive function, which is obsessively codified and publicized)—has its root in the fact that what is proposed here for the first time is a normal and collective (and hence political) organization of human life founded solely on bare life.[33]

Agamben's notion of bare life (or *homo sacer*) denotes something similar to, but more universal than, Pasolini's sense of the body as mere "merchandise." It is life (*zoē* as opposed to *bios*) that is effectively abandoned by the law, and hence may be killed (not sacrificed) with impunity.

In *Non Parlo di Salò*, Tsiolkas and Economopoulos clearly grasp these continuities when they echo the moment, near the start of Pasolini's film, at which the future victims of the four libertines are described as outside the law: "You herded, feeble creatures, destined for our pleasure; don't expect to find here the freedom granted in the outside world. You are beyond reach of any legality. No one knows you are here. As far as the world goes, you are already dead."[34] They also understand the ways in which Pasolini's film embodies a renunciation of a libidinal politics, precisely because it runs the risk of reproducing the very forms of oppression at the heart of sovereign power. At one point the Pasolini character in the play declares "the body fails at liberty every time" (29). The play uses Pasolini's career as a template for a contemporary form of political engagement, but also as a way of working through problems that Tsiolkas seems to inherit from his commitment to the confluence of radical sexual and political expression. The play works on many levels. It responds very directly to the Office of Film and Literature Classification's banning of the film in 1998, and reiterates enough of it (or its spirit) that Australian audiences unable to see *Salò* in the cinema could have treated the play as a rough substitute. It also puts Pasolini's career into an implicit dialogue with a contemporary Australian reality that seems utterly, depressingly moribund. In fact this aspect of the play constitutes one of Tsiolkas's most emphatic critiques of Australia's cultural conservatism, complacency and insularity. At the same time the play holds up the atrocities of Pasolini's film as a mirror that captures the horrifying reality that is excluded from the country's cultural and political consciousness (literally in the case of the film's banning).

Non Parlo di Salò moves between the filming of Pasolini's movie and the reflections of an Australian film student called Luke, who is outraged at the decision to ban *Salò*. In the first of these frameworks we encounter Pasolini as a character who gets to articulate the political and intellectual context of the film, but who also expresses a sense of his own redundancy in terms of this context. Tsiolkas and Economopoulos have Pasolini articulate a relatively direct and didactic defense of the film, and at these moments we can hear both Pasolini's voice (as we know it from his essays, for instance), and Tsiolkas's voice, which seems to speak through Pasolini. The sense of doubling is worth dwelling upon. It is clear that Tsiolkas has used Pasolini's thinking as a framework for his own and that in many ways he sees himself as an iteration of Pasolini. It is thus unsurprising that his own voice (in novels and essays) sounds like Pasolini's. But here that sense of indistinction is driven to a point at which the two voices are completely conflated. Pasolini becomes a persona—a mask—through which Tsiolkas can speak. Pasolini's "repudiation" becomes a mirror of the dynamic that has informed Tsiolkas's own work and a way for Tsiolkas to reflect on his own society.

> Am I a pornographer? I thought the body was the last site remaining uncontaminated by the reach of capitalist consumption. So I returned to books and stories that predated capital. *The Decameron*, *The Canterbury Tales* and *The Arabian Nights*. It was romantic. It was short-sighted. The trilogy I made now sickens me. How many millions of images of the carnal can there be? How many bodies captured, exposed, exchanged? What is it the body will not sell? I have learnt to abhor the body. I now detest youth. (*Pause*)
>
> My despair led me to de Sade. He reveals the truth that the romantic imagination is ultimately fascistic. Just like the Fascists in *Salò* who wish to recreate the world in their own image. Just as capitalism is recreating the whole world in its image. You say you see torture and abuse and pornography when you look at my film. My film is a mirror. My characters are forced to eat shit, but you yourselves do so willingly. You condemn the violence in my film but you stand idle while whole classes are eradicated. You abhor the sexual degradation of *Salò* but you acquiesce to the commodification of not only your bodies but your spirits, your souls. Even your imagination is not your own. (42)

We might think of the sections of *Dead Europe* set in rural Greece as working through the romanticism of pre-capitalist society in a way that is similar to what the Pasolini character articulates here. The peasantry offers no point of resistance to capitalism, but a latent fascism—evident in its anti-Semitism—that is every bit as bad. But we also might imagine this speech in the mouth of Tsiolkas as he talks about *The Jesus Man*: "Am I a pornographer? [...] My [book] is a mirror" (42). What emerges unmistakably is Tsiolkas's uncanny proximity to Pasolini; his doubling or mimicry of the forms of thought that defined the later stages of Pasolini's career is a way of articulating his own engagement with middle Australia. This is particularly clear when the Pasolini character evokes the obscenity of his film as both a call to arms and a way of renouncing his own body as the basis of a politics: "This film is a new beginning. It frees me from the hypocritical adulation of the bourgeoisie, it frees me from the cul-de-sac of eroticism, it liberates me from the suffocating conservatism of naturalism. I have created a nightmare and I will continue to create nightmares. I will hound the capitalists and the church and the state until my death. I will create nightmares that will expose the cannibalism of their economic miracles, the savagery of their colonial exploitations, the death stink of their democratic platitudes" (52).

The play's other *mise-en-scène* leaves us in no doubt about Tsiolkas's contempt for middle Australia. The shit eaten in the course of *Salò* echoes through critiques of Australian cultural (specifically cinematic) incompetence. "This country is shit," Mirella, Luke's mother, tells him. "Their films, their culture is shit. There's no fucking ideas, no politics, no passion. It's either naturalistic bullshit or moronic comedies with inarticulate characters. No aesthetics, no guts. It's bourgeois bullshit" (34). Luke has a degree of idealism that will see him resist his mother's plea to leave the country, but his belief that "Films can be a call to arms" leaves the banal reality of Australia's cultural malaise in place and consolidates the sense that Pasolini's world of fascistic consumers is also our own. That sexually violated bodies constitute the punctum of capitalism's horror returns us to what Žižek describes as the repressed social *jouissance* of an apparently modernized habitus. From this perspective, the foundational logic of capitalism is the routine suspension of its own moral law, a sadistic will to power that structures its processes of objectification and exploitation.

In his essay "On the Concept of Tolerance," part of Sydney PEN's "three writers project" that also includes essays on prejudice and fear by Gideon Haigh and Alexis Wright respectively, Tsiolkas approaches the "obscene underside" of neoliberalism in a way that does a great deal to clarify the conceptual underpinnings of his fiction. The essay introduces the obscene as that which liberal democracy has to bracket in order to guarantee its own coherence. It opens by evoking Ursula Le Guin's story "The Ones Who Walk Away from Omelas," in which a utopian society is founded on, as Tsiolkas puts it, "the abject suffering and oppression of a lone child."[35] The sense of a hidden cost—the "obscene underside" of the polis—functions as a figure for the inherently compromised character of liberal tolerance. "Tolerance is something liberalism identifies as intrinsic to the democratic state. We justify our continued occupation [of Iraq and Afghanistan, presumably] by claiming that only by staying can we ensure the creation of new states that will understand tolerance, the importance of freedom and equality. But in the very same breath we are also told we will not tolerate those who oppose our way of life."[36] This paradox enables Tsiolkas to highlight the discrepancies of cosmopolitanism that are tolerated in the name of economic freedom:

> we increasingly hear talk of "zero" tolerance. But in case we think this means we should abandon tolerance we are reminded that globalisation, which we must enthusiastically embrace, is to be supported because it brings freedom, opportunity and liberalisation to the whole world.

Globalisation annihilates tradition, smashes the borders of the nation state, allows the free flow of capital, ideas and trade. Globalisation celebrates diversity and tolerance. This most ruthless form of capitalism, in promising us the freedom to identify as part of a global community, makes the nation state itself obsolete; and through the marriage of capital and digital technology we are even promised that we can transcend the limitations of physical and temporal space. But when it comes to dealing with the most manifest development of this globalisation, the displacement and homelessness of millions of people around the globe, we are then told that we must secure our borders, that we have to affirm our nationhood.[37]

This situation creates exactly the division on which *Dead Europe* turns: "the fortunate, the wealthy, the democrats, are free to roam the world, but the non-citizens of the world, those without a homeland, a passport, a job, a future, a livelihood are permitted nowhere."[38] The non-citizen is the fodder of globalization, the sacrifice to the logic of the free market with its promise of "justice, freedom, liberation and whitegoods for all":

So for the women in the stinking textile factories in Indonesia, China and the Philippines, forced to piss in plastic bottles or face punishment for taking a break, they are told to wait, that prosperity is just around the corner. As for the boys and girls sold into sexual slavery in Bangkok, in Kiev, in Phnom Penh, they too are asked to wait patiently for the alleviation of their suffering. For the miners breathing in the noxious fumes of prosperity in Papua New Guinea, South Africa or Sierra Leone, their deaths, their torture, all of it is worth it for the day to come in which everyone on the globe will be able to participate in the consumerist freedom which is promised by the globalised free market.[39]

The conclusion of the essay returns us to the Le Guin story to make a point about the hidden suffering of global capitalism: "the suffering not of one person but of millions. Those who make our shirts, our toys, who pick the beans for our coffee, who process the petroleum to power our cars, who we barter with or tip or get to fuck when we holiday in their world."[40]

The movement from T-shirts to sex tourism in this passage is typical of Tsiolkas's thinking: an apparently innocuous instance of consumerism strings us along to one that foregrounds, palpably, the brutal social and economic relations underwriting consumption in general. This movement also resonates with the glimpses of a dislocated global underclass that we get in *Dead Europe*, where Isaac's vampiric monstrosity suggests the monstrosity of a mobile, cosmopolitan elite that is now at liberty to rove the planet and prey (as sex tourists among other things) upon those from the wrong side of the West's borders.

> I will wander the streets and cross the bridges over its [Amsterdam's] canals and all the while I will glory in my omnipotence [...] I will no longer be saddened by the rote masturbations of the whores parading their grotesque bodies in the clear glass windows of the brothels. I will look on at a young African woman, her cunt shaved, cupping her mammoth breasts in her hands, and it will make me laugh. She will be there for my pleasure. I will walk among schizophrenic homeless men and women and their snarls for money will appal me and I will understand the urge to wipe this wretched scum from the earth. I will enter a porn cinema and have sex with three men, a German, an Italian and a Korean: I wish to have my fill of bodies, to consume and devour. (302)

Passages like this one foreground the relationship between global economics—the forces that can launch a woman from Africa to the brothels of Amsterdam—and the tainted pleasure that circulates around the corporeality of consumption. If the use of the future tense here creates something of a rift between the narrator and the predatory subjectivity he assumes, it also seems to reflect an anxiety at the possibility of the narrative voice becoming too directly implicated in the monstrosity it nevertheless harbors within it.

As Isaac's vampiric transformation gathers momentum toward the end of *Dead Europe*, his hunger forces him to literalize Agamben's notion of bare life in his delirious and homicidal vision of the bodies that are now at his mercy. At this point, mired in the abjection of his own desire, Isaac embodies a more powerful version of the negation that we have seen in *Loaded* and *The Jesus Man*. What, in *Loaded* especially, had the ability to interrupt narratives of repressive normalcy and suspend their manifestly ideological effects is now reconfigured not as a form of nihilism, but as a form of sovereign violence; the basis of a world of pure political elements in which bodies simply prey upon each other. Isaac's statement of his belief at this point in the novel echoes Hobbes and Sade; "sombre writers of the bourgeois dawn," as Adorno and Horkheimer put it.[41]

> What I believe is that we will kill each other, that we will hurt each other. We will destroy our neighbours and we will exile them. We will sell our children as whores. We will murder and rape and punish one another. We will keep warring and we will keep hating and we will believe we

are just and righteous and faithful. We will keep killing and selling one another and we will believe that we are just and fair and good. We will pursue pleasures and destroy one another in these pursuits. We will abandon our children. We will do all this in the name of God and in the name of our nature. We will create poverty and illness and we will create obscene wealth and the depravities that arise from it. We will think ourselves just and righteous, faithful and sane. We will hate and kill and piss and shit on one another. We will continue to do so. We will create Armageddon. (379)

This passage effectively prefaces *Dead Europe*'s brutal climax, which involves Isaac's total breakdown and the subsequent erasure of his voice. In a London hotel room, Isaac succumbs at last to his demon and becomes the vampire, the predator, the Sadean sovereign that has been shadowing him throughout the novel. He rapes and then devours a comatose Russian, egged on by a depraved American businessman—"He's nothing, he's an animal [...] Destroy him, kill him, annihilate him" (380–81)—but then turns on the American as well. "Meat, blood and flesh," Isaac thinks in the grip of this frenzy, "I know then what man is. Meat. Flesh. Blood" (381). Closure comes only because Isaac is now written out of the novel's concluding moments. Near death, he is flown back to Australia, where his mother effectively saves him from the curse by taking it on herself, aware that she is strong enough to overcome or at least contain its violence.

The thought of Isaac returning to his monogamous life with his partner Colin is about as convincing as the sudden spiritual conversions in Dostoevsky's *Crime and Punishment* and *The Brothers Karamazov*. Throughout the novel, Isaac's intermittent conversations with Colin merely, though no doubt inadvertently, confirm the insularity and banality of the space marked as domestic and monogamous in Tsiolkas's libidinal cartography. At this point in his career Tsiolkas cannot seem to imagine a way of writing that is not implicated in the forces he wants to critique. That both *The Jesus Man* and *Dead Europe* involve the death or breakdown of their protagonists points to this impasse and to the inherent emptiness of forms of desire anchored to processes of objectification. In *The Jesus Man*, Tommy spirals toward increasingly extreme forms of violence as a result of the constant and corrosive encounter with this emptiness. In *Dead Europe*, Isaac's story can only terminate in exhaustion, annihilation or, as Laura Joseph provocatively puts it, the "disintegration" and "evisceration" of a "coherent identity."[12] In this sense Tsiolkas's fiction seems to literalize the schema of Freudian psychoanalysis: beyond the pleasure principle, the death drive. In both novels pornography marks the space of this empty transgression. It enables Tsiolkas to present consumer culture as antisocial if not pathogenic in its provocation of emphatically egocentric needs that—like capitalism more generally—see other people as objects, resources or props in the libidinal life of the individual. That the violence of pornography emblematizes both Tommy's and Isaac's desire brings us face to face with forms of consumption that are utterly banal and virtually ubiquitous but that also embody the necropolitical machinery of capitalism.

In "On the Concept of Tolerance," Tsiolkas's discussion of global capitalism's underside also opens up onto those ideological forces that have robbed us of "a language with which to comprehend and understand the effects of power."[43] In the absence of that language, we (the privileged citizens of industrialized societies) are thrown back on the delusional solace of our agency as consumers and forced to inhabit the inherently unstable fictions of consumer capitalism and liberal democracy in which the theology of the free market is the end point of history:

> The liberals themselves are blind to how the market now makes a lie of their claims for universality. The market tells us that we are broken, unfulfilled and that only by filling our homes, our souls, our selves with the needless junk of consumption can we ever hope to attain some approximation of the whole. But the whole is an infinite abyss that cannot be sated. We are no longer communities, no longer society, we are niches, lifestyles, we are our opportunities not our commitments.[44]

This, of course, is Tommy Stefano's story as much as it is Isaac's. What Tsiolkas calls the "infinite abyss" is precisely the emptiness embedded in the fantasies of consumer culture. This is also the point at which the pursuit of individualized pleasure morphs into a violence that registers, implicitly, the impossibility of that pleasure. With this in mind it is not hard to see how Tsiolkas's focus on pornography enables him to clarify the futility of consumer culture: pornography, in this framework, is merely the form of consumer culture that dramatizes that culture's internal dynamic. It both belongs to and tropes the hidden actuality of quotidian experience. It reveals the egocentric subjectivity incited by consumer culture and the abjection that lies in wait for it. In this sense Tsiolkas's critical orientation also seems to approach the very specific notion of "political commitment" evoked by Julia Kristeva in her discussion of Louis-Ferdinand Céline: "a *delirium* that literally prevents one from going mad," precisely because "it postpones the senseless abyss" in which the ego "drowns in the whirl of its objects and its language."[45]

But if political commitment postpones the abyss, it is also—at least in particular configurations—the platform that allows us to encounter it. Later in "On the Concept of Tolerance," Tsiolkas talks about the importance of exploring the obscene, the imperative to "look towards that defined as unspeakable, intolerable, traitorous, seditious, evil and abject in order to ensure that the violence enacted against its expression is given a voice, shaped into a memory."[16] The hint of libertarianism here also works in concert with the desire to excavate forms of subjectivity and forms of experience integral to, but often mystified or occluded altogether by, the ideological apparatus of capitalism. Hence, "the tolerance of the radical artist cannot be a liberal tolerance." On the contrary, "it is a radical, disturbing, dangerous tolerance; heretical, blasphemous, cruel. It has to speak on behalf of not only the oppressed, the imprisoned, the condemned, it also has to refute the silencing of the racist, the inhuman, the murderous and, dare I say it, even the fascistic."[17] Perhaps Tsiolkas is responding to those critics who have raised at least the possibility of reading *Dead Europe* as an anti-Semitic novel. But he is also highlighting the ways in which a liberal notion of tolerance can limit the scope and effectiveness of explicitly political fiction. His notion of a non-liberal tolerance indicates his willingness to let his fiction inhabit, and even embody, the worlds he writes about. This is central to Tsiolkas's conception of fiction. His first three novels orbit, with varying degrees of precariousness, the abyss that political commitment must both encounter and ward off as the condition of its legibility.

Tsiolkas's use of pornography and a broadly pornographic sensibility in *Dead Europe* brings us to the edge of this abyss and, for a moment perhaps, takes us just beyond it. This experience generates a powerful and emblematic distillation of contemporary social and economic relations and presents us with the ruse of political power in its most direct and unmistakable form: what underwrites the efficacy of commodity capitalism is precisely the fiction of an element banished beyond its limits. In the dark dreams of consumer culture, our fulfillment, or salvation, is tethered to the possibility of that exterior space. But in following the thread of desire to the limits of the social, we also find ourselves mired in the networks of power, knowledge and pleasure that constitute the social in the first place. The outside is the inside; the line of flight returns us to the center, to the abject ruins of consumerist fantasy. In both *The Jesus Man* and *Dead Europe*, Tsiolkas's visions of necrotic cities (European and Australian) sinking into their own filth powerfully evoke a social order weighed down by its failure to escape itself. His work approaches the death drive at the center of consumer culture and accordingly begins to expose and displace a system that assimilates millions of people—whether as subjects or objects, agents or victims—to its empty dream of enjoyment. What will remain to be seen is how he can rescue his own voice from the abyss he exposes without capitulating to the forms of bourgeois complacency his fictional Pasolini rails against.

Chapter 4

IN THE SUBURBS OF WORLD LITERATURE: FROM *DEAD EUROPE* TO *THE SLAP*

The Slap was a watershed publication in Tsiolkas's career. It transformed him from a writer of local notoriety into an international bestseller. For the first time, Tsiolkas was visible well beyond the insular confines of Australian literary space. It was possible to see him interviewed on the BBC in the United Kingdom, or to hear him on NPR in the United States. The novel won the 2009 Commonwealth Writers' Prize and was long-listed for the 2010 Booker Prize. It was also adapted for a high-profile television miniseries, which in turn became the basis of an NBC miniseries set in New York City. The success of the initial adaptation, in Australia and the United Kingdom especially, integrated the novel and its author into a broader media apparatus in which diverse forms of cultural consumption could conveniently undergird each other. As a result Tsiolkas achieved a degree of celebrity unusual for an Australian writer. One consequence of this is that he has been able to produce a discourse about his work via a proliferation of interviews and other appearances as a public intellectual. Interviews have always played an important role in framing Tsiolkas's writing. In the early stages of his career they provided a loosely autobiographical framework that foregrounded the engagements with immigrant experience, class politics and queer identity that underpin his work. By the time *The Slap* was published, this had changed a bit. The interviews that proliferated in its wake became the most influential and authoritative discourse about the novel and successfully linked it to a range of political issues that were by no means self-evident in the text itself: Australia's regressive immigration policy, the brutal treatment of asylum seekers, and a sense of what Ghassan Hage has called "Anglo decline."[1] Today, that discourse is probably the decisive context for critical appreciations of *The Slap*. It is an enviable position for a writer to be in. Few authors get to exert such a degree of control over the ways in which their work is being read and interpreted.

The Slap also embodies a departure from the sort of fiction Tsiolkas had hitherto been writing. For the first time one could read his work without being overwhelmed by the excesses of protagonists caught up in the violence of their own sexuality. Characters like Hector and Harry in *The Slap* might echo Ari, Tommy and Isaac from the earlier novels, but they are also, very clearly, creations from which Tsiolkas has a greater degree of distance. By contrast Ari, Tommy and Isaac feel more like the projections of struggles that belong to Tsiolkas as much as they do his characters. The fact that a character called Ari wanders through the opening section of *The Slap* and is vaguely recognized by Hector suggests that both character and author are glimpsing earlier versions of themselves that they have outgrown. This shift correlates with a few other noticeable formal and thematic differences. Because *The Slap* is organized around the perspectives of eight different characters, all of whom are given equal weight, the novel loses the sense of being caught up in or defined by the delirium of an individual. And although we experience the often anguished interior states of these characters, the orientation of the novel is really toward a quotidian reality that can contain this multiplicity. By contrast, the experience of reading the earlier novels was one of confronting subjectivities so volatile that they threatened to demolish the everyday altogether, an idea that was literalized in the Gothicism of *Dead Europe*, in which Isaac's story radically departs from the framework of realism and pushes through to the moment at which it explodes into violence and abjection. In *The Slap*, by contrast, the moment at which Harry has aggressive oral sex with his wife and the moment at which he imagines himself bashing Rosie both have a characteristic violence, but they also remain localized, contained in a bedroom or the imagination. They aren't moments that might potentially reconfigure an entire narrative. In this respect the actual slap at the center of the novel (when Harry slaps the child Hugo) is exceptional only by virtue of its visibility. Most social relationships in this novel are premised on the sublimation of a violence that we still hear crackling through the novel's free indirect discourse. Occasionally this violence bubbles over to form another series of slaps (sometimes figurative, sometimes literal) in which characters are confronted, rejected or rebuked. But the everyday, often mundane nature of this violence ensures that it remains contained in a narrative framework that is never in danger of being overwhelmed by the relationships it depicts. In this sense the novel maintains a sort of repose, or a sort of formal coherence, that is lacking in the earlier works. We have seen that Tsiolkas, in those early novels, repeatedly highlights the absence of viable communal and political structures. Those novels were about alienation and the forms of affect (often linked to aggression) that it generates. Their focus on individuals, however, also enabled them to accentuate alienation in the portrayal of characters that become pathological (in the case of Tommy Stefano) or abhuman (in the case of Isaac Raftis). These characters function as indexes of a broader set of social relations that are always tending toward catastrophe. Their individual fates take us to the limits of a habitus that has clearly become intolerable. In *The Slap*, by contrast, violence and abjection are nowhere near as extreme, but they are just as universally distributed. Their relationship to the material circumstances in which they occur, however, has lost some of the polemical clarity of the earlier novels, which might explain why Tsiolkas's own commentary about *The Slap*, which I will get to in a moment, is so crucial to a sense of its political investments.

We can approach the difference between *The Slap* and these earlier texts, *Dead Europe* especially, by thinking about the ways in which they construct their settings and arrange the relationship between their foregrounds and their backgrounds. This is something Kalinda Ashton has touched on in her review of *The Slap*:

> One noticeable shift in tone from the author of *Dead Europe*—a novel memorable for its capacity to *indict*—is in the realm of scale. Travels through the red light districts and slums of European cities have been replaced by gatherings in the backyards of Northcote. Prague and Venice are no longer on the horizon—instead, brick-veneer properties go for auction in Thomastown. In that respect, the book is set locally, but in a broader sense, the book interrogates precisely what 'local' might be—if, indeed, it exists any more.[2]

There is, I think, more to be said about the issue of scale that Ashton touches on here. *Dead Europe* plays out against momentous histories and political processes: European fascism, genocide, globalization and the collapse of communism. In this context the actions of characters and the characters themselves can function as indexes of these processes. At moments it is as if the historical-political background of the novel threatens to consume the foreground. At other moments, the hyperbolic depiction of individual pathology obscures any sense of a realistically or objectively verifiable context. This instability is literalized in the photographs Isaac takes, which reveal the demon in the process of possessing him, an entity that moves from the background of the narrative to the foreground as Isaac is literally captured by the violence of his own history. In *The Slap*, by contrast, this sort of movement between background and foreground is absent. The novel is also, as Ashton emphasizes, relentlessly suburban in its orientation. In this context actions take on a more restricted and even literal meaning. The background of history, even in a specifically Australian sense, has receded and become much less significant. At times it barely seems to matter at all. Characters talk about public education, economic rationalization or the misery of being "normal" in John Howard's Australia, and they are no doubt formed by a pervasive, though largely invisible sense of neoliberal governmentality, but the political also seems scaled in a way that stops it from actually consuming the characters who speak about it. As I have already suggested, Tsiolkas himself has had to supply the political backdrop that is largely implicit in the novel itself: "It's possible to see *The Slap* occurring within the space of two elections, the 'Tampa election' of 2001 and the Latham election of 2004." He goes on to talk about changes in Australia's class structure and their relationship to "extreme nationalist and racist reactions."[3] What Tsiolkas touches on here are two federal elections, both victories for the Liberal government, that consolidated a sense of the increasing conservatism of the Australian electorate, particularly around the country's immigration policy and its management of asylum seekers coming to Australia by sea.[4] Nothing of this sort, however, is needed to clarify the background of *Dead Europe*. It seems clear that the relationship between foreground and background, character and context, organizes the intensity with which we experience the political vision of particular texts. I do not mean the intensity with which characters or even narrators might speak about politics. What I have in mind here is more a matter of how form mediates the political, or of how particular texts construct the worlds that are internal to them.

Tsiolkas's first three novels could all be described as explicitly political, not because of the amount of time they spend talking about political events and processes, but because the combative ethos of his characters and the deformities of the narrative voices linked to them register, by way of both negation and reflection, the intolerability of material relations as they currently exist. In *The Slap*, by contrast, we seldom get a sense of material relations consuming or unhinging the foreground of the text. Richie, for instance, might think that world events are leading to "a violent, catastrophic and, for the human species if no other, a deservedly sadistic end,"[5] but for Isaac and Tommy this idea is lived out as a form of self-annihilation. In *The Slap*, the measured interaction between foreground and background effectively contains the political, holds it at arm's length, and prevents it from proliferating through the formal structure of the text. At moments, in fact, the foreground is so overwhelming in its everyday detail that it feels both trivial and distracting. What we have here is a middle-class world so obsessed with the struggles of individuals—its characters, the figures in its foreground—that everything else seems to drop out of view. Perhaps the ensuing sense of absence or lack is the real point of the novel. We are in a world of people trapped in the incommunicability of their subjective states. Of course these states are conditioned by social and economic processes, but these processes seldom appear above the threshold of visibility in a way that would let them motivate any kind of sustained resistance or critique. Ironically, it is precisely this aspect of the novel that enables us to recognize it as realistic, and this guarantees a basic sort of accessibility that *Dead Europe* and *The Jesus Man* may well have lacked. An important register of this difference is that *The Slap* has dispensed with the apocalyptic tenor of those novels. It takes us to a recognizable world of norms, not exceptions. In *Dead Europe* and *The Jesus Man*, by contrast, exceptions are norms, and the implicit claim of those novels is that collapsing the two generates an urgency that is evident in the fever with which they dissect their material underpinnings.

We might be able to describe this shift more articulately by looking at the particular value Theodor Adorno's thinking about aesthetics attributes to negation. In my discussion of *Loaded* I touched on the ways in which Ari's negation of prevailing social narratives registers a waning of the possibility of politics in the sense of class-based agency and activism. Adorno's work takes us in a different direction, but his thinking about aesthetic negativity powerfully explains why the unrelenting bleakness of Tsiolkas's vision in *The Jesus Man* and *Dead Europe* might have a restorative value that has been partly surrendered by *The Slap*. Adorno opens his posthumously published *Aesthetic Theory* with a gloss on the socially constituted autonomy of art (or of aesthetic experience). "Artworks detach themselves from the empirical world and bring forth another world," he writes. This other world is "opposed to the empirical world" as if it too "were an autonomous entity." This opposition to empirical reality, he believes, is a fundamental structural quality of artworks and seems to survive despite their particular content: "Thus, however tragic they appear, artworks tend a priori toward affirmation."[6] Precisely because of this autonomy, however, art leaves the empirical world untouched, and hence, in its detachment and purposelessness, it "sanctions the primacy of reality."[7] We have already come across a version of this idea in Herbert Marcuse's essay "The Affirmative Character of Culture." It is also similar to what Oskar Negt and Alexander Kluge have in mind when they discuss fantasy as a "necessary compensation for the experience of the alienated labor process," although here they recast the idea as part of an account of proletarian production that "constitutes an unconscious practical critique of alienation" and is thus sharply distinguished from its bourgeois variant.[8]

For Adorno, the problem with affirmative culture and notions of aesthetic autonomy stems from their ability to provide a kind of solace. This seems especially pronounced after World War II, which involved such a transformation in the character of empirical reality that the very idea of an imaginative retreat from it seemed tainted by its insularity: "In the face of the abnormality into which reality is developing, art's inescapable affirmative essence has become insufferable. Art must turn against itself, in opposition to its own concept, and thus become uncertain of itself right into its innermost fiber."[9] What Adorno announces here is a particular aesthetic bent in which art must constantly question its structural relationship to other forms of social and cultural production. One way in which it can do this is to disrupt its fundamental orientation to affirmation by withholding the promise of consolation. If art can still be said to contain a utopian dimension, it is evident for Adorno in its renunciation of all false utopias, its "renunciation of the semblance of reconciliation" and its corresponding commitment to the "promise of reconciliation in the midst of the unreconciled":

> This is the true consciousness of an age in which the real possibility of utopia—that given the level of productive forces the earth could here and now be paradise—converges with the possibility of total catastrophe. In the image of catastrophe, an image that is not a copy of the event but the cipher of its potential, the magical trace of art's most distant prehistory reappears under the total spell, as if art wanted to prevent the catastrophe by conjuring up its image.[10]

It is in the "negativity of collapse," Adorno believes, that art remains true to the promise of utopia: "In this image of collapse all the stigmata of the repulsive and loathsome in modern art gather."[11]

Adorno's orientation here seems resolutely modernist. He believes that the negativity of modern art, its status as a cipher of catastrophe, is what the culture industry has effectively repressed. "Authentic contemporary art" embodies a "radically darkened objectivity" that has effectively assimilated the disaster of modernity into itself.[12]

> To survive reality at its most extreme and grim, artworks that do not want to sell themselves as consolation must equate themselves with that reality. Radical art today is synonymous with dark art; its primary color is black. Much contemporary production is irrelevant because it takes no note of this and childishly delights in color.[13]

We do not have to take these comments literally to understand their point. And we do not have to position Tsiolkas alongside Samuel Beckett and Arnold Schoenberg (two constant points of orientation for Adorno) to read the bleakness of *Dead Europe* as at least an attempt to approximate something like the "radically darkened objectivity" that Adorno pits against the injustices of "cheerful art" and "entertainment."[14] What else is *Dead Europe* if not a product and an embodiment of catastrophe—a work that gradually draws disaster into itself until it is consumed by it?

Isaac's photographs of the Europe he travels through might be read as allegorizing this process. At first the demon that haunts his mother's family—

the afterimage of European anti-Semitism and an anticipation of a predatory transnationalism—appears as an isolated element in these images. Just as Isaac's family curse might be thought of as part of the background of his story, the demon is initially a figure that hovers on the edge of his experience. As Isaac's narrative progresses, however, the sense of monstrosity, abjection and violence localized in that "poisonous face mocking and malevolent" seems to colonize the vision of Europe he captures with his camera.[15] Precisely what is repressed by fantastic, fetishistic visions of Europe as a tourist destination—a continent lurching from one catastrophe to the next, a continent in a permanent state of crisis—returns in images that capture the abjection of bare life and that seem to link the victims of past genocides with the victims of globalization. Isaac's pictures of Gerry's warehouse on the outskirts of Paris, for instance, seem to superimpose images of concentration camps (images Isaac has already encountered as a tourist) onto the present of a disenfranchised labor force:

The young men in Gerry's warehouse are not laughing and joking. Their faces are contorted into death masks of sullen despair, of unbearable anguish and of never-ending grief. Their bodies are charred, blackened as if from fire and plague. Some of them have their faces turned from the camera, their bodies are limp, entwined, slumped. They are carcasses, they are meat. The warehouse is an abattoir. Those morose faces turned towards the lens are countenances pleading for a great silence: they are doomed. (303)

When Isaac's friend Sam in Cambridge comments on the images, we perhaps get a sense of the sort of novel *Dead Europe* has tried to be. Sam, stunned at the horror of Isaac's work, and clearly not in a position to grasp its accursed, supernatural provenance, forces Isaac to explain himself:

I pretended that the bodies were grafted from pornography and the vileness of the internet, and this explanation seemed to satisfy him. Of course, he exclaimed, they're montage [...] He must have assumed a thousand depravities about where I had found the models for my work. The only question he posed was of the dubious moral worth of using such traumatic real subjects. I answered that what I was doing was akin to what samplers did in utilising fragments of other people's work in their own creation; I also answered that, unfortunately, these very images were free and public on the convoluted garbage dump which was the internet. I was convincing myself as I spoke. The inert fear that had taken hold of me when I first glimpsed the photographs had now left me. Instead, I was delighted with them, aware of their disturbing

evil, excited by their ability to move and confuse people. I was proud
of them. The emotion swelled and met the ravenous call of my blood.
I was famished. (361)

Montage is not a good description of *Dead Europe*, but it does get at something of
Tsiolkas's method, which juxtaposes moments of political invective, historical
reflection, travel diary, Gothic horror and pornographic fantasy. The "garbage
dump" of contemporary history, archived in the abyss of the digital, supplies
both the sensibility of the photographs and of the novel itself, which might be
thought of as scouring the repressed of contemporary consciousness for those
waste products not readily assimilated into it. That Isaac is able to surrender
himself to the horror of his work also reflects an uncertainty about the sort
of project Tsiolkas has undertaken here. By the time the content of Isaac's
photographs spills into his reality (a process that culminates in his vision of
Armageddon as a Hobbesian war of all against all), catastrophe has effectively
consumed the novel.

     The fact that Isaac's photographs—and Tsiolkas's novel—can claim to
reflect or mirror a reality forces us to rethink what is at stake in the claims
of literary realism. The issue is especially interesting in the wake of *The Slap*,
the reception of which was informed by the sense of the novel being an
accurate, realistic evocation of middle-class Australia. In fact this idea that
Tsiolkas's recent work (*The Slap* and *Barracuda*) has a fidelity to its Australian
context is central to both its commercial and critical viability. An editorial
column in *Overland* described *The Slap* as a "snapshot of the anxieties
and compromises of a diffuse suburban middle class," and as a novel that has
"taken the temperature of our times."[16] If reality is being reflected in *Dead
Europe*—a novel full of "snapshots" in a more literal sense—it is a reality that
we are inclined to misrecognize. *Dead Europe* is, after all, a Gothic horror story,
not a work of realism. *The Slap*, by contrast, moves us firmly into a reality
that we do recognize, precisely because it eschews the "radically darkened
objectivity" of the previous novel (though what words like "recognize" and
"misrecognize" now mean is the issue). The fact that this shift coincides with
Tsiolkas's acceptance by the market and by a broad (we might even say "mass")
public seems to literalize the cultural topography Adorno's work maps out. We,
urban Australians that is, recognize ourselves. Readers overseas also recognize
urban Australia, partly because of the ways in which the novel reproduces
(sometimes with marked self-consciousness and irony) a standard repertoire of
topoi that viewers of *Neighbours* and *Home and Away* will know all too well. This
is not to say that *The Slap* is "cheerful" in the way disparaged by Adorno. Of
course it isn't. But it does suspend the relentless negativity of *Dead Europe* (and
The Jesus Man). The sense we get is that sublimation, repression and resentment

are just part of the everyday experience of modern suburban life, along with the moments at which characters fall in love or display genuine affection for each other. Instead of catastrophe we have a multitude of more modest but still corrosive failures, but these are also constantly tempered by even-handed evocations of the positive potential in complex characters. All of this is no doubt central to the novel's realism (it is a book about everyday people with everyday problems), but it is that realism that has also robbed the novel of its ability to, as Adorno would put it, summon the power of the aesthetic to ward off the impending catastrophe. In the world of *The Slap*, in fact, catastrophe has been replaced by a sense of things persisting with such intransigence that it seems pointless even to worry about them; that in itself might constitute its own sort of catastrophe. *The Slap* is critical enough to fend off complacency, yet not so critical that it might jeopardize its own consumability by radically assaulting the world in which its readers are firmly placed.

I will return to these issues in my final chapter, where I want to discuss *The Slap* and *Barracuda* as instances of literature's ambiguous relationship with the culture industry. All of this suggests a shift in Tsiolkas's work, but there is another sense in which *Dead Europe* and *The Slap* form a fairly seamless continuity across which we can see a crystallization of Tsiolkas's critique of middle Australia and his corresponding investment in a literary space or trajectory formed by his commitment to the immigrant experience. We have already seen how insistent Tsiolkas's critique of middle-class, Anglophone Australia can be. Mirella's stinging attack on Australia and Australian culture in *Non Parlo di Salò* captures a lot of the anger that is dispersed throughout Tsiolkas's writing. It also consolidates the sense in which Tsiolkas can imagine an alternative cultural space that hinges on a certain kind of foreignness that seems to insulate him against the "bourgeois bullshit" and cultural mediocrity of his immediate environment. The way in which *Dead Europe* redescribes the demography and geography of the European city is an important development of this aspect of Tsiolkas's work. The novel both evokes and displaces a phantasmatic sense of the European city as a locus of cultural capital. It works to loosen the hold that Europe might have on the Australian imagination. Isaac's father, for instance, laments the historical unreality of Australian life. He talks about "Paris and Berlin, real cities [...] in which there were people in the streets day and night," or Thessaloniki, with its two thousand years of history: "What does this country have to offer that is that old? Nothing. Fucking nothing. We are going back to real history" (6). The novel constantly measures this fantasy of Europe against its neoliberal reality, partly through Isaac's recollections of his earlier travels through the continent. On his first visit to Paris, he recalls, he was "enchanted by the beauty of the French capital": "Why couldn't our cities be more like Paris? I moaned when I got home. I detested the wide empty streets and grid-like patterns of Australia's modern metropolises. I couldn't bear the vast tentacle reach of suburbia" (277).

In a strange but I think very obvious way, *Dead Europe*'s interest in anti-Semitism and Judaism reflects this hunger for the history that is apparently lacking in the suburbs. What I am trying to evoke here has been discussed at greater length by scholars who work on Holocaust literature. The horror of European anti-Semitism, the extent of its tragedy, and the crisis in representation it evokes have generated a kind of experiential envy through which writers with no tangible relationship to those events develop a literary universe around them.[17] In Australia, Helen Darville's 1994 *The Hand that Signed the Paper* and the debate it evoked are the clearest examples of this. John Scott's *The Architect*, which constructs a compulsive, homoerotic infatuation with the specters of fascism and the city of Berlin, gives us another (more compelling) version of this sort of historical fetishism, though it also seems acutely aware of the genre in which it is working. When Ken Gelder and Paul Salzman discuss Darville's novel alongside *Dead Europe*, they seem to be glimpsing these affinities.[18] There is a sense in which the often emblematic qualities of the racial encounters in *Dead Europe* (think of Isaac's meeting with the mute Jew in Venice or the apparent significance of Gerry turning out to be both a ghost and a Jew) embody the novel's hunger for history. But *Dead Europe* also overwrites these older histories of racial violence with more contemporary forms of discrepant cosmopolitanism that cut across national spaces and produce a much more rhizomatic sense of both immigration and discrimination. In this process two things happen. Firstly, we lose any sense in which we can still invest in places like London and Paris as focal points for the sort of cultural capital that Signor Bruno rehearses when he insists to Isaac that fine literature "meant British or French literature" (140). This is something to which Lynda Ng has drawn attention when she reads the novel as dismantling the "binary between old Europe and new Australia."[19] Secondly, the term Greek-Australian is reframed not as the minor strand of a marginal, Anglophone experience, but as one more trajectory in a world of scrambled and decentered flight patterns.

By rewriting Europe in a way that effectively divests it of its claims to metropolitan centrality and symbolic prestige, the novel opens up conceptions of demography and geography that speak more directly to a decentered sort of immigrant experience that will become the basis of Tsiolkas's rewriting of suburbia in *The Slap*. As Brigid Rooney writes, *The Slap* "reinvents suburban terrain precisely through its engagement with Australia's diversifying demography and changing urban/suburban modes, in turn conditioned by global capitalism's fluid and precarious present, in what Zygmunt Bauman influentially terms 'liquid modernity.'"[20] Crucially this also involves reimagining the reality of history in such a way that can accept the actuality of the everyday rather than trying to transcend it via a fetishized vision of Europe's tragedy. If this process is about space in a literal sense, it is also about space in a more figurative way. Tsiolkas's critique of Europe as a locus of cultural capital is an important reorientation in his sense of *literary* space. Predictably, he has explained this in autobiographical terms:

> In 2005 I published a novel called *Dead Europe* that had taken me seven years to write. I have described it as my exorcising the "Europeanness" that is one aspect of my identity and consciousness as an Australian. It was a dark novel, both in its themes of recurring racism and anti-semitism, and in trying to give voice to the melancholy and loss that is at the heart of the immigrant and refugee experience. The novel was written at night, set in sombre and haunted spaces. Having finished it I wanted to be in the light again, in that vast and harsh but vivid Australian light that I miss so dearly when I have spent time away from home. Having cleaved myself of my European heritage—or so I thought—I wanted to write an Australian story, one that spoke to the Australia I knew.[21]

One novel clears the way for another. Tsiolkas needed to purge the shadow of Europe before he could write unencumbered about suburbia in Australia. A very specific sense of location is enabled by the reimagining of a broader cultural geography that effectively nullifies the gravity of Europe, partly by hollowing out its claims to cultural capital and by developing an emphatically decentered vision of our historical actuality, our contemporaneity.

The story "Tourists," in *Merciless Gods*, performs a similar sort of displacement with regard to New York. Here an Australian couple on holiday (Bill and Trina) negotiate a moment of crisis in their relationship that is brought on by Bill's casual racism, which seems to measure the distance between the insularity of Australia and the much more comfortably cosmopolitan character of the world city. The crisis is defused partly by Trina's varying attitudes to New York. "We're in New York—how can you even try to compare it to Melbourne?" she says early in the story. Later, however, she is struck by the "smug emptiness" of the art in the Whitney: it is the art appropriate to a "city that had brought an entire economy to near collapse by speculating on the value of nothing [...] none of it will survive. I don't think any of it deserves to survive."[22] The shift, which is also a repudiation of the city's cultural authority, loosens the tension between Bill and Trina sufficiently for them to deal with Bill's racism unencumbered by the hierarchical relationship between Melbourne and New York, which now appears as an abstraction capable of distorting the lives of the people caught in it.

We could think of these dynamics in the terms articulated by Pascale Casanova in her exploration of world literary space, *The World Republic of Letters*. The Europe Isaac has assimilated from his father and Signor Bruno—a Europe of auratic urban spaces with complex and layered cultural histories—would be, according to Casanova, part of the long process by which world literary space has produced its own relatively autonomous geography. This geography is both imagined and grounded in tangible, institutional structures. Because cities like London and Paris have anchored autonomous literary production since the eighteenth century, they also embody a discernible literary heritage, and a high concentration of value-determining institutions. For Casanova these institutions include an educated readership and public spaces given to literary discussion, a specialized press, prestigious publishers, an established critical culture capable of making judgments that are broadly respected and a population of celebrated authors.[23] It goes without saying that in the nineteenth century these "literary resources" were concentrated in imperial capitals, not in the cities of the new world, and not, generally, in the provinces of Europe. The aura that surrounds Paris or London, say, partly reflects the fact that for centuries writers have had to imagine their careers channeled through those cities, and have accordingly incorporated them into their work (even if only to evoke the squalor of literary failure, as in George Gissing's *New Grub Street*). As a result literature itself became a recitation of the symbolic capital that now seems evident in the mythology that attaches to certain literary cities. Hence the Serbo-Croation writer Danilo Kiš could describe his arrival in Paris as an uncanny kind of return: "I did not come to Paris as a foreigner, but as someone who goes on a pilgrimage in the innermost landscapes of his own dreams, in a *terra nostalgia*."[24] As Casanova puts it, "The cities where literary resources are concentrated, where they accumulate, become places where belief is incarnated, centers of credit, as it were."[25]

By contrast, the "suburban outskirts" of this literary geography produce acute anxiety that comes from a consciousness of having to work through various forms of institutional or cultural lack that manifest partly in anxieties about geography itself. From this perspective, what A.A. Phillips described as Australia's cultural cringe is actually a fairly objective reflection of the conditions under which Australian writers have had to work. Confronted with these conditions, writers from the peripheries nevertheless "invent their own freedom as artists," though often with a strategic ingenuity that would never occur to a writer born and bred in Paris, London or New York.[26] The way in which Mark Davis raises the issue in *The Land of Plenty* suggests exactly the ingenuity Casanova describes.

There's perhaps no greater desire among the arbiters of Australia's official culture than to have a 'great civilisation', which generally means emulating others. So, every few years, a new publication is launched that seeks to mime the cultural authority of the *New Yorker*, or the *Times Literary Supplement* or *Granta*, or the *London Review of Books*. So high-profile book reviewers affect a mock Oxbridge literati 'man of letters' persona, and eschew insight in favour of the compulsive name-dropping of great names and great books from the 'great elsewhere' of Europe and the United States. So local novelists write affected, overworked prose of the sort that they imagine will gain them a discerning audience in New York or London. So local architects continue to build provincial versions of landmark overseas buildings in what's been a long tradition of working to silhouettes first seen in established metropolitan centres, perhaps in search of similar praise and prizes (and sometimes getting them). So local television producers license overseas concepts and fulfil local-content provisions with zero imagination. So, too, conservative talkback hosts and columnists admire the take-no-prisoners hardball spin of conservative US talkshow host Rush Limbaugh, or work hard to channel the savage loopiness of US culture warrior Ann Coulter. And local conservatives, eager to remake Australian economic and social life in the image of the United States, make regular pilgrimages to the Heritage Foundation or the American Enterprise Institute, sometimes having served apprenticeships there in the first place.[27]

The passage's conflation of radically different forms of influence, and radically different cultural and political orientations is central to its ability to displace (or at least address) the hierarchies of literary space. By performing the drift from the material structures of literary space to the political failings of the people beholden to US mass media (though the slide from *Granta* to Ann Coulter is clearly absurd), Davis also opens up the space for another sort of enunciative act linked to the conviction that cities like Melbourne and Sydney do not need to emulate London and New York because, presumably, they have reached a level of maturity that cancels any sense of their cultural belatedness. Hence the fact that "more than two centuries after white settlement, Australians speak, still, to Europe, and wait for the echo to come back, understanding that echo as validation" indicates an embarrassing and regressive failure to grasp their independence and a servile reproduction of modes of cultural and political capital bound up with foreign powers.[28] The passage gives one an acute sense of how suffocating the Australian cultural scene can feel, but what makes it so interesting is the strategic urgency with which it engages with literary space in order to perform an alteration in the ways in which that space generates value. Davis does not advocate national autonomy as a response to Australian anxieties of influence. Rather he stresses the indistinction of local and global spaces, and insists that this new reality has made older cultural hierarchies anachronistic. My point is that this emphasis, which involves its own sort of fantasy about how economic conditions determine cultural production, is a strategy that performs a reorientation of the field of cultural production. It enacts the shift it purports to represent, and thus registers, by way of the urgency of its opposition, the intransigence of the structures in which Australian writers work. Put bluntly, no level of local-global fusion in the alleyways of Melbourne can change the demographic factors that differentiate the Australian and US publishing industries, but understanding that subservience to the larger market is out of step with a new cultural cartography at least offers an imaginative refusal of these conditions and the forms of evaluation tethered to them.

The relationship between *Dead Europe* and *The Slap*, I think, manifests the same sort of ingenuity Davis displays. In the former, Tsiolkas engages with and displaces precisely the cultural geography discussed by Casanova. In fact *Dead Europe*'s vision of Cambridge intellectuals, with their pomposity and poor personal hygiene, feels very close to home (it is as much Brunswick Street as it is Trinity College). It attacks what we could imagine, without too much effort, as the pretentiousness of a local "mock Oxbridge literati." The novel also dispels the myth of the metropolis—which now seems anachronistic—and resituates a sense of the contemporary (the now of both political and aesthetic experience) in terms of a decentered world of migration, marginalization and exploitation. The Australia Tsiolkas wanted to return to in writing *The Slap* is continuous with the Europe his previous novel had discovered: both imagine spaces defined by the movement of immigrants and the increasing hybridization of national formations. *Dead Europe*, in other words, makes it possible to return to the suburbs (both in the sense of a real location and the setting for a novel) with the knowledge that suburbia is one more peripheral space in a world of peripheries. If the inherently anti-suburban stance of post-war Australian writing embodies a Eurocentric modernism, Tsiolkas's return to the suburbs in *The Slap* cannot help but imply an engagement with and displacement of that legacy, and a renewed sense of Australian localities.

Part of the appeal of *The Slap*, at least for an Australian reader, is the confidence with which it manages all of this. It reminds me more of a novel like Jonathan Franzen's *The Corrections* than any of its more obvious Australian precedents, precisely because of its lack of embarrassment at being mired in the quotidian. This lack of embarrassment is a direct consequence of the way in which the novel presupposes a relationship between the space its represents and the space in which it circulates. In both, the everyday has become so deracinated and culturally decentered that it no longer evokes the geographical conceptions of cultural capital that might lead us to imagine the Australian suburb as a cultural wasteland lacking the historical actuality of Paris, London or Berlin. These are not the suburbs of a Patrick White novel or of George Johnston's *My Brother Jack*, which are constantly measured against the promise of Europe or visions of cultural alterity concentrated in an inner-city bohemia, spectralized immigrant populations, Indigenous Australia, or art itself. That map no longer seems to be operative. Instead the suburbs exist on a vast, non-hierarchical continuum that presupposes a constant blurring of the national and the international, the local and the global. That is not to say that the suburbs as Tsiolkas represents them in *The Slap* are not mundane and claustrophobic. They are both those things, and at times the novel evokes such a sense of being suffocated in the everyday that it seems continuous with the very banality it wants to represent. The point is that other places and other cultural formations either are not apparent, or they do not offer an alternative. When the novel turns to London via the backstory of Connie's father, there is no sense of a cultural or spatial hierarchy. The confidence of the novel's portrayal of a multicultural, Australian city is related to the way in which it has abandoned an older form of Eurocentricism.

But what emerges when a novelist like Tsiolkas—one given to polemic and to fiction as a form of critique—commits himself to this vision of the suburb? Perhaps we should start with the title and most obvious premise of the novel: the slap. This fleeting moment of aggression in which an adult slaps a three-year-old child at a backyard barbeque both disrupts the surfaces of suburban complacency and reveals the tensions that in fact structure it. It is the device that organizes relationships (or non-relationships) between characters, and in doing so unifies what in actuality is a fairly sprawling, decentered sort of book. That violence effectively forms the novel and the interactions in it is important. In fact many of Tsiolkas's characters, even the ones that emerge as relatively likeable, seem to be constantly prone to moments of racism or sexism that flare up out of the depths of psyches related to the reader in free indirect discourse. Beneath the surfaces of multicultural Australia, in other words, the violence that wells up at the moment of the slap seems like a constant facet of a society composed of alienated individuals trapped by prejudices, resentments and animosities that are largely beneath the threshold of communicability.

Having said that, much of the novel is quite focused in its violence, and this focus seems central to its advocacy of multiculturalism and its polemical relationship to older conceptions of suburbia as predominantly Anglo-Celtic. This is something to which Mandy Treagus has drawn attention. Highlighting the ways in which the novel "queers" middle Australia, Treagus discusses Rosie and Gary (the parents of Hugo, the slapped child) as embodiments of "'traditional' white Australians who have not thrived in Howard's Australia," and whose resulting paranoia drives much of the novel. For Treagus these characters embody some of the racism that fuelled the Cronulla riots of 2005, and this seems to explain the fact that they are generally unsympathetically depicted.[29] Tsiolkas himself has been very clear about wanting to do "the antithesis of *Neighbours*," which means replacing the "white face" that still dominates representations of the Australian suburbs with the reality of Australian multiculturalism.[30] This does not happen, however, just because the novel seems to reflect the reality beyond it. On the contrary, *The Slap* also has a strong performative element. It acts out the event of displacement, which is to say that it contains the very narrative of multicultural transformation that is also posited as its condition of possibility, and this involves a form of textual violence; restorative violence perhaps, but violence nonetheless. We saw in *The Jesus Man* that Tommy's phantasmic insertion of himself into scenarios involving racialized sexual violence, in which black men destroy white women, could be read as an attempt to connect the immigrant experience to the experience of Indigenous Australians. In a way *The Slap* continues something of the sadism of that relationship in its treatment of Rosie, the archetypal blonde Australian whose infantilizing and overly protective mothering practices touch off a much wider range of animosities directed at an increasingly anachronistic version of white Australia. If *Loaded* and *The Jesus Man* had constructed anguished, minoritized characters who move against the vast, largely silent backdrop of Anglo-Australia, *The Slap* constructs a world in which white Australians constitute one more minority in a demographic vision that no longer has a dominant national identity linked to narrow conceptions of natality and ethnicity. But the novel cannot simply assume this. It has to enact it at the level of its content in order to foreground the historical context (the moment of transition) out of which its own eventfulness emerges.

Interestingly Tsiolkas has drawn attention to precisely this aspect of the novel by clarifying what he sees as the text's real political force. Like his referencing of the "Tampa election" and the "Latham election," this is another key moment at which Tsiolkas has been able to explain the political stakes of the text:

> the slap that I wanted to deliver with that book was to a culture in Australia that had literally made me sick, sick to the stomach. A middle class culture that struck me as incredibly selfish and ungenerous; in fact maybe that's the specific word I should use, ungenerous. And I thought I wanted to try and write [...] a book that painted that culture. That represented that culture. And to do that, honestly, I had to put myself in the middle of it. I also had to put my Greekness in the middle

of that book. Because I didn't feel separate from the things that were disgusting me […] I've said it before that the real slap for me in the book and the most difficult part of that book to write is actually a confrontation that happens with one of the Anglo characters, Rosie, who's the mother of the child who gets slapped, and an Aboriginal man. It is he, I think, whom [sic] delivers the real slap in the book. When he says: 'you're no good. Your people, your world is no good. I don't want you to have anything to do with my family. I don't want you to have anything to do with my life.'[31]

This would probably come as a shock to the multitude of reading groups that have fervently debated the ethics of smacking spoilt children. The comments are characteristically confessional and they do point to the fact that the novel's animosity is fairly evenly spread. At the same time though they also get at a representational problem that is fundamental to the novel and that complicates the politics around its displacement of Australia's "white face." Put simply, the way in which the novel evokes ethnicity is caught between realism and allegory, between an attempt to evoke the flux of lived, multicultural experience and emblematic evocations of ethnicity, like the one in the passage just quoted, in which characters become, essentially, ethnic types.

Allegory, of course, is a perfectly feasible representational form, and an allegorical encounter between an Anglo-Celtic character and an Indigenous Australian character can make a powerful, polemical point about a longer history of racism, neglect and abuse. But the realism of the novel—and realism is its dominant mode—works against this sense of encounters between characters standing for broader historical processes. The tension consolidates but also compromises the normative value of the novel's multiculturalism. On the one hand, the novel's realism insists on a multicultural world in which characters might have diverse cultural and ethnic backgrounds but are never subsumed by the stereotypes once associated with these backgrounds. The force of realism is precisely that it dispels stereotypes, or sees through the fictions of racially inflected ideologies. On the other hand, this realistically evoked world is underpinned by the centrality of the allegorical encounter with an "Anglo" character who also, in the broader scheme of the novel, embodies the anti-suburban ethos rejected by the novel's unembarrassed embrace of a quotidian Australian reality. As a result *The Slap* is constantly creating moments at which the political eventfulness of its multiculturalism is subsumed by a suburban landscape that itself feels like the same stifling, banal, aspirational place Australian literature knows all too well, but now merely with different and more diverse markers of identity, and no possibility of resistance. At these moments, the novel's evocation of an anachronistic white

Australia, which in *The Slap* is both working-class and oddly bohemian, feels strained in its attempt to capture a broader dynamic linked to a conservative exploitation of race as the basis of an electoral "wedge" politics, precisely because it is the "Anglo" characters who embody a kind of discontent that is directed primarily at suburbanization. Multiculturalism, in other words, also necessitates displacing the anti-suburban ethos that Tsiolkas's early novels shared with figures like Patrick White and George Johnston. In this respect it also involves a form of resignation or surrender to the everyday. This process reflects the overdetermined character of multiculturalism in the novel. *The Slap*'s multicultural sensibility is continuous with Tsiolkas's critique of Australia's colonial legacy and the forms of racism that continue to undergird its immigration policy, but it is also central to the novel's engagement with its own sense of literary space and its negotiation of its place in a broader literary geography. What I want to highlight here is the curious way in which these two projects inform, but also unsettle, each other.

* * * * *

The actual political processes lingering in the background of the novel are complex and have been discussed at great length by some very articulate commentators and theorists (Tsiolkas among them). At stake is the way in which successive Australian governments have used notions of race and, relatedly, anxieties about immigration to manage the rapid neoliberal rationalization of the economy. The creation of a large population of economically disenfranchised Australians in rural areas and on the outer-suburban fringes of large cities has generated a discontent that the conservatives have masterfully mobilized in the interests of what Ghassan Hage calls "paranoid nationalism." As "hope" becomes scarce, Hage argues, the nation becomes more worried and less able to care for or open itself to others.

> The caring society is essentially an embracing society that generates hope among its citizens and induces them to care for it. The defensive society, such as the one we have in Australia today, suffers from a scarcity of hope and creates citizens who see threats everywhere. It generates worrying citizens and a paranoid nationalism. This brings us to the final problematic around which the issue of caring has been thought about and articulated: the institutionalisation of a culture of *worrying* at the expense of a culture of caring under the rule of John Howard's Liberal Party.[32]

As numerous commentators on the left have pointed out, the rise of Pauline Hanson and One Nation in the mid-1990s embodied a virulently racist politics that attributed scarcity itself to assaults on a (fictive) Anglo-Australian core. Mark Davis evokes Richard Sennett's discussion of *ressentiment* to explain this:

> *Ressentiment* seems an accurate enough word to describe the sense of disenfranchisement and betrayal felt by many of the people who supported Pauline Hanson's One Nation Party in the late 1990s and early 2000s, or perhaps many of the young men who rioted in Cronulla in 2005. It was convenient, in a way, for those of us who are safely 'inside' the democratic system to accuse them of simple racism when the realities are undoubtedly more complex. What looks like simple racism can also be a reaction to the 'spectre of uselessness', as Sennett calls it, that can haunt those who haven't succeeded in a social meritocracy: 'The spectre of uselessness ... intersects with the fear of foreigners, which, beneath its crust of simple ethnic and race prejudice, is inflected with the anxiety that foreigners may be better armed for the tasks of survival'.[33]

Howard's Liberal Party, Davis also explains, effectively marginalized One Nation by incorporating its agenda and preying on the paranoia it had evoked. As a result race became "*the* political weapon that could be used to destroy the political assumptions and traditional class allegiances of postwar consensus politics."[34] As Mark Latham himself puts it, "The political skill of the Howard Government lies in its ability to appeal to outsiders, even though the government itself is part of the ruling elite."[35] What Hage, Davis and Latham all point to here is something very similar to the world opened up by Tsiolkas through figures like the Kennett Boy (from *Who's Afraid of the Working Class*) and Tommy Stefano: both are marginalized characters who seem to be at the mercy of their *ressentiment*. The narrative of paranoid nationalism these commentators set out reached its nadir, of course, in the Howard Government's exploitation of the *Tampa* crisis to mobilize an electoral victory bound up with border control, national security and the ruthless disregard for the lives of refugees seeking asylum in Australia. The subsequent implementation of an appalling immigration policy premised on a form of thanatopolitics directed at virtually everyone outside the enchanted realm of Australian (or perhaps broadly "Western") citizenship reflects the normalization of racism as a part of Australian political life, and the intractable problems of a political system that tethers rights and legal protection to the stamps in one's passport.

These processes are an indispensible part of the background Tsiolkas has evoked to contextualize *The Slap*. That background, however, probably gets its most thorough treatment in "On the Concept of Tolerance," published the same year as *The Slap*. In that essay Tsiolkas offers his most sustained account of how Hansonism mobilized anxieties about multiculturalism to displace an older language of class conflict. Firstly, it imagined Australia as culturally monolithic in a way that marginalized both immigrant and Indigenous experience: "Conflict, contradiction, change—the very stuff of living history is abandoned."[36] Secondly, it produced a fiction of an imperiled, Anglo-Celtic subject—the "battler"—that rewrote class divisions as ethnic divisions in order to mobilize a politics based on racial enmity:

> the battler could be working class or an aspiring bourgeoisie, a maverick entrepreneur, a straight-talking millionaire journalist. When the battler, however, stepped over the line, when they erupted into violence on the sands of Cronulla, when they beat a young Sudanese-Australian to death in the far-eastern suburbs of Melbourne, they stopped being part of who we are and instead became ugly, became the mob.[37]

Interestingly, Tsiolkas's more recent engagements with immigration and multiculturalism have also acknowledged how neoliberalization has created a paradox at the heart of this set of issues. It is now precisely the beneficiaries of economic rationalization who embody a cosmopolitanism capable of accommodating difference:

> The reality is that there isn't "one nation" that makes up Australia, only competing notions of "nationhood". There is the cosmopolitan, educated nation of the inner cities and the parochial, anxious communities of the urban fringes and the bush. Asylum seeker rights are easily understood and supported by cosmopolitan Australians. We are well-travelled, we are not suspicious of multiculturalism and we are confident of processing and adjusting to change. At the same time, we rubbish their McMansions while gentrification makes the inner city unaffordable, and we castigate them for their cashed-up lack of generosity while it is in fact their kids mixing with the children of refugees.[38]

The passage indicates an anxiety at how its own cosmopolitanism is economically implicated in gentrification, the property market and the perpetuation of inequality. At the same time the passage cannot help but present cosmopolitanism as a kind of cultural capital lacking on the fringes or in the bush. This sense of cultural capital also haunts *The Slap*. On the one hand, the novel is committed to exploding the myth of suburbia as an Anglo-Celtic space and to normalizing an inclusive multiculturalism. On the other hand, multicultural difference is itself flattened into this vision of a privileged cosmopolitanism that, at so many moments in the novel, recasts the hollowed-out signifiers of difference as markers of distinction that reproduce a homogenous, aspirational bourgeois habitus with little relationship to the experiential content of multicultural difference.

The way in which *The Slap* marks characters in terms of their ethnicity is partly what generates this problem. In the scene that Tsiolkas claims is the real slap in the novel, an interaction between an "Anglo" character (Rosie) and an "Aboriginal" character (Bilal) is at the center of the novel's political vision. The rejection of middle or Anglo-Australia marks a break (a slap) that seems to gesture toward a future that might be able to wriggle free of its debilitating entanglements with Australia's colonial past. As I have already pointed out, the strategy here, at least according to the way Tsiolkas glosses it, is allegorical. The characters seem to wear their ethnicity (as they would a costume) in a way that enables them to stand for much broader entities (the phrase "white face," with its uncomfortable echoes of "black face," suggests this). By this reckoning, characters function as synecdoches for larger populations. This is made clear by Tsiolkas in a *Guardian* interview that also touches on this key moment of racial confrontation and emphasizes that the "Anglo" character here is a "white woman who's kind of our idea of Australia—a Home and Away idea."[39] Elsewhere in the novel, this sense of characters wearing ethnicity enables them to disidentify with a pervasive sense of malaise that attaches to middle Australia. Consider the ostensibly Jewish character, Anouk. In the wake of the controversy generated by *Dead Europe* and the sense of that novel not quite separating itself from the stereotypes it explores, the inclusion of a sympathetic Jewish character in *The Slap* obviously is not going to pass unnoticed. Contemplating Rosie, Bilal (who has converted to Islam) and his "white Muslim wife" Shamira, Anouk thinks that all three have tried to shed their pasts and grow "new, vastly different skins."

> She glanced over at Aish and she was suddenly convinced that her friend was thinking exactly the same thoughts. It was a shared moment in which they were both pitying and ridiculing the experiences of the three true authentic Australians. Aish and herself, they had real pasts, real histories. Jewish, Indian, migrant; it all meant something, they had no need to make things up, to assume disguises. (71)

It is hard to know exactly what to do with this sort of passage. It clearly conveys the reflections of a character, not the reflections of a narrator and certainly not the reflections of the author. And yet the strangeness with which Anouk emerges in this novel as Jewish (and with which Aish emerges as Indian, for that matter) leads one to suspect that it is precisely a sort of verbal disguising that creates the aura of cultural or ethnic identity. Put simply, there is almost nothing Jewish about Anouk other than the fact we are told she is Jewish. It is as if the term itself functions as an emblem, a sign, a costume or a verbal fetish. This is underlined by the fact that she comes from Perth, has no family around her, and can thus live in Melbourne without any of the rhythms of Jewish life or any connection to the city's large and culturally vibrant Jewish population. Of course all of that is plausible enough, but to see how these choices implicate the novel's multicultural ambition, we only have to imagine a scenario in which we are not explicitly told that Anouk is Jewish, but in which we see her attend synagogue, or even contemplate the possibility. It is an issue that does not appear in the novel's evocation of Greek-Australians, because those identities are so settled in a more expansively imagined universe. In this respect the section of the novel devoted to Manolis is terrific in the pathos of its evocation of old age, lost friendships and lost time. Here the fact of being Greek is inseparable from the novel's complex evocation of a broader habitus through which identity emerges as so much more than what is contained by the term "Greek." But this is not how other identities are developed, and for this reason the novel's attempt to be panoramic in its evocation of the multicultural also produces a sense of superficiality that is clear in the possibility of referring to the "Jewish," the "Anglo" or the "Aboriginal" characters.[40]

I have no doubt that marking an Anglo identity that has been, historically, unmarked, is an important and legitimate strategy in the novel's performance of multiculturalism. But if we return to Tsiolkas's sense of the interaction between Rosie and Bilal being at the center of the novel, we can see how this strategy creates ambiguities with which this novel has to wrestle. The fact that Tsiolkas's characters wear particular ethnic identities does not mean that ethnicity becomes a totalizing form of characterization. In fact the opposite is more often the case: these identities seem almost ephemeral or interchangeable. It does not matter much who is what so long as we perceive that people are different, and that difference has become a norm. The idea that an Aboriginal character confronting an Anglo character can carry the propitiousness of a historical or political rupture, however, is really only plausible if we assume that characters are subsumed into the identities ascribed to them: the terms "Aboriginal" and "Anglo" have to stand for larger processes that are more important than the complexities of the individuals to which they attach. And remember, it is Tsiolkas's commentary on the novel that insists we read it in this way. It is for this reason that the Anglo couple—Rosie and Gary (the parents of Hugo, the slapped child)—seem so overdetermined in this novel. The emergence of the novel's multicultural sensibility depends on an artful and allegorical displacement of the centrality of the "Anglo," which in turn becomes the object of a great deal of the novel's sublimated aggression. In this respect the novel constantly reminds us of the representational violence from which white Australians have been historically exempted and for which they have been historically responsible. The fact that it is Rosie who summons the law in order prosecute Harry, the man who slapped her child, seems to reflect the increasingly abject situation into which she and her husband have sunk. The absurdity of this recourse to legal protection suggests something like the ruins of a once privileged white experience.

The novel constantly returns to this sense of white abjection in a way that would be problematic in the case of virtually any other identity. As we follow Gary and Rosie through the novel, abjection moves from fleeting and unobtrusive remarks to a much more thorough imposition of the sort of racial typology that Anglo-Australia has used to think about a wide range of other populations. We might even say that this aspect of the novel is one of its technologies of recognition, in so far as it allows Anglo-Celtic Australians to see how the mechanisms of colonial and postcolonial biopolitics that underpin their privilege have treated Indigenous peoples and various immigrant groups. "*Australezi*, what do you expect? It's in their blood!" Hector's mother is wont to say when confronted with Gary's drunkenness (21). Later Harry's wish to see "vermin" like Rosie and Gary "sterilized" is clearly obscene, but his racialized vision of an anachronistic demographic actually does anticipate the way in which their story plays out: "On the cocaine high he had fantasised about a bullet in each of their brains. There was no need. It would be a waste of bullets. They were scum. He and Rocco and Sandi weren't even part of the same species. They were as far above them as the moon was from the earth. There was nothing for him to do. The future would exact its revenge" (135). Harry embodies a familiar sort of bourgeois aggression directed at an apparently feckless working class, though now there is a racialized intensity that carries within it broader histories of discrimination. But the aggression he articulates does inform other moments in the novel at which Rosie and Gary appear as the waste products of demographic and economic changes that have left them in its wake. That Gary's impractical artistic ambitions, like his left-wing identifications, reflect a refusal of his actuality suggests this, while Rosie's relationship with Hugo and his persistent breastfeeding suggest a broader sort of infantilization. We can hear a strong echo of Hage's account of the relationship between infantilized social expectations and paranoid nationalism here. As Hage writes, "the newly marginalised are not used to their state of marginality [...] They live in a state of denial, still expecting that somehow, their nation and their 'national identity' will be a passport to hope for them. 'Deep down', they know that their national society is no longer 'servicing' them, but like a child whose mother has stopped feeding her, the very idea of such a reality is too hard to accept and to think."[41] It is not hard to read Hugo's breastfeeding in *The Slap* as somehow indexical of the broader state of infantilization embodied by his parents.

This immaturity, however, also refers to older, Eurocentric anxieties about suburbia. Together Rosie and Gary embody a refusal to accommodate the suburban ethos embraced by virtually every other character in the novel. In fact it is in them that we see the relics of the anti-suburban outlook the novel has renounced. Gary's resistance to suburbia is also a resistance to the structures of family that anchor Hector and Aish, Bilal and Shamira, and, though more problematically, Harry and Sandi. The fact that family and the property market seem to be quite tightly bound up in this novel also raises a question about how to situate the novel's attempt to accommodate suburban life. When Rosie accompanies Bilal and Shamira on a house-hunting expedition to Thomastown, some of these issues are apparent:

> The unrelenting flat suburban grid of the northern suburbs surrounded them. The further they drove, the more Rosie thought the world around them was getting uglier, the heavy grey sky weighing down on the landscape, crushing down on them. The lawns and nature strips they passed were yellowing, grim, parched. The natural world seemed leached of colour […] She understood her husband's resistance to even thinking about living here, to settling into this dreary suburban emptiness. But it was all they could afford. (246–47)

"Three hundred friggin' thousand dollars. For this dump, for this distillation of banal, ugly suburbia?" (249), Rosie thinks as she wanders through the drab, two-bedroom house Bilal and Shamira will eventually buy. This relationship to property, accentuated in the television adaptation of the novel in which middle-class characters inhabit visions of what the Australian media routinely refers to as "property porn," is one of the novel's most recognizable indexes of social marginalization. If Harry's homicidal rage does not take care of Rosie and Gary, the future, distilled in the tension between the property market and an anachronistic vision of bohemia, almost certainly will.

It is Gary's alcoholism, though, that embodies the novel's most obvious attempt to defamiliarize the racial thinking that has historically underpinned white Australia. When Rosie thinks about her husband's drinking, it is in terms of an explicitly eugenicist framework that reminds us of how protectorate administrators once talked about Indigenous Australians.

> She wondered if it was possible to protect Hugo from his ancestry. Increasingly it was said that mental disease, alcoholism, addiction, it was all genetic. How could she protect him from the microscopic particles of his biological destiny? Her own father's alcoholism hadn't been congenital, the sickness had not run in his family. His drinking had a

cause, it was an effect. The man had lost his job, his house, his wife, and finally his children. But the sickness *was* in Gary's blood. His father had been a drunk. As had his mother. And his grandparents as well. They were probably drunks all the way back to the first convict ship. She almost laughed. He was an exemplary Australian, her husband. She recalled a conversation during dinner from over a decade ago, when Hector had expounded how Australian drinking differed from all other cultures in its extremity, in its lack of conviviality, in the way it centred on the pub bar and not the dinner table. She had blushed then, as she blushed every time she remembered the occasion. How Hector had been able, without any malice in his tone and distaste in his demeanour, to fill that word, *Australian*, with such derision. (256)

When Bilal insists on separating his family from Rosie and Gary—the moment Tsiolkas has put at the center of the novel—he echoes, albeit ambiguously, these sentiments: "I just want to protect my family," he tells Rosie. "I don't think you're any good, Rosie. Sorry, it's just your mob. You've got bad blood. We've escaped your lot, me and my Sammi" (288). The fact that Rosie's section of the novel concludes with Gary passed out on the lounge-room floor, where he has shat himself, seems emblematic of a broader sense of shame, infantilization and abjection that attaches to both of them. If, as Tsiolkas insists, Bilal's rejection of Rosie is the real slap in the novel, then we are forced to see her and her status as "Anglo" embodying an idea of whiteness in excess of the text's realism. At the same time though, it is hard to avoid the feeling that multicultural Australia in *The Slap* is a thoroughly aspirational middle-class society that has merely managed to accommodate a diversity made visible in the signifiers of difference. Despite the novel's best intentions, its progressive vision of a multicultural Australia is almost impossible to distinguish from an aspirational, bourgeois habitus that, in the greater scheme of Tsiolkas's work, is clearly regressive. From this perspective, the stupidity of Gary's artistic aspirations and the egotism of his loathing of suburbia remain the only real forms of disidentification left in the novel, other than the hopefulness of the younger characters (Connie and Richie) who, it is fairly clear, will also eventually have to learn to renounce their idealism and accommodate the everyday. In this respect that fleeting appearance of the Ari character at the novel's opening (in the section devoted to Hector) is almost a piece of misdirection. In *The Slap*, it is Gary and Rosie who embody Ari's antipathy to suburbia, but now that antipathy seems to have lost pretty much all of its topicality and is clearly presented as a kind of immaturity. At this point we can see how the novel's renegotiation of its literary space and its engagement with the politics of multiculturalism overdetermine the question of "whiteness" in a way that generates something not quite aligned with its intentions. Tsiolkas's vision of the multicultural suburb displaces the racial fictions of Anglo-Australia but also the possibility of a resistant, anti-suburban ethos that, it turns out, is deeply beholden to the Eurocentrism of traditional conceptions of literary space.

For this reason *The Slap* develops a cultural politics much more ambivalent and complex than the discourse around it suggests. Having said that, I don't think the immediate strategic value of the novel's treatment of ethnicity can be overstated. Its decentering of the Anglo-Celtic and its propagation of a much more cosmopolitan vision is exactly what a country mired in a regressive debate over immigration needed, and still needs. The novel's insistence on shattering the myth of Australia as white or Anglo-Celtic is a positive contribution to that debate. *The Slap* tries to accommodate readers to the possibility of a national space that has successfully transcended residual notions of racial exclusivity. Its success has a lot to do with that vision, but it is a vision that is also inseparable from the fraught ways in which the novel renegotiates the literary space in which it appears. This renegotiation might be the novel's real and lasting achievement. As Casanova has pointed out, aesthetics and politics constitute the two poles of interpretation that obscure the orientation of writers and their works to the literary space in which they circulate. *The Slap*'s management of ethnicity is what enables it to constitute the eventfulness of its suburban orientation. Its multiculturalism emerges hand in hand with this reimagining of the suburb. If Gary's abject conclusion signals the end of a predicable, bohemian refusal of the everyday, it also suggests the shift in perspective that enables Tsiolkas to produce an ostensibly political novel whose resistance to the world it depicts feels, at moments, so tenuous.

Chapter 5

THE POLITICS OF THE BESTSELLER:
THE SLAP AND *BARRACUDA*

Towards the end of *Barracuda*, Tsiolkas's troubled protagonist, Danny Kelly, finds a dog-eared copy of *David Copperfield*. He has already read the book, but he opens it nevertheless and rereads the opening lines, which have always struck him with a "visceral force": "*Whether I shall turn out to be the hero of my own life, or whether that station will be held by anybody else, these pages must show.*" The sentence forces him to reflect on his own disgrace. He continues to read, but nothing other than the quandary of this opening sentence seems to stay with him: "He couldn't think how anyone but himself could be the hero of his own life, but he knew that he wasn't a hero."[1] Later (years later in the story but a mere forty-odd pages as we read the novel), Danny returns to Dickens. After an angry but cathartic confrontation with his working-class father, Danny realizes that his father "was a good man": "It struck him with the force of revelation, exultation, light flooding through him. His father was a good man. His father was the hero of his own life" (459). These moments are, thematically speaking, at the center of the novel. They also orient *Barracuda* to a fairly conventional sense of character development. This is a *Bildungsroman* in the tradition of *David Copperfield* or *Great Expectations*, yet it also takes a metafictional approach to the genre. For *Barracuda* to emerge as a *Bildungsroman*, Danny has to learn to reconstruct the ruins of his own life into a narrative that can take him beyond the anger and alienation that has largely defined him. This also means that he has to develop a passion for reading, for the pleasures of language and for the sort of temporality that narrative can provide. From this perspective, *Barracuda* is, first and foremost, a novel about the medium of literature and its profoundly restorative function. In chapter 1 I suggested that Tsiolkas's first novel, *Loaded*, rejected the form of the *Bildungsroman* and the vision of cultural education as a mode of social integration that it implies. That Tsiolkas's most recent novel, published almost twenty years later, recuperates a genre so antithetical to the early part of his career indicates its own kind of narrative arc and suggests the ways in which Tsiolkas's conception of how literature might relate to its social context has undergone a gradual but pronounced shift.

If this sounds like a throwback (and perhaps it is), it also needs to be stressed that this narrative about narrative's redemptive ability plays out against other forms of media that feel deceptive, corrosive and finally damaging. At the start of his story, Danny Kelly is a young, working-class kid from an immigrant background. He is also a champion swimmer. He gets a scholarship to an elite private school and encounters the class-based prejudices of kids who have grown up in extremely affluent parts of Melbourne like Toorak and Armadale, but his ability as a swimmer carries him through all of this to the point at which he is on the cusp of greatness. But after the rise comes the fall. His failure to win a medal at the Pan Pacific Games in Fukuoka triggers a humiliating breakdown driven by simmering class-based resentment. What follows is the rapid disintegration of his career. He drops out of school and gets a job in a supermarket while his former schoolmates all go on to university. On the night of the opening ceremony of the Sydney Olympics in 2000—a moment that he had always imagined would belong to him—he gate-crashes a party being held by Martin Taylor, one of his former friends on the school swimming team, gets drunk and beats Taylor's face into a bloody pulp with the help of a broken glass. The moment of violence, which will land Danny in prison and represents the nadir of his story, but also the possibility of redemption, is characteristically overdetermined. It is informed by resentment, rage and Danny's own sense of failure. But behind all of this is the much broader problem of Danny's inability to locate himself except through the phantasmagoria of the mass media, with its orientation to huge sporting events as spectacular, though obviously hollow, representations of the nation. The night of the opening ceremony, a night that virtually all Australians will recall, catalyzes Danny's fall and highlights the damage implicit in the mediatization of the nation and the self as a component of it. If the notion of *Bildung*, which I discussed in chapter 1, orients to the unfolding of innate capacities until they manifest in a compatibility with the objective social context external to them, the media spectacle as Tsiolkas presents it here reads like a parody of that process of incorporation and harmonization. Danny can only be assimilated into the phantasmagoria of the nation through profoundly damaging forms of alienation that erode the stability of the self and its relationship to its habitus.

How does Tsiolkas establish this sense of alienation? To begin with, the novel is organized in a non-linear manner. In this sense its structure is not unlike the split-frame technique used by *Dead Europe* to such great effect. We move between Danny's life as a swimmer and his life after prison. In the first part of the novel these two halves of Danny's experience are related in different voices. We move from the third-person voice of what feels like a young adult novel to Danny's more mature and reflective first-person voice. In the second part this structure is inverted. The movement is probably essential to the readability of the novel. Precisely because of the way in which the worlds of school and swimming close around Danny's sense of himself, the parts of the novel that recount Danny's swimming career feel claustrophobic and run the risk of being too invested in the forms of experience the novel clearly sets out to displace. Driven by anger, competitiveness and egotism, Danny's early incarnations seem to be grasping at forms of identification that undermine his ability to stabilize an ethically centered sense of self. These identifications correspond to a creeping sense of abjection that coheres in the novel's ability to recreate media spectacles most Australians will have seen. The section of the novel that describes Danny and his family watching Kieren Perkins win a gold medal at the Atlanta Olympics works like this. It is a moment deeply embedded in recent Australian memory. Many of us felt elated watching it. But there is something disturbing about the detail with which Tsiolkas recreates it. It is as if repetition in the medium of a novel is also a form of demystification, and once events like this have been reformed in this way, ossified in fiction, we cannot help feeling compromised by the importance they have (or once had) in the formation of national life: "It was Perkins, Kowalski, Smith. It was gold for Australia, it was silver for Australia" (80). The syntax here pushes the voice of television commentary into the free indirect discourse that relates Danny's thoughts. As a result, we get an unmistakable sense of a character's interior space filling up with the linguistic junk of the mass media spectacle and of experience being commandeered by televised sport. Something like autonomy is being surrendered to an abjectly instrumentalized form of distraction that, for the reader at least, feels nauseatingly insular. The novel's meticulous recreation of the opening ceremony in Sydney has the same effect. As Danny watches it, aware of how thoroughly he has been excluded from the pageant of the nation, he is still capable of rehearsing the folklore of Australia's sporting prowess.

> The stadium was in darkness and a woman in a wheelchair held the Olympic torch aloft. Dan knew that the old lady was Betty Cuthbert and the woman pushing the wheelchair was Raelene Boyle. 'Cuthbert,' whispered Dan, 'you were at Melbourne and Rome; and Boyle, you won silver in Mexico City.' He stretched out a finger, as if to touch the screen. 'I know how you were cheated in Montreal,' he continued whispering. 'I think I can imagine what it cost you not to go to Moscow.' (282)

The solemnity of these moments is partly what makes them feel so awkward. They remind us of the airless world of Australian childhoods compulsively oriented to television sets and the sporting mythologies they perpetuated. Even though Danny's hatred of what he calls the "golden boys" (white, privileged athletes, made for their role in the media spectacle) indicates a degree of skepticism, the early parts of his story are defined by his near total absorption in this world.

But from his vantage point as an ex-swimmer, he also realizes that the future he thought was his is gone: "It was all dust" (284). In its absence, he has to confront his own essential hollowness. By not being there at the 2000 Olympics, "he was nothingness itself, he had failed to exist," except as a vessel tormented by the persistence of the media spectacle that proceeds without him:

> he had shut his eyes and though he was trying to shut out the sound, the world had rushed in, he couldn't stop it, it seeped into him and through him and around him: darting specks of red and yellow light were criss-crossing the darkness behind his shut eyelids, they made the bodies whole and they conjured up the athletes. He opened his eyes and there, in close-up, was Kieren Perkins, waving to the fevered crowd, and as the camera began to pan across the Australian team, that group of golden boys and golden girls, he knew that he had to inhale, he had to open his lungs, and so he turned and was fighting for breath, pushing and shoving and kicking and elbowing until he had broken through the deafening mass, and was on the footpath, in the open air. There wasn't a car in sight, there was no one on the street—not one other being to share his humiliation. He was alone and wretched in the world. (278)

To overcome this sense of hollowness and the violence it engenders, Danny also has to learn how to reconstruct his own life as a different sort of narrative, one grounded ultimately in family and a recuperative sense of charity, rather than in the egotistical gratification of celebrity and the mass spectacle. It is for this reason that Danny's developing passion for literature is important. Words, language and ultimately narrative become forms of self-discovery and empowerment that enable him to take back his life. At times this feels like a form of escapism that allows Danny to forget his own shame and to lose himself in Dickens, Eliot, Hardy, Dostoevsky, Tolstoy, Zola, Balzac, Hugo and Stendhal. But it is also clear that Tsiolkas wants us to see language as a medium essential to our capacity for meaningful and autonomous self-fashioning. Danny discovers that books can be woven into corporeal experience, that language can order time and space, that it can reclaim the past and reanimate memory. If we are going to become the heroes of our own lives, we need lives that are our own, that are built out of our own experiences, our own proximities and intimacies, not mediated by forces beyond us or oriented to largely imagined horizons of collectivity. By the time Danny can atone for his crime and reclaim a sense of agency, he has also reoriented his life to his own experiences of family, intimacy, and care for others. This story also hinges on the recognition that subjectivity's ethical horizon is inseparable from the mutual reciprocity of community and a broader notion of self-sacrifice and charity.

It is, without doubt, Tsiolkas's most optimistic statement and his most decisive move away from the apocalyptic tone of his earlier novels. It is also a statement that seems to embody a kind of repose, a leaning toward humility that segues into a broader discourse about immaturity in Australia. In a 2013 essay on asylum seekers, Tsiolkas uses the Greek word *amorphoté* to describe a disposition that he perceives as deeply related to the climate of prejudice around the nation's failure to address the cruelty of its current immigration policy. The background here will be well known, at least to Australians, and broadly intuitable by most other people living in the West. The unwillingness of successive Australian governments to process the asylum claims of refugees arriving by boat has led to a humanitarian catastrophe where, in most cases, legitimate asylum seekers are incarcerated in a legal limbo on Nauru and on Manus Island in Papua New Guinea. The policy of refusing to allow boats carrying these people to land on Australian soil has also increased the danger and the death toll of the journey from Indonesia to Australian waters. This shameful history speaks to the larger issue of racial animosity in Australia and the cynical use of race by conservative Australian governments as a "wedge" to divide the electorate against itself. It is in this context that so much of Tsiolkas's recent writing and thinking needs to be understood. His evocation of the word *amorphoté*, a word used by his parents, enables him to evoke a broad range of political and cultural failings implicated in the ruthless and paranoid treatment of a global underclass: "How do I translate this Greek word? Literally, it means to be uneducated but this is inadequate. My parents were not educated people; born to peasant families, they didn't undergo secondary schooling. What Mum and Dad were referring to was a code of behaviour, a civility that they believed Australians lacked."[2] It is a civility, Tsiolkas goes on to suggest, bound up with compassion, generosity and kindness. Comparing the efforts of the Asylum Seeker Resource Centre with the demeaning, Kafkaesque administration of the Refugee Review Tribunal, he gives us a further sense of what the word might mean. It is not a lack of academic education but "barbarity, pure and simple"; the barbarity of ignorance, or prejudice, and of a failure to think and feel beyond an often violent and xenophobic egotism. That the word *amorphoté* allows Tsiolkas to claim the mantle of *Bildung* (or something like it) not as the imposition of an Anglo (or Anglo-Germanic) tradition of bourgeois assimilation, but as part of his own cultural inheritance, is important. The word evokes, by way of opposition, a form of maturation not contaminated by any prior association with hegemonic educational structures. Instead it points to a sense of social inclusivity premised on thinking beyond restrictive notions of ethnicity and citizenship.

The orientation to charity and self-sacrifice manifest in Danny's decision to work in disability rehabilitation (he cares for men suffering acquired brain damage) feels like a decisive move beyond the *amorphoté* that seems to characterize his life once his dreams of becoming a great swimmer are bound up with the privileged world of private school education, which is very clearly a world of barbarity: insularity, ignorance, class- and race-based prejudice. That the men Danny cares for are located on a kind of biopolitical threshold is also important. They all have diminished intellectual capacity and a limited ability to maintain themselves. They are all on the margins of society, which jeopardizes their claims to social inclusion and recognition. The novel does not dwell on the broader political and theoretical subtexts here. To do so would be heavy-handed. But at a time when the Australian state has become so exclusionary, Danny's gravitation to this threshold clearly has a broader range of historical resonances and associations. It indicates a rejection of the phantasmagoria of national inclusion that he once believed was manifest in media spectacles of parading athletes and a commitment to the very populations most minoritized by these fantasies of able-bodied normalcy. One does not have to do too much imaginative work to think about the spectacle of the 1936 Olympics in Berlin and the German state's almost simultaneous liquidation of what, in the terminology of fascism, was called *lebensunwertes Leben* (life not fit to be lived). Tsiolkas has not made these associations explicit. It is perhaps an exaggeration to say that they haunt the novel. Nevertheless the association between the national spectacle and the novel's visions of damaged, marginalized men in the precarious care of the welfare system suggests some sort of continuity here. This becomes clearer when we remember the climate of racism and racially motivated paranoia in which the novel was written. *Amorphoté*, in this sense, might suggest a broader sort of ethical failure in which restrictive conceptions of the person, personhood or the citizen also administer potentially fatal forms of social exclusion that are continuous with the idea of legal death that we have seen in *Non Parlo di Salò*.

At this point, *Barracuda* could be read as speaking to a kind of impasse in the way the Australian left has tried to develop a totalizing vision of the country's political landscape. As Mark Davis has argued, the ascendency of the New Right in Australian political life has driven current policies on immigration and the treatment of asylum seekers, and it has also eroded the forms of egalitarianism on which Australian society is apparently based. The neoliberal creation of a disadvantaged population (the unemployed and the underemployed), Davis suggests, enabled the rise of One Nation and the subsequent wedge politics of the Howard government. As we saw in the previous chapter, the cultural politics accompanying this process of marginalization seems to be visible in the ways in which *The Slap* frames Rosie and Gary. Their resentment reflects their sense of having being excluded from what, elsewhere in the novel, looks like a prosperous middle class. Davis explains this process by appealing to a notion of rights displaced by the logic of the marketplace.

> In meritocratic societies, democracy, in fact, tends to become a matter of difference between insiders and outsiders who need to be managed, and whose equally disenfranchised sub-groups tend to be warring and set against each other (again, as at Cronulla). This shift is from an egalitarian democracy to a market democracy that is explicitly anti-egalitarian, and from a rights model of citizenship towards a model that understands citizenship as the exercise of market opportunities.[3]

The reference to the Cronulla riots here links a popular sort of racism to these processes of market rationalization. Elsewhere in Davis's work a "politics of cruelty" manifest in the government's administration of detention centers for asylum seekers (with the 2001 *Tampa* incident in the foreground) is also underwritten by these processes of domestic disenfranchisement.[4] What I see as an impasse here relates to a somewhat nostalgic investment in a "rights model of citizenship," which misconstrues a cause of the problem for a solution. As Hannah Arendt so convincingly argued in *The Origins of Totalitarianism*, the very entanglement of rights and citizenship, the virtual impossibility of disassociating the two, ensures that those without citizenship—refugees who are stateless—also enter the space of the political under the sign of an erasure.[5] Giorgio Agamben glosses Arendt's argument when he writes that:

> the figure that should have embodied human rights more than any other—namely, the refugee—marked instead the radical crisis of the concept. The conception of human rights based on the supposed existence of a human being as such, Arendt tells us, proves to be untenable as soon as those who profess it find themselves confronted for the first time with people who have really lost every quality and every specific relation except for the pure fact of being human.[6]

It is precisely this entanglement of rights and citizenship that underpins the "politics of cruelty," and that lingers behind the victimization of dislocated populations that we see in *Dead Europe*. Against this context, Tsiolkas's critique of *amorphoté* and his interest in the sort of selfless maturity that was once the domain of the nineteenth-century *Bildungsroman* announces an ethical orientation that can gesture at a progressive political vision precisely because it can also bypass the precise terms of the impasse that an investment in the rights of citizenship is now confronting. I do not mean this as a criticism. On the contrary, the ability to gesture at an ethical horizon unencumbered by these problems is one of the things that a writer of fiction is licensed to do. In fact, *Barracuda*'s investment in charity and care feels like an allegorization of the position Ghassan Hage sets out in *Against Paranoid Nationalism*, in which he opposes a "worrying" nation to a "caring" one. As we saw in the previous chapter, "worrying" in this sense points to forms of anxiety and to competition for the scarce resource of hope that have been co-opted into a xenophobic, paranoid consensus. "Caring," in contrast, suggests an openness to alterity that has moved beyond the panic induced by notions of scarcity.[7] As Danny Kelly refashions himself around a selfless surrender to an ethic of care, he also replaces the fiction of the nation with an orientation to the very people most at risk of falling out of the magic circle of rights-based citizenship; those with diminished physical and intellectual capacity who, as Arendt puts it in regard to the stateless, "have lost all distinctive political qualities and have become human beings and nothing else."[8]

At this point, the novel also recasts Tsiolkas's habitual interest in abjection. Readers of the earlier novels will be familiar with the ways in which abjection organizes the transgressive forms of sexuality that Tsiolkas explores. This is one of the most commented-upon aspects of his work, and we see it again in *Barracuda*, though now in a more stylized manner. In prison, Danny discovers his homosexuality through a relationship that is literally mediated by the exchange of bodily secretions: pieces of tissue paper containing semen, urine and fecal matter. These exchanges structure his relationship with his lover Carlo, but their orientation to the abject also anticipates the boundary that Danny will need to cross when he becomes a caregiver later in the novel. For perhaps the first time in Tsiolkas's work, the topos of abjection is taken beyond the realm of the sexual, and becomes a part of the everyday routine of caring that requires a certain kind of self-surrender. One would not be wrong to hear echoes of Patrick White, for whom abjection implies a wide-ranging kind of openness to the other, often in the form of care or hospitality. What ultimately emerges here are the multiple senses in which one can move beyond the limits of an atomized, egotistical self. In prison, Danny tells us, words free his imagination and enable him to "soar up and beyond walls and concrete and steel." Being "pierced and entered" by Carlo is also a moment of transcendence; it "liberates me from my will" (205). The sense of giving himself to others with which Danny's story of maturation concludes has to be understood as more or less continuous with these other ways in which the self is overcome or obliterated. Self-discovery is also self-renunciation. The process of becoming the hero of one's own life involves giving up on any conception of the "hero" mediated by the spectacle, by the technologies of the market, or the norms of an aspirational bourgeoisie.

Read in this way, as a self-conscious *Bildungsroman* pitted against other forms of cultural mediation, *Barracuda* very clearly circulates a claim about its own value as literature, and about the value of novel reading to a broader sense of public maturation. It is no coincidence that Danny's maturation is also characterized by a refusal of mass and digital media: "He preferred the silence, the loneliness that was comfort; he didn't want uproar and infinite noise [...] In reading he found solitude. In reading he could dispel the blare of the world" (330). What Tsiolkas has in mind here has nothing to do with the professional practices of literary critics or scholars. Instead it orients to a more informal, autodidactic relationship to books. This orientation can be contextualized in a number of ways. We have seen that the discourse Tsiolkas has produced around *The Slap* effectively politicizes that novel partly by stressing the insular, egotistical limits of middle-class consciousness. *Barracuda* is also written in that vein of critique. We have also seen that Tsiolkas is very interested in the ways in which different media forms construct experience, and that this issue has formed one of the persistent thematic threads of his writing. His work on cinema has stressed the often utopian qualities of that medium and its ability to evoke corporeal experiences that might not readily find other forms of expression. *Loaded* and *The Jesus Man* offer up specific media ecologies organized around popular music, the Walkman, television and pornography. *Barracuda* continues this interrogation of media forms, but here, for the first time really, we get a very clear sense of literature's ability to consolidate a sense not of political dissidence, but of social responsibility pitted against the mass spectacle. This is all the more striking given the ways in which Tsiolkas's early fiction cultivated forms of negativity that either reject social incorporation or reveal its deeply pathological dimensions.

The idea of maturation set out in Danny's story corresponds to the way in which maturity has become a trope in Tsiolkas's own critical reception. Peter Craven's review of *Merciless Gods*, for instance, conjures this framework. It is as if Tsiolkas himself has become a character in a *Bildungsroman*. With *Merciless Gods*, Tsiolkas has "kicked on" and "developed." The "ugly-ugly quality" of his early work has settled into something as "traditional as a story by Somerset Maugham or Henry James." It is lavish praise from one of Australia's most respected critics. What it suggests is that Tsiolkas's arrival as a "master" is also a repudiation of the raw, visceral and decidedly immature qualities that made his early work so compelling.[9] It is not hard to see this as a trade-off between the aesthetic and the political, between a kind of belletristic respectability and a youthful rebelliousness. It is true that many of the stories in *Merciless Gods* have a kind of formal accomplishment and economy lacking in the earlier novels, but it is also important to grasp this as a consequence of how many of these stories ("The Hair of the Dog," "Saturn Returns," "Genetic Material" and "The Disco at the End of Communism," for instance) displace or redescribe the dissident elements that dominated the earlier work. There is a pattern here: a narrator or a central character cares for a dying family member or remembers one who is already deceased. This pattern establishes the primacy of filial relationships and essentially reconciles them with political and/or subcultural currents that run counter to the logic of reproductive futurity and the middle-class family.

In "The Hair of the Dog," for instance, a son recalls the wild literary career of his alcoholic mother: her often autobiographically driven writing was "undisciplined," obsessed with the "euphoria that comes with drinking," and characterized by "righteous fury" but devoid of "genuine kindness." It is also, at moments, "perverse" and informed by an "unrepentant eroticism."[10] But the crucial point here is that the elegiac tone of the story keeps its distance from this sort of writing: it is a story about remembrance, not rebelliousness. It is tempting to read this as a model for how Tsiolkas's own writing has matured precisely through its ability to displace its earlier investments; to look back on them and to articulate them without allowing them to subsume or infect the narrative perspective. In "The Disco at the End of Communism," a successful, middle-class family man mourns and eulogizes his politically radical brother, who had previously turned his back on his family. In "Saturn Returns," a son participates in the euthanasia of his AIDS-afflicted father. In "Genetic Material" a son helps his father, who is stricken with Alzheimer's disease, masturbate (and then tastes his semen). All of these stories are intensely moving, partly because their formal economy is secured by a narrative perspective that expresses a desire for reconciliation. This involves displacing or reframing political and sexual elements that, in other contexts, one might expect to be resistant to the harmonizing ethos of the *Bildungsroman* form. In *Barracuda*, Danny's investment in family feels similar. A productive and nurturing relationship with family members suggests reconciliation with the social body more broadly conceived and an attenuation of the earlier sense of class difference that produces an intractable and destructive kind of rage.

Maturity in *Barracuda* is, however, not without a vague feeling of disquiet, if only because the milieu of university-educated leftism that Danny encounters through his friends Demet and Luke feels conventional to the point of parody. Take Demet, for instance. Like Danny, she is from a working-class, immigrant background. By the time Danny reencounters her after his release from prison, she is working on a PhD and comfortably ensconced in a long-term lesbian relationship. Together with Danny's Scottish boyfriend Clyde, she rehearses diatribes about Australia's conservatism that feel numbingly propositional: "We are parochial and narrow-minded and we are racist and ungenerous and we occupy this land illegitimately and we're toadies to the Poms and servile to the Yanks" (401–02). A few pages later, as the discussion drifts to the "moralism" of the middle classes, Danny realizes that he and Demet have both become middle-class themselves, but are haunted by the fact that "the middle class wasn't worth it" (408). It is a telling moment at which we can glimpse Tsiolkas reflecting on a context in which maturation feels like a particularly bourgeois achievement that reduces the political to the status of platitudes over dinner.

For Craven, it is the formal qualities of *Merciless Gods* that integrate Tsiolkas into the space of the nation. Gone is the "Greek gay boy who used to bawl and brag about his sexuality and ethnicity with such clamour and self-regard." The sense of particularity here is dispelled with the claim that "everyone in the country who cares about fiction" should read the collection's opening story.[11] At least in regard to *The Slap* and *Barracuda*, however, this stress on formal accomplishment as the basis of national integration drastically misconstrues the way in which Tsiolkas's fiction has positioned itself. We have seen that *Barracuda*'s embrace of the literary corresponds to its deep (and deeply critical) relationship to the mass media. The orientation to other, popular forms of media is also, very clearly, a central organizing feature of *The Slap*. I will discuss *The Slap*'s engagement with television soap operas in a moment, but first it should be stressed that what really creates a continuity between *The Slap* and *Barracuda* and separates those two novels from Tsiolkas's earlier work is the unmistakable sense that both are thoroughly and self-consciously integrated into a popular media landscape, rather than defined in opposition to it, even though both take issue with the ways in which television mediates experience. What I mean by this is that both seem to have put aside the idea that literature might define itself through its refusal to engage with other forms of social and cultural production that are more obviously permeated by the logic of the market: a refusal that might be evident in stylistic opacity, abstraction, experimentation or the intransigence of the word in relationship to its propositional translatability. Instead, both novels firmly anchor themselves in the space of popular media consumption, where they assert claims about their political value relative to other media forms with which they are competing and with which they are in dialogue. This reorientation of the literary toward the popular seems quite representative of the way in which Australian writing has responded both to a changed political climate since the beginning of the so-called war on terrorism and to a cultural climate, almost simultaneous with it, in which the viability of literary fiction seems increasingly threatened by the homogenizing forces of the market. These circumstances have made the kind of autonomy that apparently typified an older form of modernism increasingly problematic in Australia.

This is what Mark Davis has called the "decline of the literary paradigm": "Literary journals such as *ABR* and *Meanjin* and the book pages of broadsheet newspapers have set themselves up as nostalgic guardians of a (mid-list) literary culture at odds with both the 'postmodernist' academy and the new commercial imperatives. Their valorisation of old-fashioned notions of aesthetics and artistic autonomy can be understood as part of an attempt to recover art as a space sealed off from market forces."[12] The increasing marginalization of these older notions of aesthetic autonomy, at least in so far as they inform the calculations and practices of the Australian publishing industry, seemed to find a fairly dramatic confirmation in the *Australian*'s so-called "Patrick White hoax" of July 2006. Chapter 3 of White's *The Eye of the Storm* was submitted to a representative group of editors and publishers under the name Wraith Picket. The responses indicated that the Nobel Prize winner's chances of getting published today would be very slim indeed, at least in Australia. One might lament this, but it also seems clear that during the early part of the twenty-first century the marginalization of a conception of value linked to modernist aesthetics, or to a broader philological investment in the autonomy of literary language, has reinvigorated both contemporary Australian fiction and criticism. In the last chapter I suggested that the shift from *Dead Europe* to *The Slap* embodies a reorientation away from residual notions of cultural capital to a new willingness to embrace the quotidian dimension of Australian experience. A novel like *Barracuda*, so clearly directed at a mass reading public, reflects something similar. This movement also seems to be in keeping with a renewed sense of the political urgency around fiction. Opposition to current regimes of national security and border control has generated a robustly political literature that is also mindful of its accessibility and implicitly understands that its efficacy cannot be separated from issues of readership and circulation. A politically effective literature, in other words, might also have to be a commercially successful one. Hence the once unlikely, and for some uncomfortable, proposition that today, at least in Australia, renouncing the aesthetic autonomy, or negativity, that defined the resistant qualities of modernism might be central to consolidating a sense of literature's political engagement. This is the new, and paradoxical, politics of the bestseller.

In the first decade of the new century, Linda Jaivin's *The Infernal Optimist*, Andrew McGahan's *Underground* and Richard Flanagan's *The Unknown Terrorist* (dedicated to the former Guantanamo Bay inmate David Hicks) all pointed to this shift away from the aesthetic as a form of resistance and toward a much more direct and sometimes didactic engagement with a contemporary political climate defined by neo-conservative, neo-imperialist and narrowly nationalist approaches to both foreign policy and domestic issues. What distinguished these novels (all published in 2006) from other novels that shared their political commitment was the fact that their engagements seem to emerge alongside their appropriation of popular idioms and genres. All, in other words, at least implicitly phrase their claims to political effectiveness through a refusal of autonomous aesthetic forms and a reproduction of what might be called (after Jacques Rancière) the "popular *gestus*."[13] What Richard Flanagan had to say about *The Unknown Terrorist* is very revealing in this regard. The author of *Gould's Book of Fish*, a work of magical realism and self-conscious literariness, had abandoned any hint of formal complexity in order to maximize the political efficacy of his new novel:

> The sentences are short, the words are small, and I want the reader to pass through the words as the eye does through a window, and see straight into the story. I wanted it to be one of those books people read in one or two sittings and feel like they have been in a car smash and their life ever after is a little changed. I wanted it to be a Trojan horse of a book, a book that everyone would want to read, but having read it, some ideas escape into the citadels of suburban lounge rooms and people once more begin to think and question.[14]

I am using the phrase "popular *gestus*" to describe this sort of strategic populism, because it is just as clear that none of the novels I am talking about belong easily or naturally to what Ken Gelder has called the "field" of popular fiction (though they do not quite belong to the field of literature as Gelder discusses it either).[15] They all allude to the popular in a gestural, performative or strategic manner without necessarily occupying or embodying it in a way that implies an understanding of the logics of genre or a relationship to fan-based networks of circulation and validation.

The popular orientation of these novels was echoed in critical work around the same time. In an *Overland* essay that also appeared in 2006, Gelder himself calls for a fiction that engages with commercial logics in order to generate a popular critique of neoliberalism, a "critical political realism" that refuses the rarefied and elitist conception of aesthetics that he brands "Tory style."[16] *The Slap* and *Barracuda* represent a development—even a heightening—of this ethos, and in fact the latter's account of "Cunts College" largely accords with what Gelder has in mind when he talks about Tories. Dismantling residual forms of cultural capital and institutional privilege is an important aspect of a literary politics for both Gelder and Tsiolkas (though one suspects that Gelder, unlike Tsiolkas, would also place a figure like Adorno in the Tory camp). Though *The Slap* and *Barracuda* are critical of popular media forms, they both offer versions of the literary that have emptied themselves of virtually any possibility of aesthetic alterity. Rather, the literary becomes one more form of popular media, though one that can engage with other media in a critical or correctional manner, and offer a much more restorative way of constructing experience. For a critic like Gelder, this also makes the literary more democratic and hence more able to actualize a progressive politics. Yet it also integrates novels into an industrial model of cultural production in which the political is dependent on the commercial. The questions here about aesthetics, politics and the market cannot be resolved by polarized conceptions of value that oppose "elite" culture to "popular" culture. Rather—and I think Tsiolkas's most recent work demonstrates this— relationships between literary aesthetics, the political and the commercial form a sort of constellation that moves forward via a series of stops and starts, or checks and balances. Critique, we might say, is now also a process of compromise: a kind of strategic instrumentalization.

The operative term here might be middlebrow. It is a concept that has long been used to designate the insipid compromises of bourgeois taste, but as Beth Driscoll's work demonstrates, it can also describe a much more complex and topical cultural formation. For Driscoll, the term middlebrow designates a series of relationships between texts and the forms of media that help them circulate; it also designates relationships between readers and the texts they consume that are, in many instances, functions of the media vectors out of which these texts emerge. Middlebrow texts repudiate suppositions about the autonomy of the literary precisely because they are visibly integrated into "commercial distribution networks" and "new media formats." They also orient to middle-class notions of recreation, but at the same time imply a qualitative dimension evident in the earnestness, reverence and emotional investment that readers bring to them. Stories of "personal growth and moral redemption" seem ideally suited to solicit this sort of disposition.[17] There is little doubt that *The Slap* and *Barracuda* both conform to this model. In fact, the *Bildungsroman* form embodied in the latter seems exemplary in its ability to consolidate the range of middlebrow identifications Driscoll discusses.

Because the concept of the middlebrow, as Driscoll points out, stresses commercial dynamics and forms of mediation that are exterior to the field of the literary as it is traditionally conceived, it also demands a much more interdisciplinary approach to the texts it describes. *The Slap* and *Barracuda* have to be understood as media events that set in motion processes and dynamics that are best elucidated through the fields of cultural studies and media studies. Both texts generate meaning by virtue of their interactions with other media forms. Both appropriate the strategies and the topoi of these forms, and both are tethered very closely to the increasing visibility of Tsiolkas himself as a public intellectual, if not a literary celebrity. This shift in methodology reflects the ways in which these texts have surrendered their claims to an autonomy that would place them in the domain of the philological. Some of the approaches and concepts that are useful here have been set out by the work of Graeme Turner, John Hartley and McKenzie Wark, among others who have investigated the function of celebrity in the Australian media. We have already looked at the way in which Hartley's seminal sense of a "postmodern public sphere" moves away from a traditional Habermasian model of the bourgeois public sphere to posit the political potential of otherwise disparaged forms of popular culture anchored around celebrities. In a related vein, McKenzie Wark has argued that celebrities essentially mediate the cultural commons in that they supply communal points of orientation.

> Australians have many different ways of thinking and feeling, but nevertheless share a cyberspace within which cultural differences are not only negotiated and adjudicated, but creatively combined. The most visible signs of this process are celebrities. They embody not just the particular culture from which they come, they embody also something beyond. We may not like the same celebrities, we may not like any of them at all, but it is the existence of a population of celebrities, about whom to disagree, that makes it possible to constitute a sense of belonging.[18]

As Graeme Turner, Francis Bonner and David Marshall write, the blurring of the space between private and public spheres is central to this process.[19] Tsiolkas, almost since the beginning of his career, has made a point of turning his private life out to the public. As early as *Jump Cuts*, there is a clear assumption that his private life is the stuff of public circulation. And while this was in the interests of interrogating the structural underpinnings of our notions of private and public spheres, it is also clear that the strategy lent itself to Tsiolkas's growing visibility.

Against this background, literary celebrities—Tsiolkas, Anna Funder, Tim Winton and Richard Flanagan, for instance—occupy a sort of liminal position that allows them to draw on the extended circulation created by market technologies without quite surrendering a residual sense of cultural capital that is still associated, however tenuously, with the literary. As Brigid Rooney explains, the ability of writers to function as non-expert political commentators hinges on "a commitment to literary-field-related values of freedom and autonomy."[20] Though she does also stress the ability of writers simply to communicate lucidly, it is without doubt the authority of autonomy (or its ghost) that underpins the ability of writers to speak credibly about politics. This authority is inherited from or through residual conceptions of how literature has functioned in Western societies. Rooney's summary of how Tim Winton's work circulates gets at the possibilities of this formation but also hints (perhaps unintentionally) at the depressingly propositional quality of middlebrow writing:

> His novels orient themselves to a new "middlebrow" readership, to those seeking a quality reading experience but unwilling or unable to invest the time required for more arcane, difficult or inaccessible texts. Winton's fiction embraces a broad readership, offering accessibility and quite immediate reward. Yet it bears the traces of an older literary disposition, referencing its cultural inheritance.[21]

Whether this is a cause for celebration or not remains up in the air. We are all no doubt more comfortable with figures like Flanagan and Winton mediating a non-expert sense of the political than with figures like Sophie Lee or Kylie Minogue (two of John Hartley's examples of postmodern celebrity). But the idea that Australian literary culture is now less and less invested in producing writing that grasps the aesthetic itself as a mode of resistance surely represents a kind of impoverishment bound up with the renunciation of possibilities that exceed instrumentalization.

Today Tsiolkas, perhaps more so than any other Australian writer, occupies this liminal position at which commercial technologies and a trace-memory of aesthetic autonomy seem to coexist. It is a liminality that also seems to be explicitly thematized in his work. As Mandy Treagus has argued, *The Slap* sets out to "queer the divisions between the literary and the popular."[22] What she means by this crystallizes in the novel's dialogue with suburban soap operas like *Neighbours* and *Home and Away*. This is something numerous critics have commented upon and that Tsiolkas himself has made central to the discourse around the novel. As Kalinda Ashton puts it:

> There's more than a whiff of soap opera in the structure and form of *The Slap*. With its epic span and its domestic focus, the book suggests what *Neighbours* could be—if that show was populated with Aborigines who had redeemed themselves through Islam; if episodes featured bisexual AIDS-afflicted men being good parents; if the characters were Indian, Serbian, Greek, Jewish and Arabic [sic]; if they swallowed pills at backyard barbecues, experimented with the consolatory sexual excitements of shampoo bottles, and let their school kids experiment with ecstasy, anti-Bush posters and same-sex baths with no palpable ill-effects.[23]

While Ashton seems to present this as an endorsement of the novel's subversive energy, it is difficult not to read an anxiousness about how the literary might be compromised by its proximity to mass media forms, even as the novel offers a definitive rejection of their cultural insularity. *The Slap*, of course, raises this issue almost as its opening gambit. Anouk is an aspiring novelist but also makes a living as a scriptwriter for a television soap opera. The sense of her having being coopted by the culture industry provokes the ire of Gary who, as we have seen, remains invested in a vision of art as some sort of resistance to bourgeois respectability. "That's not how real families are," Gary accuses her. Of course it isn't, it's commercial television, she tells him. The argument continues and its tone lingers through the opening scenes of the novel.

> "But you're perpetrating bullshit that has an influence on millions of people around the world! Everyone thinks that Australian families are exactly like those on the show. Don't you want to do something better with your writing?"
>
> "I do. That's why I work as a scriptwriter on the show. To make money to pay for the writing I do want to do."[24]

The section of the novel devoted to Anouk continues to be informed by this opposition between a literature that is critical or realistic and a commercial television industry that perpetuates the mythology of the Australian suburb: "She knew what she wrote was infantile and moronic. She knew that she assisted in exporting stupidity to the world" (55).

This initial referencing of the ways in which the Australian suburb has been represented and exported is obviously a way of announcing the context into which the novel is intervening. *The Slap* will revise the myths of a racially insular suburbia by presenting the reality of its multiculturalism and of the manifold conflicts that beset an aspirational bourgeoisie. But it would also be disingenuous to claim that the novel is simply oppositional in relationship to the soap operas it evokes. In fact the popularity of *Neighbours* and *Home and Away*, in the United Kingdom especially, was probably an important condition for the novel's international reception. Its legibility as a critical intervention depended on that prior infatuation with the infantile mythologies of Australian television and the forms of celebrity that it spawned. If *The Slap* were being critical of these mass media forms, in other words, it also asserted a fundamental continuity with them. The novel was part of a dialogue with a recognizable universe of everyday media, rather than the assertion of an unbreachable divide between the space of the literary and the culture industry. Given this proximity, it was probably no surprise that the novel was adapted so seamlessly into television. As Glyn Davis has written, "the structure of the book—eight chapters, all of similar length, each with a different character as the focus—neatly translates into eight episodes of television drama." Davis goes on to explain the particular economy at stake in this:

> this narrative format fits a dominant production process often utilized in the creation of serial or series television drama, in which individual characters are accorded pre-eminence in distinct episodes. Not only does this working method allow for a team of writers to graft separately on the scripts for individual episodes, threading these together with series narratives built or inserted during roundtable meetings, but it also provides actors with sustained periods in the spotlight (and, conversely, less intensive periods of filming). [25]

The congruence between the structure of the novel and the production process that would adapt it into a television series suggests that *The Slap*'s commercial viability might have always been dependent on its relationship to other forms of media. Rather than the space of the literary being one that stubbornly refuses its incorporation, the contemporary, commercial novel seems to have already anticipated networks of appropriation and recirculation premised on a constant translation of one media form into another: the novel realizes itself as television, which in turn enables it to find a broader audience partly driven by its association with the celebrity actors appearing on the cover of its subsequent editions.

There is nothing especially unusual about this. Today the popularity of "classic" literature (particularly the *Bildungsromane* of the nineteenth century) depends to a large degree on these networks of adaptation that turn canonical texts into period cinema or "quality" television, forms that attempt to preserve the symbolic capital that once distinguished literary texts from the mass media. That the television adaptation of *The Slap* would cast Melissa George, formerly of *Home and Away*, as Rosie, marks the irony of these relationships. On the one hand, it measures the distance between the miniseries and the soap operas it complicates. Viewers can see that George is performing a revision of the sort of character she once played in *Home and Away*, materializing Tsiolkas's sense that Rosie represents the clichéd vision of white Australia *The Slap* was trying to displace. On the other hand, it enables the miniseries to draw on its relationship to the soap opera format and the recognizability of the celebrities it created. This feels very much of a piece with visions of a postmodern public sphere, in which mass circulation, mediated by the appeal of television personalities, enables what are in effect quite minimal, yet broadly distributed, moments of critical reflection. The sense of these moments being minimal stems from the limits of the medium itself (quality television does not do critical theory). Yet precisely because they are minimal, they circulate very widely and effectively.

The Slap's relationship to the world of soap operas was not the only way in which the novel asserted an ambiguous relationship to the forms of the culture industry. While Tsiolkas has spoken at length about the relationship between the novel and a political vision linked to multiculturalism, immigration and the residual racism of Australian society, the reality is that, at least initially, the popularity of the novel owed a lot to the spurious topicality of its opening incident when Harry slaps Hugo. As James Ley writes, the "novel's initial point of conflict is perfectly targeted."[26] Should he or shouldn't he have slapped the child? That the characters in the novel themselves spend an enormous amount of time agonizing over this reflects the way in which the novel was discussed in the reading groups to which it seemed ideally adapted, precisely because it could orient to an issue that readers were able to discuss without any prior expertise or without having to perform any kind of interpretive work. The issue seems ideally calibrated to Driscoll's conception of the middlebrow, because it enables one to bring a kind of emotional investment, linked to the semblance of an ethical dilemma, to recreational reading. There is a tabloid quality to the way in which this unfolded: a sense of controversy, or topicality, bound up with an issue that evokes strong feelings, and that touches a wide segment of the population. The slap here in fact reminds one of the way in which John Hartley discusses "the kiss" as both an example of and a metaphor for the diverse ways in which popular media disseminate meaning. Kisses, Hartley writes, are "very like meanings, being soft, fleeting, immensely important, sometimes telling the truth, sometimes not, sometimes holding the universe still for a moment, sometimes betokening very little; always highly coded according to socio-cultural, historical and political systems for both performers and observers, and always marking, changing and renewing the boundaries between public and private."[27] A kiss, like a slap, constructs a vector in which a diverse range of non-expert opinion can be mobilized, and this in turn constitutes precisely the sense of belonging that McKenzie Wark attributes to the culture of media celebrity. Just as Harry is worried about reporters from *A Current Affair* camping out on his lawn, one could easily imagine this sort of issue coming up in the context of tabloid television. The way *Barracuda* orients to familiar mass media stories about swimming stars and their personal travails is very similar. Tabloid coverage of Grant Hackett trashing his Melbourne penthouse or his misadventure in Crown Casino, Kieren Perkins's divorce and, not least, Ian Thorpe's well-documented battle with depression and addiction prior to his coming out supply a discursive framework and a context of reception for Danny's story. Both novels work hard to overcome what feels like an initial marketing hook linked to idioms and forms that presuppose a mass readership. Both do that with a fair degree of success, and yet it is hard to shake the feeling that what is new and noteworthy about these novels is the strategic awareness with which they have navigated their relationship to the marketplace and to the obsessions of the mass media.

How skeptical should we be about all of this? Does an orientation to the marketplace involve a heightening of the political potential of cultural production or a form of concision that limits the ways in which we communicate about and understand our world? The idea that modernity engenders the autonomy of aesthetic experience and then systematically undermines it in the interests of ideology, homogeneity and the universality of market value is one of the great organizing narratives of critical theory. We see it most obviously in Theodor Adorno's account of a culture industry that erodes the possibility of both high art and popular culture. We also see it in Pascale Casanova's analysis of world literary space, in which commercial literary production constitutes a direct threat to the "independence of the world of letters":

> What is being played out today in every part of world literary space is [...] a struggle between the commercial pole, which in each country seeks to impose itself as a new source of literary legitimacy through the diffusion of writing the mimics that style of the modern novel, and the autonomous pole, which finds itself under siege not only in the United States and France but throughout Europe, owing to the power of international publishing giants.[28]

In Australia these tensions between the autonomous pole and the commercial pole of literary production are perfectly clear. The sometimes vehement debates about the relationship between the popular and the political orient to these tensions. But so too do the much more pragmatic considerations of publishers, editors and agents in a market that feels increasingly besieged. At the same time, the recent emergence of a number of independent presses represents a healthy (though still precarious) resistance to the erasure of autonomy without which literature risks hollowing itself out and becoming one more form of instrumentalization.

The sense of maturity that *Barracuda* develops through its orientation to the *Bildungsroman* is reflected in Tsiolkas's own career, which has, since the publication of *Dead Europe*, become more oriented to a public sphere that is increasingly difficult to distinguish from the marketplace. The middlebrow dimension of this seems hard to deny, but as Brigid Rooney has shown us, the middlebrow has a political dimension that should not be underestimated. Tsiolkas's success as what Rooney would call a "literary activist" has moved his work into a zone where its viability seems contingent on a fundamental redefinition of its formal orientation. I do not think there is any doubt that the anarchic thrill of his earlier writing has gone. But perhaps these are the compromises one must accept if one wants to speak and be heard. And perhaps it is precisely this thrill, this pleasure, that must be tempered in the interests of the political.

.

Conclusion

AESTHETIC AUTONOMY AND THE POLITICS OF FICTION

I was deep into the writing of this book when *Barracuda* was published. The appearance of that novel consolidated what was, for me at least, an unexpected change in the trajectory of Tsiolkas's career. We have seen how emphatically the early part of Tsiolkas's career oriented to the figure of Pasolini and the problem of imagining constituencies and ways of being not yet incorporated into the circuits of capitalism and neoliberal desire. For both Pasolini and Tsiolkas, the possibility of remaining outside these circuits produced a visceral intensity that would also, ultimately, be the basis upon which atomized subjects are assimilated into the hedonism of consumer society and global capitalism. In Tsiolkas's first three novels this impasse is reproduced with increasing degrees of urgency until, finally, Isaac Raftis in *Dead Europe* confronts the complete breakdown of his character at the moment that he becomes the monstrous embodiment of a sexualized sovereignty that concentrates alienated, egotistical and violently exploitative drives. The arc that connects *Loaded*, *The Jesus Man* and *Dead Europe* is a despairing one. These novels constitute Tsiolkas's trilogy of negation, or of annihilation. They explore and confront the limits of a model of subjectivity that promises transgression only to find itself back at the center of the very system it hoped to negate and destroy. It is for this reason that life for Tommy and Isaac becomes quite literally intolerable.

The Slap, of course, is a very different kind of novel, but not one that offers any clear path beyond the pessimism of the early texts. The promise of multiculturalism is ultimately hollowed out by the aspirational, middle-class structures in which it appears. It is a novel in which the sheer facticity of the everyday wins out and marginalizes any serious or sustained resistance to it. That Tsiolkas himself has had to explicate the political backdrop of the novel so insistently reflects the fact that, without the furious negativity of the earlier texts, *The Slap* is, politically speaking, a fairly nebulous sort of undertaking. Its realism, we could say, embodies an attenuation of its political engagement. *Barracuda*, however, feels quite different. Because of the clarity with which it embraces the *Bildungsroman* form, it also offers a way beyond both negativity and the tyranny of the everyday. It points to an ethical horizon oriented to a productive engagement with a social habitus in which characters can choose to remake themselves on the basis of a politics of care, charity, inclusion and selfless surrender to the claims of the other. This not only constitutes Tsiolkas's most optimistic statement but also suggests perhaps his most tangible engagement with the political realities that have become increasingly clear since the rise of the New Right in the mid-1990s. What I have in mind here involves the development of exclusive forms of biopolitical governmentality that insist on drawing distinctions between lives that are worth nurturing and lives that can be abandoned to poverty, violence and environmental degradation, or incorporated into a state of exception that affords no legal protection or recourse.

The model of *Bildung* set out in *Barracuda* is calibrated to address these structures. It evokes the kind of self-fashioning that might become the basis of a public culture capable of engaging with the utterly inhumane policy formations that dominate Australian political life today. The narrative is continuous with nineteenth-century notions of the novel as a form of moral education, but it also revises them for a new set of political realities. On the one hand, it presents a narrative in which a character reconciles himself with the social whole, but on the other, this sense of reconciliation is based on a reconceptualization of the social that moves away from incorporative fictions of the nation and the mass media and toward an embrace of society's most threatened and excluded constituents. The social, in other words, comes into focus only by opening its boundaries to those on its margins or beyond its limits. *Barracuda* begins with a restrictive or exclusionary vision of the nation, one bound up with the jingoism of sport, and ends up turning it inside out. In this process we can perhaps read Tsiolkas's own narrative of maturation. Following Pasolini down the paths of semen has led to a kind of ethical transformation in which the *Bildungsroman*—paradoxically perhaps—is once again central.

I do not think we are disparaging Tsiolkas's achievement to describe *Barracuda*—and *The Slap* for that matter—as middlebrow in the sense elucidated by Beth Driscoll or by Brigid Rooney when she uses the term to talk about Tim Winton. These novels are accessible and content-driven. They seem to have found their way to a mass audience based on the assumption that they reflect our lives back to us. At the same time, however, the term middlebrow, even as Rooney uses it, cannot help but sound like a reservation, at least for someone who makes a living teaching literature. This is because the institutional history of literary studies has been, by and large, defined by notions of aesthetic experience that have always been imagined as antithetical to commercial and governmental logics. Tsiolkas's strongest statements of artistic intent reinforce this sense of writing as a form of resistance or dissent that draws its political potential from its autonomy. In "On the Concept of Tolerance" his evocation of aesthetic radicality turns on his vision of the novelist rejecting the propositional language of political power and embracing instead everything that seems to be outside its range: "It is this motivation for dissent and resistance that convinces me that artists are not necessarily good politicians, because the urge to speak the unspeakable, the unpopular, the uncompromising, the dangerous and the seditious is what art, but not politics, can countenance."[1] This orientation to alterity is, for Tsiolkas, finally associated with blasphemy:

> This is a position beyond the bourgeois politeness that taints the liberal's conception of free speech, and also a position at odds with the redemptionist hope that defines the socialist and feminist ideal of art. It asks that the writer and the artist always exist in a position of readiness to opposition, a consciousness that we live in a state of emergency; not an emergency as articulated to us by politicians or the media but as a concrete reality that defines our past and present and our potential. This is not to say that the artist cannot hold an opinion, express a political opinion, join a movement, take on a faith. But we are required, I believe, to always look towards that defined as unspeakable, intolerable, traitorous, seditious, evil and abject in order to ensure that the violence enacted against its expression is given a voice, shaped into memory.[2]

There is little doubt that this vision of the blasphemous writer is as much about aesthetics as it is about political engagement. It evokes the Pasolini who imagined an existence resistant to capitalist incorporation, and then, when he realized that such an existence was impossible, conjured the nightmare of its absence, but it also seems to evoke a long line of *poètes maudits* who embodied what Marion Campbell, in a brilliant elegy to aesthetic radicality, calls the "twinning of poetry and revolution."[3]

Strangely, however, it is precisely this heretical ethos, albeit in an attenuated form, that underpins the viability of the sort of middlebrow writing Brigid Rooney sees as activist. The space of the middlebrow, as she suggests, allows the ghost of the aesthetic to linger (as a kind of authorizing stamp) over forms of writing that have largely rejected the aesthetic disposition. The sort of writing Rooney explores does seem to have a currency in Australia that it might not quite have in other national spaces. This has to do with the ways in which Australian cultural institutions have overdetermined the relationship between the political and the aesthetic. There are a number of aspects to what I have in mind here. Firstly, realism has always been a privileged term in the field of Australian literature. It is tightly linked to the emergence of a national literature and to a kind of working-class populism (associated with people like Henry Lawson and William Lane). These positive connotations persisted through the twentieth century with figures like Frank Hardy and still inform a contemporary sense of how literature organizes social and political engagement. By contrast, abstraction, experimentation and stylistic opacity have tended to be associated with an imported aesthetic formation that is both Eurocentric and elitist. Secondly, the apparently populist orientation of the realist text has also segued into a sense of its commercial viability. Today, Australian publishing has very little tolerance for novels that try to complicate the relationship between form and content or that try to privilege the former over the latter. Literary novels that function as mirrors (those that let us see ourselves) or that simply tell stories in a purely propositional manner are the norm. At moments these two frameworks, the one political and the other commercial, come together, as in Ken Gelder's call for a socially engaged realism, a "critical political realism in contemporary Australian fiction," that works through commercial logics.[1] It is hard to object to this, though one still feels, intuitively perhaps, that a novel like Marion Campbell's *Konkretion*, precisely because of its stubborn refusal of commercial logics and its corresponding evocation of the relationship between aesthetic experimentation and political radicality, continues to mark the possibility of an alterity that has become all the more urgent for being so obviously untimely. The populism that lingers behind the confluence of politics and commerce, by contrast, has something distinctly defeatist about it. As Adorno put it, the bourgeois' "love of people as they are stems from his hatred of what they might be."[5]

The third factor in play here involves a general move away from the aesthetic disciplines within higher education and a corresponding embrace of forms of academic work that are much more pragmatically or instrumentally invested in their material contexts. There are a number of arguments motivating this move. The idea that the aesthetic is a bulwark against instrumentality has been complicated by a long tradition of left-oriented thinkers who have also pointed out the ways in which it reinforces a bourgeois consensus precisely around its withdrawal from direct political engagement. More damning, though, was Pierre Bourdieu's seminal account of how aesthetic appreciation functions as a mode of cultural capital that reflects and reinforces deeply entrenched, class-based distinctions.[6] Both of these strands appear in Australian cultural studies, in which a democratically oriented interest in everyday life and a broad, anthropological conception of culture have also highlighted the specific interests underpinning residual conceptions of cultural value. One of the things that has emerged quite powerfully in this context is an interest in the actual political efficacy of cultural production and critique.

This interest finds perhaps its clearest articulation in Ian Hunter's work on the relationship between aesthetics and governmentality. For Hunter, the aesthetic ethos is a form of self-fashioning that presupposes a kind of lack. "At the center of this ethic," he writes, "lies a powerful technology for *withdrawing* from the world as a sphere of mundane knowledge and action. In fact the aesthete does not pursue knowledge or 'worldly' activity as such, having subjected them to a problematization that makes them ethically worthless. Instead, he or she seeks to prepare or cultivate the kind of self that will be worthy of enlightened knowledge and action in an indefinitely deferred future."[7] According to Hunter this "technology" is ambiguously situated with regard to the forms of governmentality that developed throughout the nineteenth century. On the one hand, it belongs to them in so far as it anchors both an educational apparatus oriented to teachers who embody precisely the ethical disposition it assumes and interpretive procedures that endlessly rehearse this disposition. On the other hand, because the governmental itself is part of the incomplete social order at odds with an idealized notion of human actualization, it is also the site that cannot be occupied in any sustained manner.

> It is precisely this new "governmentalized" form of society that the aesthetic ethos constitutes as the "mechanical," "alienated," "ordinary," and "mundane" world to be transcended. And it does so not by engaging with the governmental organization of this world but by constituting it as the site on which the self must call itself into question; that is, by using it as a domain of experience to be subjected to continuous ethical problematization as the means of constituting oneself as the subject of a higher mode of being.[8]

In contrast Hunter opens up the possibility of ethical action formed through a pragmatic engagement with governmental structures, not a withdrawal from them in the interests of an immaterial horizon that anchors an aesthetic experience of the world.

These poles help us grasp what sort of writer I think Tsiolkas has become with the publication of *Barracuda*. The attempt to present a model of self-fashioning that hinges on literary appreciation—and on learning the lessons of selflessness it teaches—is evident in Danny's story. But this is not a matter of aesthetic withdrawal. On the contrary, it orients to very tangible ways of being in the world, of working with and relating to others. At the same time Tsiolkas's novel offers itself as part of a larger conversation about the ways in which media forms construct our experience. It does not eschew the commercial. In fact it seems to embrace commercial logics in the interests of maximizing the effectiveness and reach of its intervention. There is no sense in which the commercial compromises its ethical investments. The text no longer seeks to withdraw from or refuse the social whole. Rather it seeks to expand its communicative potential by integrating itself into commercial structures and media networks. Today Tsiolkas's work seems inseparable from broader considerations around circulation, mediatization, the creation of politicized readerships and the role of literature in opinion formation.

This does not mean that we can simply do without the possibility of imagining the sort of withdrawal Hunter discusses or that the dominance of middlebrow forms and structures can exhaust a sense of the literary. Tsiolkas's viability as a public voice and a bankable commercial prospect rests, paradoxically, on a persistent sense of him as a heretical, blasphemous figure; the writer who, at the beginning of his career, evoked the ghost of Pasolini and refused to censor his own anger or his desire. Today that earlier incarnation haunts the sort of literary space Tsiolkas now inhabits. The idea that Tsiolkas has become a sort of double of himself might be one of the consequences of this. Of course even the most ardent pragmatist still dreams of the utopian possibility of a freedom from material structures and relations. But dreams, as the narrator of Roberto Bolaño's *Distant Star* tells us, have a habit of turning into nightmares. Tsiolkas knows this as well as anyone.

NOTES

Preface

1   Tom Shone, "Novel of the Year? Get Ready for *The Slap*," *Sunday Times*, Culture Section, 9 May 2010, 10–11.
2   Shone, "Novel of the Year? Get Ready for *The Slap*," 11.
3   Sasha Soldatow and Christos Tsiolkas, *Jump Cuts: An Autobiography* (Milsons Point, NSW: Random House, 1996), 282.
4   Quoted in Ian Syson, "Smells Like Market Spirit: Grunge, Literature, Australia," *Overland* 142 (Autumn 1996): 22.
5   The Wheeler Centre for Books, Writing and Ideas, an arts organization dedicated to fostering literary culture, was founded in 2010, after Melbourne was named the second UNESCO city of literature in 2008.
6   James Ley, "A Furious Moralist," *Australian Book Review* 306 (November 2008): 9–10.

Introduction: Pasolini's Ashes

1   Walter Benjamin, *Charles Baudelaire: A Lyric Poet in the Era of High Capitalism*, trans. Harry Zohn (London: Verso, 1997), 117
2   Miriam Bratu Hansen, *Cinema and Experience: Siegfried Kracauer, Walter Benjamin, and Theodor W. Adorno* (Berkeley: University of California Press, 2012), 306 n18.
3   Oskar Negt and Alexander Kluge, *The Public Sphere and Experience: Toward an Analysis of the Bourgeois and Proletarian Public Sphere*, trans. Peter Labanyi, Jamie Owen Daniel, and Assenka Oksiloff (Minneapolis: University of Minnesota Press, 1993), 6–7.
4   See Jürgen Habermas, *The Structural Transformation of the Public Sphere: An Inquiry into a Category of Bourgeois Society*, trans. Thomas Burger with Frederick Lawrence (Cambridge, MA: MIT Press, 1991), for the decisive statement of this position.
5   Negt and Kluge, *The Public Sphere and Experience*, xlvi.
6   Sasha Soldatow and Christos Tsiolkas, *Jump Cuts: An Autobiography* (Milsons Point, NSW: Random House, 1996), 285.
7   Pheng Cheah, "Mattering," *Diacritics* 26.1 (Spring 1996): 112.
8   Christos Tsiolkas, *The Devil's Playground* (Sydney: Currency Press, 2002), 3–4.
9   Tsiolkas, *The Devil's Playground*, 5.
10   Tsiolkas, *The Devil's Playground*, 8.
11   Tsiolkas, *The Devil's Playground*, 16.
12   Soldatow and Tsiolkas, *Jump Cuts*, 11.
13   Elizabeth Grosz, *Volatile Bodies: Toward a Corporeal Feminism* (Bloomington: Indiana University Press, 1994), x–xi.

14 Tsiolkas, *The Devil's Playground*, 31.

15 Slavoj Žižek, Speech Delivered at Liberty Plaza (9 October 2011), accessed 29 December 2014, http://www.criticallegalthinking.com.

16 Tsiolkas, *The Devil's Playground*, 28, 31.

17 Tsiolkas, *The Devil's Playground*, 60.

18 Roberto Esposito, *Living Thought: The Origins and Actuality of Italian Philosophy*, trans. Zakiya Hanafi (Stanford, CA: Stanford University Press, 2012), 206.

19 Esposito, *Living Thought*, 206–7.

20 Robert S.C. Gordon, *Pasolini: Forms of Subjectivity* (Oxford: Clarendon Press, 1996), 2–3.

21 Pasolini's film was initially banned in Australia in 1976. The ban was overturned in 1993, sparking an ongoing debate. In 1998, the Office of Film and Literature Classification reinstituted the nationwide ban. In 2010 a classification review board approved a DVD release.

22 Soldatow and Tsiolkas, *Jump Cuts*, 204–5.

23 Soldatow and Tsiolkas, *Jump Cuts*, 85.

24 Wallace P. Sillanpoa, "Pasolini's Gramsci," *MLN* 96.1, Italian Issue (January 1981): 122.

25 Esposito, *Living Thought*, 211.

26 Pier Paolo Pasolini, "Repudiation of the Trilogy of Life," in *Heretical Empiricism*, trans. Ben Lawton and Louise K. Barnett (Washington D.C.: New Academia Publishing, 2005), xvii. The "Repudiation" was originally published in *Trilogia della vita* (Milan: Garzanti, 1995) and was added to this later edition of *Heretical Empiricism* in 2005.

27 Pasolini, "Repudiation," xvii–xviii.

28 Pasolini, "Repudiation," xix.

29 Pasolini, "Repudiation," xix.

30 Maurizio Viano, "The Left According to the Ashes of Gramsci," *Social Text* 18 (Winter 1987–88): 54.

31 Pier Paolo Pasolini, *Poems*, trans. Norman MacAfee (New York: Random House, 1982), 11.

32 Jacques Derrida, *Specters of Marx: The State of the Debt, the Work of Mourning, and the New International*, trans. Peggy Kamuf (London: Routledge, 1994), xix.

33 Soldatow and Tsiolkas, *Jump Cuts*, 151.

34 Soldatow and Tsiolkas, *Jump Cuts*, 153.

35 Negt and Kluge, *The Public Sphere and Experience*, 33.

36 Christos Tsiolkas, "Me and My Country, Where to Now?" Interview with Heather Taylor Johnson. *Meanjin* 72.1 (March 2013): 180–81.

37 Christos Tsiolkas, "On the Concept of Tolerance," in Tsiolkas, Gideon Haigh and Alexis Wright, *Tolerance, Prejudice and Fear* (Crows Nest, NSW: Allen and Unwin, 2008), 47.

38 John Hartley, "The Sexualization of Suburbia: The Diffusion of Knowledge in the Postmodern Public Sphere," in Roger Silverstone ed., *Visions of Suburbia* (London: Routledge, 1997), 181.

39 See Brigid Rooney, *Literary Activists: Writer-Intellectuals and Australian Public Life* (St. Lucia, QLD: University of Queensland Press, 2009), 186–87.

1. The Down-Curve of Capital: *Loaded*

1 Christos Tsiolkas, *Loaded* (Sydney: Vintage Books, 1995), 2. Hereafter cited parenthetically in the text.

2 Pheng Cheah, *Spectral Nationality: Passages of Freedom from Kant to Postcolonial Literatures of Liberation* (New York: Columbia University Press, 2003), 41, 45.

3 Cheah, *Spectral Nationality*, 40.

4 Cheah, *Spectral Nationality*, 168.

5 Jed Esty, *Unseasonable Youth: Modernism, Colonialism, and the Fiction of Development* (Oxford: Oxford University Press, 2012), 3.

6 Esty, *Unseasonable Youth*, 5–6. Esty is drawing on seminal discussions by Franco Moretti and M.M. Bakhtin. See Moretti, *The Way of the World: The Bildungsroman in European Culture*, trans. Albert Sbraglia (London: Verso, 2000) and Bakhtin, "The *Bildungsroman* and its Significance in the History of Realism (Toward a Historical Typology of the Novel)," in *Speech Genres and Other Late Essays*, trans. Vern W. McGee (Austin: University of Texas Press, 1986), 10–59.

7 Christos Tsiolkas, Interview with Glenn D'Cruz, in Glenn D'Cruz ed., *Class Act: Melbourne Workers Theatre 1987–2007* (Carlton: Vulgar Press, 2007), 149.

8 Christos Tsiolkas, "On the Concept of Tolerance" in Tsiolkas, Gideon Haigh and Alexis Wright, *Tolerance, Prejudice and Fear* (Crows Nest, NSW: Allen and Unwin, 2008), 29–30.

9 Lee Edelman, *No Future: Queer Theory and the Death Drive* (Durham, NC: Duke University Press, 2004), 2.

10 Edelman, *No Future*, 6.

11 Pheng Cheah, "Humanity in the Field of Instrumentality," *PMLA* 121.5 (October 2006): 1556.

12 Fredric Jameson, *Postmodernism, or the Cultural Logic of Late Capitalism* (Durham, NC: Duke University Press, 1991), 44.

13 Jameson, *Postmodernism*, 54, 53.

14 See, for instance, Marc Augé, *Non-Places: An Introduction to Supermodernity*, trans. John Howe (London: Verso, 2009).

15 Christos Tsiolkas, "Into a Liquid Ether," *Age*, 14 June 2008, 18–19. Muñoz draws on the utopian impulse of the Frankfurt School and the work of Ernst Bloch to reconceptualize queerness as the basis of a concrete utopia, as a "longing that propels us onward, beyond romances of the negative and toiling in the present." It is "that thing that lets us feel that this world is not enough, that indeed something is missing." See José Esteban Muñoz, *Cruising Utopia: The Then and There of Queer Futurity* (New York: New York University Press, 2009), 1. Whereas Edelman dispels futurity and temporality, Muñoz embraces both, though he is careful to distinguish queer and straight conceptions of time.

16 Sneja Gunew, *Haunted Nations: The Colonial Dimensions of Multiculturalism* (London: Routledge, 2004), 105.

17 Ian Syson, "Smells Like Market Spirit: Grunge, Literature, Australia," *Overland* 142 (Autumn 1996): 22.

18 Syson, "Smells Like Market Spirit," 22.

19 Fabio Vighi, "Pasolini and Exclusion: Žižek, Agamben and the Modern Sub-Proletariat," *Theory, Culture and Society* 20.5 (October 2003): 101.

20 Pier Paolo Pasolini, "Repudiation of the Trilogy of Life," in *Heretical Empiricism*, trans. Ben Lawton and Louise K. Barnett (Washington, D.C.: New Academia Publishing, 2005), xvii.

21 Pasolini, "Repudiation," xvii–xviii.

22 Pasolini, "Repudiation," xviii–xix.

23 Pier Paolo Pasolini, "Heart," trans. Juliana Schiesari, in Beverly Allen, ed., *Pier Paolo Pasolini: The Poetics of Heresy* (Saratoga, CA: Anma Libri and Co., 1982), 123.

24 Interviews with Tsiolkas in John Vasilakakos, *Christos Tsiolkas: The Untold Story* (Ballan, VIC: Connorcourt Publishing, 2013), 94, 108.

25 Christos Tsiolkas, "Me and My Country, Where to Now?" Interview with Heather Taylor Johnson. *Meanjin* 72.1 (March 2013): 182.

26 Tsiolkas, "Me and My Country, Where to Now?," 183.

2. Inside the Machine: From *Loaded* to *The Jesus Man*

1 Anja Schwarz, "Mapping (Un-)Australian Identities: 'Territorial Disputes' in Christos Tsiolkas' *Loaded*," in Anke Bartels and Dirk Wiemann eds., *Global Fragments: (Dis) Orientation in the New World Order* (Amsterdam: Rodopi, 2007), 22.

2 Elizabeth McMahon, "Lost in Music," *Meanjin* 59.2 (2000): 169.

3 One Nation, led federally by Pauline Hanson, rose to prominence in the mid-1990s with an aggressive resistance to multiculturalism, focused largely on Asian immigration and what it saw as a discriminatory prioritizing of Indigenous Australian communities. John Howard became prime minister of Australia in 1996, when his Liberal-National coalition defeated Paul Keating's Labor Party. In the same election, Hanson won the seat of Oxley.

4 Michel de Certeau, *The Practice of Everyday Life*, trans. Steven Randall (Berkeley: University of California Press, 1984), 118.

5 de Certeau, *The Practice of Everyday Life*, 101.

6 See Walter Benjamin, *Charles Baudelaire: A Lyric Poet in the Era of High Capitalism*, trans. Harry Zohn (London: Verso, 1973), 34–66.

7 Ivan Cañadas, "A Sin That Dare Not Speak its Name: Class and Sexuality in Christos Tsiolkas's *Loaded* and Ana Kokkinos's *Head On*," *Overland* 177 (Summer 2004): 44.

8 Cañadas, "A Sin That Dare Not Speak its Name," 46.

9 Ben Authers, "'I'm Not Australian, I'm Not Greek, I'm Not Anything': Identity and the Multicultural Nation in Christos Tsiolkas's *Loaded*," *JASAL* 4 (2005): 133.

10 Sasha Soldatow and Christos Tsiolkas, *Jump Cuts: An Autobiography* (Milsons Point, NSW: Random House, 1996), 45. The problem raised here is something Tsiolkas has recently returned to in a *Monthly* essay entitled "Whatever Happened to the Working Class?", where he writes that "a politics of rights, classically liberal and universalist, has never been adequate to addressing the conflicts between labour and capital." See *The Monthly*, May 2014, accessed 20 June 2014, http://www.the monthly.com.au.

11 Authers, "'I'm Not Australian, I'm Not Greek, I'm Not Anything,'" 134.

12 Authers, "'I'm Not Australian, I'm Not Greek, I'm Not Anything,'" 143.

13 Authers, "'I'm Not Australian, I'm Not Greek, I'm Not Anything,'" 143.

14 Paul Dawson, "Grunge Lit: Marketing Generation X," *Meanjin* 56.1 (March 1997): 119.

15 Philippa Hawker, "Loaded on the Back Streets," *Age*, Saturday Extra, 22 December 1995, 7.

16 Jane Sullivan, "*Three Dollars* Leaves the Rest Behind," *Age*, Agenda, 12 July 1998, 20.

17 McKenzie Wark, *Celebrities, Culture and Cyberspace: The Light on the Hill in a Postmodern World* (Annandale, NSW: Pluto Press, 1999), 230.

18 Wark, *Celebrities, Culture and Cyberspace*, 231.

19 Christos Tsiolkas, *Loaded* (Sydney: Vintage Books, 1995), 19.

20 Schwarz, "Mapping (Un-)Australian Identities," 23.

21 McMahon, "Lost in Music," 172, 169, 168, 166.

22 See Wark, *Celebrities, Culture and Cyberspace*, 232.

23 Christos Tsiolkas, "Mix-Tape: The Technology of a Passion" (2006), *Meanjin* 69.4 (Summer 2010): 139.

24 Herbert Marcuse, *Negations: Essays in Critical Theory*, trans. Jeremy J. Shapiro (Boston: Beacon Press, 1968), 95.

25 Tsiolkas, "Mix-Tape," 140.

26 Tsiolkas, *Loaded*, 133.

27 See Hans Magnus Enzensberger, *Zig Zag: The Politics of Culture and Vice Versa* (New York: The New Press, 1997), 304–17.

28 Christos Tsiolkas, *The Jesus Man* (Sydney: Random House, 1999), 5–6. Hereafter cited parenthetically in the text.

29 This kind of identification occurs elsewhere in Tsiolkas's work. We see it in the story "Petals," originally written in Greek and translated by Tsiolkas himself. The narrator of the story, an imprisoned Greek immigrant harassed by the racism of the other inmates, imagines his release as a flight from whiteness: "I will go to the desert. Black I will become." See *Merciless Gods* (Crows Nest, NSW: Allen and Unwin, 2014), 85.

30 This narrative of sexual excess, guilt and self-annihilation plays out in a different idiom in the short story "Porn 3," where Ghassan, an Urdu-speaking character and, presumably, a Muslim, is drawn into a world of assignations and sex clubs, which he sees as an expression of Western decadence: "their decadence, their sadism, their brutality, their filth: it had infected him, it was in his blood" (*Merciless Gods*, 322). The story concludes with Ghassan as a suicide bomber, "bringing the fire" to the corruption that has consumed him.

31 For Philippa Hawker the book was both "infuriating" and "exhilarating"; for Peter Blazey "marvelous and frightful." This sense of a productive ambivalence, which tended to endorse the book, was balanced by Owen Richardson's dismissal of its "humorless, mawkish narcissism." See Philippa Hawker, "Books – Paperbacks," *Age*, Saturday Extra, 14 September 1996, 8; Peter Blazey, "From Breathless to a Scream," *Weekend Australian*, Review Section, 3 August 1996, 8; and Owen Richardson, "Cappuccino Chat: Light, Fluffy and Not Much Substance," *Age*, Agenda, 20 October 1996, 7.

32 Soldatow and Tsiolkas, *Jump Cuts*, 47–48.

33 Soldatow and Tsiolkas, *Jump Cuts*, 48–49. In one of the interviews conducted by John Vasilakakos, Tsiolkas replays this scenario, or one quite similar to it: "The big challenge was moving from the City to a new school and a new suburb in Blackburn that was very different to the one I was used to. It was a horrible time. I didn't like myself, I didn't like my body, I didn't like the world I was in, and it was the first time in my life that I felt real loneliness. I felt bereft of where I was in the world and felt I was evil and dirty, because of the sexual fantasies and thoughts I had. It was a very difficult time. Everything became really dirty over that period. It took me a long time to be able to make friends." See John Vasilakakos, *Christos Tsiolkas: The Untold Story* (Ballan, VIC: Connorcourt Publishing, 2013), 19.

34 Christos Tsiolkas, *The Devil's Playground* (Sydney: Currency Press, 2002), 19–20.

35 Soldatow and Tsiolkas, *Jump Cuts*, 153.

36 Vasilakakos, *Christos Tsiolkas*, 84.

37 See Friedrich Kittler, *Discourse Networks 1800/1900*, trans. Michael Metteer with Chris Cullens (Stanford, CA: Stanford University Press, 1990), 304.

38 Julian Meyrick, "Introduction," *Melbourne Stories: Three Plays* (Sydney: Currency Press, 2000), 3.

39 Meyrick, "Introduction," 3.

40 Julian Meyrick, "*Who's Afraid of the Working Class?*: An Impressionistic History," in Glenn D'Cruz ed., *Class Act: Melbourne Workers Theatre 1987–2007* (Melbourne: Vulgar Press, 2007), 136.
41 Alan Filewood and David Watt, "Melbourne Workers Theatre: The Meat in the Sandwich," in Glenn D'Cruz ed., *Class Act*, 31–32.
42 See Tsiolkas, *Merciless Gods*, 226–46.
43 See Vasilakakos, *Christos Tsiolkas*, 93.
44 Christos Tsiolkas, "Suit" (from *Who's Afraid of the Working Class?*) in *Melbourne Stories: Three Plays* (Sydney: Currency Press, 2000), 11.
45 Tsiolkas, "Suit," 12.

3. The Pornographic Logic of Global Capitalism: *Dead Europe*

1 Slavoj Žižek, *The Metastases of Enjoyment: Six Essays on Women and Causality* (London: Verso, 1994), 54–85.
2 Žižek, *The Metastases of Enjoyment*, 56.
3 Adams is summarizing, by way of critique, the position set out by Catherine MacKinnon in *Only Words* (Cambridge, MA: Harvard University Press, 1993). See Parveen Adams, *The Emptiness of the Image: Psychoanalysis and Sexual Difference* (London: Routledge, 1996), 65.
4 Loren Glass, *Counter-Culture Colophon: Grove Press, the* Evergreen Review *and the Incorporation of the Avant-Garde* (Stanford, CA: University Press, 2013), 111.
5 See Glass, *Counter-Culture Colophon*, 101–44, for a fascinating discussion of the relationship between obscenity and the marketing of modernist and avant-garde writing.
6 Fredric Jameson, *Postmodernism, or the Cultural Logic of Late Capitalism* (Durham, NC: Duke University Press, 1991), 4.
7 J.G. Ballard, *Crash* (1973; repr., London: Vintage, 1995), iii.
8 Emily Apter, "Weaponized Thought: Ethical Militance and the Group Subject," *Grey Room* 14 (Winter 2004): 19–20.
9 Christos Tsiolkas, "'What Does Fiction Do?' On *Dead Europe*: Ethics and Aesthetics." Interview with Catherine Padmore. *Australian Literary Studies* 23.4 (December 2008): 452–53.
10 See, for instance, Lynda Ng, "*Dead Europe* and the Coming of Age in Australian Literature: Globalisation, Cosmopolitanism and Perversity," *Australian Humanities Review* 54 (May 2013): 120–35, accessed 18 December 2014, http://www.australianhumanitiesreview.org; Michael Vaughan, "'What's Haunting *Dead Europe*?' Trauma Fiction as Resistance to Postmodern Governmentality," *JASAL* 11.2 (2011): 1–10, accessed 18 December 2014, http://www.nla.gov.au; Liz Shek-Noble "'There Were Phantoms': Spectral Shadows in Christos Tsiolkas's *Dead Europe*," *JASAL* 11.2 (2011): 1–13, accessed 18 December 2014, http://www.nla.gov.au; and Andrew McCann, "Discrepant Cosmopolitanism and the Contemporary Novel: Reading the Inhuman in Christos Tsiolkas's *Dead Europe* and Roberto Bolaño's *2666*," *Antipodes* 24.2 (2010): 135–41.
11 Anthony Macris, "Hubris is Not a Dirty Word," *Bulletin*, 25 May 1999, 115.
12 Cameron Woodhead, "Hard-Core Saga of Fraternal Frustration," *Age*, Saturday Extra, 29 May 1999, 8.
13 Christos Tsiolkas, "Politics, Faith and Sex." Interview with Patricia Cornelius. *Overland* 181 (Summer 2005): 24.

14 Christos Tsiolkas, "Me and My Country, Where to Now?" Interview with Heather Taylor Johnson. *Meanjin* 72.1 (March 2013): 181. Tsiolkas has returned to this moment in his life a number of times: "There was a choice, I remember, right after *The Jesus Man* where I thought, do I give up writing and do something else, and I didn't make that choice. I made a choice to write and I'm really glad I did, but the experience of shame and humiliation is a really important thing to go through." See John Vasilakakos, *Christos Tsiolkas: The Untold Story* (Ballan, VIC: Connorcourt Publishing, 2013), 91.

15 James Clifford, "Traveling Culture," in Lawrence Grossberg, Cary Nelson and Paula A. Treichler eds., *Cultural Studies* (London: Routledge, 1992), 108.

16 Michael Davidson, "On the Outskirts of Form: Cosmopoetics in the Shadow of NAFTA," *Textual Practice* 22.4 (December 2008): 735.

17 Shameem Black, *Fictions Across Borders: Imagining the Lives of Others in Late Twentieth-Century Novels* (New York: Columbia University Press, 2010), 9.

18 Pheng Cheah, *Inhuman Conditions: On Cosmopolitanism and Human Rights* (Cambridge, MA: Harvard University Press, 2006), 2.

19 Cheah, *Inhuman Conditions*, 2–3.

20 Cheah, *Inhuman Conditions*, 263.

21 Cheah, *Inhuman Conditions*, 31–32. See also Saskia Sassen, *The Global City: New York, London, Tokyo* (Princeton, NJ: Princeton University Press, 1991), on which Cheah is drawing here.

22 Cheah, *Inhuman Conditions*, 11.

23 Tsiolkas's problematic relationship to Judaism has, with good reason, been the focus of a considerable critical debate. As Graham Huggan writes, *Dead Europe*'s "central ploy" is to "take the great phobic structures underlying Western vampire discourse—anti-Semitism, fascistic nationalism, ethnic absolutism, homophobia—and, by dismantling their myth of origin, to use them to reflect on the ravaged history of the West itself." Huggan goes on to say that he has "no wish to rescue *Dead Europe* from the inevitable charge of anti-Semitism," which indicates his ambivalence about the success of this ploy. See Huggan, "Vampires, Again," *Southerly* 66.3 (January 2006): 197, 199. In an interesting discussion of the novel, Eleni Pavlides evokes works of Nazi propaganda such as *Der Ewige Jude* to demonstrate that Syd's relationship to pornography is another anti-Semitic stereotype. See Pavlides, *Un-Australian Fictions: Nation, Multiculture(alism) and Globalization, 1988–2008* (Newcastle upon Tyne: Cambridge Scholars Publishing, 2013), 114–16. Catherine Padmore has also written at length about the role of anti-Semitism in the novel. See "Future Tense: *Dead Europe* and Viral Anti-Semitism," *Australian Literary Studies* 23.4 (2008): 434–45. Of the reviews to raise this issue the two most often discussed are Robert Manne's "Dead Disturbing: A Bloodthirsty Tale that Plays with the Fire of Anti-Semitism," *The Monthly*, June 2005, 50–53, and Les Rosenblatt's "A Place Where Wolves Fuck," *Arena* 79 (2005): 46–48. Manne's review is probably the most accusatory piece of criticism written about the novel.

24 Huggan, "Vampires, Again," 192.

25 See Huggan, "Vampires, Again," 196, and Ken Gelder and Paul Salzman, *After the Celebration: Australian Fiction 1989–2007* (Carlton: Melbourne University Press, 2009), 226.

26 Christos Tsiolkas, *Dead Europe* (Sydney: Vintage, 2005), 203. Hereafter cited parenthetically in the text.

27 Tsiolkas, "Me and My Country, Where to Now?", 183.

28 Pier Paolo Pasolini, "A Study in the Anthropological Revolution in Italy," trans. Juliana Schiesari, in Beverly Allen ed., *The Poetics of Heresy* (Saratoga, CA: Anma Libri and Co., 1982), 113.
29 Pier Paolo Pasolini, "Coitus, Abortion, Power's False Tolerance, the Conformism of Progressives," trans. Juliana Schiesari, in *The Poetics of Heresy*, 117.
30 Pier Paolo Pasolini, "Heart," trans. Juliana Shiesari, in *The Poetics of Heresy*, 123, 126.
31 Gideon Bachmann, "Pasolini on de Sade: An Interview During the Filming of *The 120 Days of Sodom*," *Film Quarterly* 29.2 (Winter 1975–1976): 40.
32 Giorgio Agamben, *Homo Sacer: Sovereign Power and Bare Life*, trans. Daniel Heller-Roazen (Stanford, CA: Stanford University Press, 1998), 134.
33 Agamben, *Homo Sacer*, 135.
34 Christos Tsiolkas and Spiro Economopoulos, *Non Parlo di Salò* (Hobart: Australian Script Centre, 2005), 24. Hereafter cited parenthetically in the text.
35 Christos Tsiolkas "On the Concept of Tolerance," in Tsiolkas, Gideon Haigh and Alexis Wright, *Tolerance, Prejudice, and Fear* (Crows Nest, NSW: Allen and Unwin, 2008), 1. Interestingly Elizabeth Povinelli has recently used the same Le Guin text as an extended allegory for neoliberalism. See *Economies of Abandonment: Social Belonging and Endurance in Late Liberalism* (Durham, NC: Duke University Press, 2011), 1–6.
36 Tsiolkas, "On the Concept of Tolerance," 4–5. The square brackets are mine.
37 Tsiolkas, "On the Concept of Tolerance," 5–6.
38 Tsiolkas, "On the Concept of Tolerance," 6.
39 Tsiolkas, "On the Concept of Tolerance," 21.
40 Tsiolkas, "On the Concept of Tolerance," 55.
41 Adorno and Horkheimer use the phrase to refer to Machiavelli, Hobbes and Bernard Mandeville, though Sade, too, clearly belongs in this company. See *Dialectic of Enlightenment*, trans. John Cumming (New York: Continuum, 1991), 90.
42 Laura Joseph, "Gardening in Hell: Abject Presence and Sublime Present in *Dead Europe* and *The Vintner's Luck*," *JASAL* Special Issue: The Colonial Present (2008): 107–8.
43 Tsiolkas, "On the Concept of Tolerance," 25.
44 Tsiolkas, "On the Concept of Tolerance," 38.
45 Julia Kristeva, *Powers of Horror: An Essay on Abjection*, trans. Leon S. Roudiez (New York: Columbia University Press, 1982), 136–37.
46 Tsiolkas, "On the Concept of Tolerance," 48.
47 Tsiolkas, "On the Concept of Tolerance," 49.

4. In the Suburbs of World Literature: From *Dead Europe* to *The Slap*

1 Ghassan Hage, *White Nation: Fantasies of White Supremacy in a Multicultural Society* (Annandale, NSW: Pluto Press, 1998), 179–231.
2 Kalinda Ashton, "Forms of Hunger and Hysteria: Recent Australian Fiction," *Overland* 194 (Autumn 2009): 93.
3 Christos Tsiolkas, Interview with Belinda Moneypenny and Jo Case (30 October 2008), accessed 18 December 2014, http://www.readings.com.au. Also quoted in Glyn Davis, "*The Slap*'s Resonances: Multiculturalism and Adolescence in Tsiolkas' Australia," *Interactions: Studies in Communication and Culture* 3.2 (2012): 176.
4 The first of these elections, the "Tampa election," refers to the government's refusal, in late August 2001, to allow the Dutch container ship *MV Tampa*, which had rescued

438 refugees from a stricken vessel, into Australian waters. As the standoff escalated, with Australian soldiers called in to prevent the ship approaching Christmas Island, the Howard government introduced its Border Protection Bill 2001, which consolidated its hard-line stance on immigration. In November that year Howard's Liberal-National coalition increased its majority in federal parliament. The *Tampa* refugees were eventually taken by the Australian navy to Nauru. *Sydney Morning Herald* polling revealed that the Australian electorate strongly supported the government's stance. See Mark Davis, *The Land of Plenty: Australia in the 2000s* (Carlton, VIC: Melbourne University Press, 2008), 220. For more detail on the development of Australia's appalling immigration policy see David Marr and Marian Wilkinson, *Dark Victory* (Crows Nest, NSW: Allen and Unwin, 2005). The second election Tsiolkas mentions, the "Latham election," refers to Mark Latham, leader of the Labor opposition between 2002 and 2005. Latham contested the 2004 federal election, which played out in the shadow of the government's cynical manipulation of the *Tampa* blockade, partly on the pledge to withdraw Australian troops from Iraq. Again the Liberal-National coalition won the election with an increased majority.

5   Christos Tsiolkas, *The Slap* (Crows Nest: Allen and Unwin, 2008), 428. Hereafter cited parenthetically in the text.

6   Theodor Adorno, *Aesthetic Theory*, trans. Robert Hullot-Kentor (Minneapolis: University of Minnesota Press, 1997), 1.

7   Adorno, *Aesthetic Theory*, 2.

8   Oskar Negt and Alexander Kluge, *The Public Sphere and Experience: Toward an Analysis of the Bourgeois and Proletarian Public Sphere*, trans. Peter Labyani, James Owen Daniel and Assenka Oksiloff (Minneapolis: University of Minnesota Press, 1993), 33.

9   Adorno, *Aesthetic Theory*, 2.

10 Adorno, *Aesthetic Theory*, 33.

11 Adorno, *Aesthetic Theory*, 32–33.

12 Adorno, *Aesthetic Theory*, 19.

13 Adorno, *Aesthetic Theory*, 39.

14 Adorno, *Aesthetic Theory*, 40.

15 Christos Tsiolkas, *Dead Europe* (Sydney: Random House, 2005), 157. Hereafter cited parenthetically in the text.

16 "Editorial," *Overland* 196 (Spring 2009): 5

17 Geoffrey Hartman has used the term "memory envy" to get at the way in which writers internalize public images of the Holocaust. See Hartman, *Scars of the Spirit: The Struggle Against Inauthenticity* (New York: Palgrave, 2002), 79–80.

18 See Ken Gelder and Paul Salzman, *After the Celebration: Australian Fiction 1989–2007* (Carlton: Melbourne University Press, 2009), 216–27.

19 For Ng, this dismantling happens on two levels. Firstly, Tsiolkas "extends the binary beyond its usual parameters; Europe here is not simply the Old World representing culture, wisdom and civilization, but rather a *dead* Europe, its people merely ghostlike spectres who are physically and spiritually adrift in a world with no future. By contrast, Australia here should become the land of the living, but with a nod towards the processes of globalisation, Tsiolkas's novel is set in a world where the distance between Europe and Australia is rapidly diminishing." Secondly, he "outlines the increasing congruence between Australia and Europe," in a way that stresses political and cultural continuities rather than geographical distance. See Ng, "*Dead Europe* and the Coming of Age in Australian Literature: Globalisation, Cosmopolitanism and Perversity,"

Australian Humanities Review 54 (2013): 121–22, accessed 18 December 2014, http://www.australianhumanitiesreview.org.

20 Brigid Rooney, "Colonising Time, Recollecting Space: Steven Carroll's Reinvention of Suburbia," *JASAL* 13.2 (2013): 1, accessed 18 December 2014, http://www.nla.gov.au.

21 Christos Tsiolkas, "Christos Tsiolkas on How He Wrote *The Slap*," *Guardian*, 16 January 2014, accessed 18 December 2014, http://www.theguardian.com.

22 Christos Tsiolkas, *Merciless Gods* (Crows Nest, NSW: Allen and Unwin, 2014), 48, 64–65.

23 Pascale Casanova, *The World Republic of Letters*, trans. M.B. DeBevoise (Cambridge, MA: Harvard University Press, 2004), 15.

24 Quoted in Casanova, *The World Republic of Letters*, 28.

25 Casanova, *The World Republic of Letters*, 23.

26 Casanova, *The World Republic of Letters*, 43

27 Mark Davis, *The Land of Plenty: Australia in the 2000s* (Carlton, VIC: Melbourne University Press, 2008), 185.

28 Davis, *The Land of Plenty*, 186.

29 Mandy Treagus, "Queering the Mainstream: *The Slap* and 'Middle' Australia," *JASAL* 12.3 (2012): 5, accessed 18 December 2014, http://www.nla.gov.au. On 11 December 2005 Cronulla beach in Sydney was the scene of a violent demonstration driven by Anglo-Australian xenophobia, which in the week before had been directed at people of Lebanese and broadly Middle Eastern background by text messages that recirculated on talkback radio.

30 Christos Tsiolkas, "Christos Tsiolkas: 'There's a Tameness to the Modern Novel.'" Interview with Elizabeth Day, *Observer*, 29 October 2011, accessed 18 December 2014, http://www.theguardian.com.

31 Nikos Papastergiadis, "Hospitality, Multiculturalism and Cosmopolitanism: A Conversation between Christos Tsiolkas and Nikos Papastergiadis," *Journal of Intercultural Studies* 34.4 (2013): 389.

32 Ghassan Hage, *Against Paranoid Nationalism: Searching for Hope in a Shrinking Society* (Annandale, NSW: Pluto Press, 2003), 3.

33 Davis, *The Land of Plenty*, 91. Davis is quoting Richard Sennett's *The Culture of New Capitalism* (New Haven, CT: Yale University Press, 2006), 90.

34 Davis, *The Land of Plenty*, 46.

35 Mark Latham, *From the Suburbs: Building a Nation from Our Neighbourhoods* (Annandale, NSW: Pluto Press, 2003), 21.

36 Christos Tsiolkas, "On the Concept of Tolerance," Tsiolkas, Gideon Haigh and Alexis Wright, *Tolerance, Prejudice and Fear* (Crows Nest, NSW: Allen and Unwin, 2008), 13.

37 Tsiolkas, "On the Concept of Tolerance," 15.

38 Christos Tsiolkas, "Strangers at the Gate: Making Sense of Australia's Fear of Asylum Seekers," *The Monthly* 93 (September 2013), accessed 18 December 2014, http://www.themonthly.com.au.

39 Aida Edemariam, "Christos Tsiolkas: 'There's Love in this Book,'" *Guardian*, 6 August 2010, accessed 18 December 2014, http://www.theguardian.com.

40 This is something Melissa Denes has commented upon: "Australian critics (and British and American ones) have praised the novel for its dissection of contemporary post-John Howard Australia, and it's true that Tsiolkas assembles a diverse cast. What he doesn't do is make their ethnicity, faith or class count for much, or venture very far into these different worlds: Hector's friend Bilal is an Aboriginal Muslim, with a white wife, but it is left to the reader to guess how much Islam and his race mean to him, how they

combine and diverge." See Melissa Denes, "Freakazoid. Review of *The Slap*," *London Review of Books* 32.16 (19 August 2010): 28.

41 See Hage, *Against Paranoid Nationalism*, 21. This is also something that Lucy Hopkins has gestured at in her discussion of Rosie as the novel's "central gatekeeper of childhood innocence." See "'The Bad Man's Going to Jail': The Ethics and Politics of Childhood in *The Slap*," in Peter Marks ed., *Literature and Politics: Pushing the World in Certain Directions* (Newcastle: Cambridge Scholars Publishing, 2012), 178–90.

5. The Politics of the Bestseller: *The Slap* and *Barracuda*

1 Christos Tsiolkas, *Barracuda* (Sydney: Allen and Unwin, 2013), 418. Hereafter cited parenthetically in the text.

2 Christos Tsiolkas, "Strangers at the Gate: Making Sense of Australia's Fear of Asylum Seekers," *The Monthly*, September 2013, accessed 18 December 2014, http://www.themonthly.com.au.

3 Mark Davis, *The Land of Plenty: Australia in the 2000s* (Melbourne: Melbourne University Press, 2008), 92.

4 Davis, *The Land of Plenty*, 220–22.

5 See Hannah Arendt, *The Origins of Totalitarianism* (New York: Harcourt Brace Jovanovich, 1973), 267–302.

6 Giorgio Agamben, *Means without Ends: Notes on Politics*, trans. Vincenzo Binetti and Cesare Casarino (Minneapolis: University of Minnesota Press, 2000), 19.

7 Ghassan Hage, *Against Paranoid Nationalism: Searching for Hope in a Shrinking Society* (Annandale, NSW: Pluto Press, 2003), 3.

8 Arendt, *The Origins of Totalitarianism*, 302.

9 Peter Craven, "The Evolution of a Master Spelt Out with Perfect Poise," *Age*, "Spectrum" Section, 15 November 2014, 37.

10 Christos Tsiolkas, *Merciless Gods* (Crows Nest, NSW: Allen and Unwin, 2014), 70–73.

11 Craven, "The Evolution of a Master Spelt Out with Perfect Poise," 37.

12 Mark Davis, "The Decline of the Literary Paradigm," *Heat* 12 New Series (2006): 103.

13 Jacques Rancière, *The Philosopher and His Poor*, trans. John Drury, Corinne Oster and Andrew Parker (Durham, NC: Duke University Press, 2003), 191. For a fuller discussion of how these novels appropriate popular forms, see Andrew McCann, "Professing the Popular: Political Fiction circa 2006," *Australian Literary Studies* 23.2 (October 2007): 43–57.

14 Richard Flanagan, "Writing *The Unknown Terrorist*," *ABC Radio National Book Show*, 23 November 2006, accessed 13 January 2015, http://www.abc.net.au. Also quoted in Brigid Rooney, *Literary Activists: Writer-Intellectuals and Australian Public Life* (St. Lucia, QLD: University of Queensland Press, 2009), 181.

15 See Ken Gelder, *Popular Fiction: The Logics and Practices of a Literary Field* (London: Routledge, 2004), 11–39.

16 Ken Gelder, 'Politics and Monomania: The Rarefied World of Contemporary Australian Literary Culture," *Overland* 184 (Spring 2006): 52, 48.

17 What I am offering here is a simplification and condensation of Driscoll's considered and patient mapping of the middlebrow. See Beth Driscoll, *The New Literary Middlebrow: Tastemakers and Reading in the Twenty-First Century* (New York: Palgrave Macmillan, 2014), 5–44, which offers a comprehensive introduction to the middlebrow and its various characteristics.

18 McKenzie Wark, *Celebrities, Culture and Cyberspace: The Light on the Hill in a Postmodern World* (Annandale, NSW: Pluto Press, 1999), 33.
19 Graeme Turner, Frances Bonner and P. David Marshall, *Fame Games: The Production of Celebrity in Australia* (Cambridge: Cambridge University Press, 2000), 12. *Fame Games* is the most thorough overview of this field and the most detailed account of its industrial minutiae.
20 Rooney, *Literary Activists*, 183.
21 Rooney, *Literary Activists*, 186–187.
22 Mandy Treagus, "Queering the Mainstream: *The Slap* and 'Middle Australia,'" *JASAL* 12.3 (2012): 6, accessed 18 December 2014, http://www.nla.gov.au.
23 Kalinda Ashton, "Forms of Hunger and Hysteria: Recent Australian Fiction," *Overland* 194 (Autumn 2009): 93.
24 Christos Tsiolkas, *The Slap* (Sydney: Allen and Unwin, 2008), 30–31. Hereafter cited parenthetically in the text.
25 Glyn Davis, "*The Slap*'s Resonances: Multiculturalism and Adolescence in Tsiolkas' Australia," *Interactions: Studies in Communication and Culture* 3.2. (2012): 175.
26 James Ley, "A Furious Moralist," *Australian Book Review* 306 (November 2008): 9.
27 John Hartley, *Popular Reality: Journalism, Modernity, Popular Culture* (London: Arnold, 1996), 4–5.
28 Pascale Casanova, *The World Republic of Letters*, trans M.B. DeBevoise (Cambridge, MA: Harvard University Press, 2004), 169.

Conclusion: Aesthetic Autonomy and the Politics of Fiction

1   Christos Tsiolkas, "On the Concept of Tolerance," in Tsiolkas, Gideon Haigh and Alexis Wright, *Tolerance, Prejudice and Fear* (Crows Nest, NSW: Allen and Unwin, 2008), 47.
2   Tsiolkas, "On the Concept of Tolerance," 48.
3   Marion May Campbell, *konkretion* (Crawley: University of Western Australia Publishing, 2013), 20.
4   Ken Gelder, "Politics and Monomania: The Rarefied World of Contemporary Australian Literary Culture," *Overland* 184 (Spring 2006): 52.
5   Theodor Adorno, *Minima Moralia*, trans. E.F.N. Jephcott (London: Verso, 2002), 25.
6   See Pierre Bourdieu, *Distinction: A Social Critique of the Judgement of Taste*, trans. Richard Nice (Cambridge, MA: Harvard University Press, 1984).
7   Ian Hunter, "Aesthetics and Cultural Studies," in Lawrence Grossberg, Cary Nelson and Paula A. Treichler eds., *Cultural Studies* (London: Routledge, 1992), 354.
8   Hunter, "Aesthetics and Cultural Studies," 362.

BIBLIOGRAPHY

Adams, Parveen. *The Emptiness of the Image: Psychoanalysis and Sexual Difference*. London: Routledge, 1996.

Adorno, Theodor. *Aesthetic Theory*. Trans. Robert Hullot-Kentor. Minneapolis: University of Minnesota Press, 1997.

———. *Minima Moralia*. Trans. E.F.N. Jephcott. London: Verso, 2002.

Adorno, Theodor and Max Horkheimer. *Dialectic of Enlightenment*. Trans. John Cumming. New York: Continuum, 1991.

Agamben, Giorgio. *Homo Sacer: Sovereign Power and Bare Life*. Trans. Daniel Heller-Roazen. Stanford, CA: Stanford University Press, 1998.

———. *Means without Ends: Notes on Politics*. Trans. Vincenzo Binetti and Cesare Casarino. Minneapolis: University of Minnesota Press, 2000.

Apter, Emily. "Weaponized Thought: Ethical Militance and the Group Subject." *Grey Room* 14 (Winter 2004): 6–22.

Arendt, Hannah. *The Origins of Totalitarianism*. New York: Harcourt Brace Jovanovich, 1973.

Ashton, Kalinda. "Forms of Hunger and Hysteria: Recent Australian Fiction." *Overland* 194 (Autumn 2009): 93–96.

Augé, Marc. *Non-Places: An Introduction to Supermodernity*. Trans. John Howe. London: Verso, 2009.

Authers, Ben. "'I'm Not Australian, I'm Not Greek, I'm Not Anything': Identity and the Multicultural Nation in Christos Tsiolkas's *Loaded*." *JASAL* 4 (2005): 133–45.

Bachmann, Gideon. "Pasolini on de Sade: An Interview During the Filming of *The 120 Days of Sodom*." *Film Quarterly* 29.2 (Winter 1975–1976): 39–45.

Bakhtin, M.M. *Speech Genres and Other Essays*. Trans. Vern W. McGee. Austin: University of Texas Press, 1986.

Ballard, J.G. *The Atrocity Exhibition*. 1970. London: HarperCollins, 2006.

———. *Crash*. 1973. London: Vintage, 1995.

Benjamin, Walter. *Charles Baudelaire: A Lyric Poet in the Era of High Capitalism*. Trans. Harry Zohn. London: Verso, 1973.

Black, Shameem. *Fictions Across Borders: Imagining the Lives of Others in Late Twentieth-Century Novels*. New York: Columbia University Press, 2010.

Blazey, Peter. "From Breathless to a Scream." *Weekend Australian*, Review Section, 3 August 1996, 8.

Bollen, Jonathan, Adrian Kiernander and Bruce Parr. *Men at Play: Masculinities in Australian Theatre since the 1950s*. Amsterdam: Rodopi, 2008.

Bourdieu, Pierre. *Distinction: A Social Critique of the Judgement of Taste*. Trans. Richard Nice. Cambridge, MA: Harvard University Press, 1984.

Burroughs, William. *The Wild Boys*. 1969. New York: Grove Press, 1992.

Campbell, Marion May. *Konkretion*. Crawley: University of Western Australia Publishing, 2013.

Cañadas, Ivan. "The Sin That Dare Not Speak its Name: Class and Sexuality in Christos Tsiolkas's *Loaded* and Ana Kokkinos's *Head On*." *Overland* 177 (Summer 2004): 44–47.

Casanova, Pascale. *The World Republic of Letters*. Trans. M.B. Debevoise. Cambridge, MA: Harvard University Press, 2004.

Cheah, Pheng. "Humanity in the Field of Instrumentality." *PMLA* 212.5 (October 2006): 1552–57.

———. *Inhuman Conditions: On Cosmopolitanism and Human Rights*. Cambridge, MA: Harvard University Press, 2006.

———. "Mattering." *Diacritics* 26.1 (Spring 1996): 108–39.

———. *Spectral Nationality: Passages of Freedom from Kant to Postcolonial Literatures of Liberation*. New York: Columbia University Press, 2003.

Clifford, James. "Traveling Culture." In Lawrence Grossberg, Cary Nelson and Paula A. Treichler eds. *Cultural Studies*. London: Routledge, 1992. 96–116.

Craven, Peter. "The Evolution of a Master Spelt Out with Perfect Poise." *Age*, Spectrum, 15 November 2014, 37.

D'Cruz, Glenn ed., *Class Act: Melbourne Workers Theatre 1987–2007*. Carlton: Vulgar Press, 2007.

Davidson, Michael. "On the Outskirts of Form: Cosmopoetics in the Shadow of NAFTA." *Textual Practice* 22.4 (December 2008): 733–56.

Davis, Glyn. "*The Slap*'s Resonances: Multiculturalism and Adolescence in Tsiolkas' Australia." *Interactions: Studies in Communication and Culture* 3.2 (2012): 173–86.

Davis, Mark. "The Decline of the Literary Paradigm in Australian Publishing." *HEAT* 12 New Series (2006): 91–108.

———. *The Land of Plenty: Australia in the 2000s*. Carlton, VIC: Melbourne University Press, 2008.

Dawson, Paul. "Grunge Lit: Marketing Generation X." *Meanjin* 56.1 (March 1997): 119–25.

de Certeau, Michel. *The Practice of Everyday Life*. Trans. Steven Randall. Berkeley: University of California Press, 1984.

Denes, Melissa, "Freakazoid. Review of *The Slap*." *London Review of Books* 32.16 (19 August 2010): 26–28.

Derrida, Jacques. *Specters of Marx: The State of the Debt, the Work of Mourning, and the New International*. Trans. Peggy Kamuf. London: Routledge, 1994.

Edelman, Lee. *No Future: Queer Theory and the Death Drive*. Durham, NC: Duke University Press, 2004.

Edemariam, Aida. "Christos Tsiolkas: 'There's Love in this Book,'" *Guardian*, 6 August 2010, accessed 18 December 2014, http://www.theguardian.com.

Enzensberger, Hans Magnus. *Zig Zag: The Politics of Culture and Vice Versa*. New York: The New Press, 1997.

Esposito, Roberto. *Living Thought: The Origins and Actuality of Italian Philosophy*. Trans. Zakiya Hanafi. Stanford, CA: Stanford University Press, 2012.

Esty, Jed. *Unseasonable Youth: Modernism, Colonialism, and the Fiction of Development*. Oxford: Oxford University Press, 2012.

Filewood, Alan and David Watt, "Melbourne Workers Theatre: The Meat in the Sandwich." In Glenn D'Cruz ed. *Class Act: Melbourne Workers Theatre 1987–2007*. Carlton: Vulgar Press, 2007. 30–58.

Flanagan, Richard. *The Unknown Terrorist*. Sydney: Picador, 2006.

———. "Writing *The Unknown Terrorist*." ABC Radio National *Book Show*, 23 November 2006, accessed 13 January 2015, http://www.abc.net.au.

Gelder, Ken. "Politics and Monomania: The Rarefied World of Contemporary Australian Literary Culture." *Overland* 184 (Spring 2006): 48–56.

———. *Popular Fiction: The Logics and Practices of a Literary Field*. London: Routledge, 2004.

Gelder, Ken and Paul Salzman. *After the Celebration: Australian Fiction 1989–2007*. Carlton: Melbourne University Press, 2009.

Glass, Loren. *Counter-Culture Colophon: Grove Press, the* Evergreen Review *and the Incorporation of the Avant-Garde*. Stanford, CA: Stanford University Press, 2013.

Gordon, Robert S.C. *Pasolini: Forms of Subjectivity*. Oxford: Clarendon Press, 1996.

Grosz, Elizabeth. *Volatile Bodies: Toward a Corporeal Feminism*. Bloomington: Indiana University Press, 1994.

Gunew, Sneja. *Haunted Nations: The Colonial Dimensions of Multiculturalism*. London: Routledge, 2004.

Guyotat, Pierre. *Eden Eden Eden*. Trans. Graham Fox. 1970. London: Creation Books, 2003.

Habermas, Jürgen. *The Structural Transformation of the Public Sphere: An Inquiry into a Category of Bourgeois Society*. Trans. Thomas Burger. Cambridge, MA: MIT Press, 1991.

Hage, Ghassan. *Against Paranoid Nationalism: Searching for Hope in a Shrinking Society*. Annandale, NSW: Pluto Press, 2003.

———. *White Nation: Fantasies of White Supremacy in a Multicultural Society*. Annandale, NSW: Pluto Press, 1998.

Hansen, Miriam Bratu. *Cinema and Experience: Siegfried Kracauer, Walter Benjamin, and Theodor W. Adorno*. Berkeley: University of California Press, 2012.

Hartley, John. *Popular Reality: Journalism, Modernity, Popular Culture*. London: Arnold, 1996.

———. "The Sexualization of Suburbia: The Diffusion of Knowledge in the Postmodern Public Sphere." In Roger Silverstone ed. *Visions of Suburbia*. London: Routledge, 1997. 180–216.

Hartman, Geoffrey. *Scars of the Spirit: The Struggle Against Inauthenticity*. New York: Palgrave, 2002.

Hawker, Philippa. "Books – Paperbacks." *Age*, Saturday Extra, 14 September 1996, 8.

———. "Loaded on the Back Streets." *Age*, Saturday Extra, 22 December 1995, 7.

Hopkins, Lucy. "'The Bad Man's Going to Jail': The Ethics and Politics of Childhood in *The Slap*." In Peter Marks ed. *Literature and Politics: Pushing the World in Certain Directions*. Newcastle: Cambridge Scholars Publishing, 2012. 178–90.

Huggan Graham. "Vampires, Again." *Southerly* 66.3 (January 2006): 192–204.

Hunter, Ian. "Aesthetics and Cultural Studies." In Lawrence Grossberg, Cary Nelson and Paula A. Treichler eds., *Cultural Studies*. London: Routledge, 1992. 347–72.

Jaivin, Linda. *The Infernal Optimist*. Sydney: Fourth Estate, 2006.

Jameson, Fredric. *Postmodernism, or, the Cultural Logic of Late Capitalism*. Durham, NC: Duke University Press, 1991.

Joseph, Laura. "Gardening in Hell: Abject Presence and Sublime Present in *Dead Europe* and *The Vintner's Luck*." *JASAL* Special Issue: The Colonial Present (2008): 105–13.

Kittler, Friedrich. *Discourse Networks 1800/1900*. Trans. Michael Metteer with Chris Cullens. Stanford, CA: Stanford University Press, 1990.

Kristeva, Julia. *Powers of Horror: An Essay on Abjection*. Trans. Leon S. Roudiez. New York: Columbia University Press, 1982.

Latham, Mark. *From the Suburbs: Building a Nation from Our Neighbourhoods*. Annandale, NSW: Pluto Press, 2003.

Ley, James. "A Furious Moralist." *Australian Book Review* 306 (November 2008): 9–10.

Macris, Anthony. "Hubris is Not a Dirty Word." *Bulletin*, 25 May 1999, 115.

MacKinnon, Catherine. *Only Words*. Cambridge, MA: Harvard University Press, 1993.

Manne, Robert. "Dead Disturbing: A Bloodthirsty Tale that Plays with the Fire of Anti-Semitism." *The Monthly*, June 2005, 50–53.

Marcuse, Herbert. *Negations: Essays in Critical Theory*. Trans. Jeremy J. Shapiro. Boston: Beacon Press, 1968.

Marr, David and Marian Wilkinson. *Dark Victory*. Crows Nest, NSW: Allen and Unwin, 2005.

McCann, Andrew. "Discrepant Cosmopolitanism and the Contemporary Novel: Reading the Inhuman in Christos Tsiolkas's *Dead Europe* and Roberto Bolaño's *2666*." *Antipodes* 24.2 (December 2010): 135–41.

———. "Professing the Popular: Political Fiction circa 2006." *Australian Literary Studies* 23.2 (October 2007): 43–57.

McMahon, Elizabeth. "Lost in Music." *Meanjin* 59.2 (2000): 166–77.

Meyrick, Julian. "Introduction." *Melbourne Stories: Three Plays*. Sydney: Currency Press, 2000. 3–6.

———. "*Who's Afraid of the Working Class?*: An Impressionistic History." In Glenn D'Cruz ed. *Class Act: Melbourne Workers Theatre 1987–2007*. Melbourne: Vulgar Press, 2007. 136–47.

Moretti, Franco. *The Way of the World: The Bildungsroman in European Culture*. Trans. Albert Sbraglia. London: Verso, 2000.

Muñoz, José Esteban. *Cruising Utopia: The Then and There of Queer Futurity*. New York: New York University Press, 2009.

Negt, Oskar and Alexander Kluge. *The Public Sphere and Experience: Toward an Analysis of the Bourgeois and Proletarian Public Sphere*. Trans. Peter Labanyi, Jamie Owen Daniel and Assenka Oksiloff. Minneapolis: University of Minnesota Press, 1993.

Ng, Lynda. "*Dead Europe* and the Coming of Age in Australian Literature: Globalisation, Cosmopolitanism and Perversity." *Australian Humanities Review* 54 (May 2013): 120–35, accessed 18 December 2014, http://www.australianhumanitiesreview.org.

Padmore, Catherine. "Future Tense: *Dead Europe* and Viral Anti-Semitism." *Australian Literary Studies* 23.4 (December 2008): 434–45.

Papastergiadis, Nikos. "Hospitality, Multiculturalism and Cosmopolitanism: A Conversation between Christos Tsiolkas and Nikos Papastergiadis." *Journal of Intercultural Studies* 34.4 (2013): 387–93.

Pasolini, Pier Paolo. "Coitus, Abortion, Power's False Tolerance, the Conformism of Progressives." Trans. Juliana Schiesari, in Beverly Allen ed. *Pier Paolo Pasolini: The Poetics of Heresy*. Saratoga, CA: Anma Libri and Co., 1982. 116–21.

———. "Heart." Trans. Juliana Schiesari, in Beverly Allen ed. *Pier Paolo Pasolini: The Poetics of Heresy*. Saratoga, CA: Anma Libri and Co., 1982. 122–26.

———. *Poems*. Trans. Norman MacAfee. New York: Random House, 1982.

———. "Repudiation of the Trilogy of Life." In *Heretical Empiricism*. Trans. Ben Lawton and Louise K. Barnett. Washington, DC: New Academia Publishing, 2005. xvii–xx.

———. "A Study in the Anthropological Revolution in Italy." Trans. Juliana Schiesari, in Beverly Allen ed. *Pier Paolo Pasolini: The Poetics of Heresy*. Saratoga, CA: Anma Libri and Co., 1982. 112–15.

Pavlides, Eleni. *Un-Australian Fictions: Nation, Multiculture(alism) and Globalization, 1988–2008*. Newcastle upon Tyne: Cambridge Scholars Publishing, 2013.

Povinelli, Elizabeth. *Economies of Abandonment: Social Belonging and Endurance in Late Liberalism*. Durham, NC: Duke University Press, 2011.

Rancière, Jacques. *The Philosopher and His Poor*. Trans. John Drury, Corinne Oster and Andrew Parker. Durham, NC: Duke University Press, 2003.

Richardson, Owen. "Cappuccino Chat: Light, Fluffy and Not Much Substance." *Age*, Agenda, 20 October 1996, 7.

Rooney, Brigid. "Colonising Time, Recollecting Space: Steven Carroll's Reinvention of Suburbia." *JASAL* 13.2 (2013): 1–16, accessed 18 December 2014, http://www.nla.gov.au.

———. *Literary Activists: Writer-Intellectuals and Australian Public Life*. St. Lucia, QLD: University of Queensland Press, 2009.

Rosenblatt, Les. "A Place Where Wolves Fuck." *Arena* 79 (2005): 46–48.

Sassen, Saskia. *The Global City: New York, London, Tokyo*. Princeton, NJ: Princeton University Press, 1991.

Schwarz, Anja. "Mapping (Un-)Australian Identities: Territorial Disputes in Christos Tsiolkas' *Loaded*." In Anke Bartels and Dirk Wiemann eds. *Global Fragments: (Dis) Orientation in the New World Order*. Amsterdam: Rodopi, 2007. 13–27.

Shek-Noble, Liz. "'There Were Phantoms': Spectral Shadows in Christo Tsiolkas's *Dead Europe*." *JASAL* 11.2 (2011): 1–13, accessed 18 December 2014, http://www.nla.gov.au.

Shone, Tom. "Novel of the Year? Get Ready for *The Slap*." *Sunday Times*, Culture Section, 9 May 2010, 10–11.

Sillanpoa, Wallace P. "Pasolini's Gramsci." *MLN* 96.1, Italian Issue (January 1981): 120–37.

Sullivan, Jane. "*Three Dollars* Leaves the Rest Behind." *Age*, Agenda, 12 July 1998, 20.

Syson, Ian. "Smells Like Market Spirit: Grunge, Literature, Australia." *Overland* 142 (Autumn 1996): 21–26.

Treagus, Mandy. "Queering the Mainstream: *The Slap* and 'Middle' Australia." *JASAL* 12.3 (2012): 1–9, accessed 18 December 2014, http://www.nla.gov.au.

Tsiolkas, Christos. *Barracuda*. Crows Nest, NSW: Allen and Unwin, 2013.

———. "Christos Tsiolkas on How He Wrote *The Slap*." *Guardian*, 16 January 2014, accessed 18 December 2014, http://www.theguardian.com.

———. "Christos Tsiolkas: 'There's a Tameness to the Modern Novel.'" Interview with Elizabeth Day. *Observer*, 29 October 2011, accessed 18 December 2014, http://www.theguardian.com.

———. *Dead Europe*. Milsons Point, NSW: Vintage, 2005.

———. *The Devil's Playground*. Sydney: Currency Press, 2002.

———. Interview with Belinda Moneypenny and Jo Case, 30 October 2008, accessed 18 December 2014, http://www.readings.com.au.

———. Interview with Glenn D'Cruz. In Glenn D'Cruz ed. *Class Act: Melbourne Workers Theatre 1987–2007*. Carlton: Vulgar Press, 2007. 148–55.

———. "Into a Liquid Ether." *Age*, 14 June 2008, 18–19.

———. *The Jesus Man*. Milsons Point, NSW: Vintage, 1999.

———. *Loaded*. Sydney: Vintage Books, 1995.

———. "Me and My Country, Where to Now?" Interview with Heather Taylor Johnson. *Meanjin* 72.1 (March 2013): 178–88.

———. "Mix-Tape: The Technology of a Passion." *Meanjin* 69.4 (Summer 2010): 136–41.

———. "On the Concept of Tolerance." In Tsiolkas, Gideon Haigh, and Alexis Wright, *Tolerance, Prejudice, and Fear*. Crows Nest, NSW: Allen and Unwin, 2008. 1–56.

———. "Politics, Faith and Sex." Interview with Patricia Cornelius. *Overland* 181 (Summer 2005): 18–25.

———. *The Slap*. Crows Nest, NSW: Allen and Unwin, 2008.

———. "Strangers at the Gate: Making Sense of Australia's Fear of Asylum Seekers." *The Monthly*, September 2013, accessed 18 December 2014, http://www.themonthly.com.au.

————. "Suit." (from *Who's Afraid of the Working Class?*) In *Melbourne Stories: Three Plays*. Sydney: Currency Press, 2000. 11–102.

————. "'What Does Fiction Do?' On *Dead Europe*: Ethics and Aesthetics." Interview with Catherine Padmore. *Australian Literary Studies* 23.4 (December 2008): 446–62.

————. "Whatever Happened to the Working Class?" *The Monthly*, May 2014, accessed 20 June 2014, http://www.the monthly.com.au.

Tsiolkas, Christos and Sasha Soldatow. *Jump Cuts: An Autobiography*. Milsons Point, NSW: Random House, 1996.

Tsiolkas, Christos and Spiro Economopoulos. *Non Parlo di Salò*. Hobart: Australian Script Centre, 2005.

Turner, Graeme, Frances Bonner and P. David Marshall. *Fame Games: The Production of Celebrity in Australia*. Cambridge: Cambridge University Press, 2000.

Vasilakakos, John. *Christos Tsiolkas: The Untold Story*. Ballan, VIC: Connorcourt Publishing, 2013.

Vaughan, Michael. "'What's Haunting *Dead Europe?*' Trauma Fiction as Resistance to Postmodern Governmentality." *JASAL* 11.2 (2011): 1–10, accessed 18 December 2014, http://www.nla.gov.au.

Viano, Maurizio. "The Left According to the Ashes of Gramsci." *Social Text* 18 (Winter 1987–88): 51–60.

Vighi, Fabio. "Pasolini and Exclusion: Žižek, Agamben and the Modern Sub-Proletariat." *Theory, Culture and Society*, 20.5 (2003): 99–121.

Wark, McKenzie. *Celebrity, Culture and Cyberspace: The Light on the Hill in a Postmodern World*. Annandale, NSW: Pluto Press, 1999.

Woodhead, Cameron. "Hard-Core Saga of Fraternal Frustration." *Age*, Saturday Extra, 29 May 1999, 8.

Žižek, Slavoj. *The Metastases of Enjoyment: Six Essays on Women and Causality*. London: Verso, 1994.

————. Speech Delivered at Liberty Plaza, 9 October 2011, accessed 29 December 2014, http://criticallegalthinking.com.

INDEX

Lightning Source UK Ltd.
Milton Keynes UK
UKOW04n2159230615

254010UK00007B/43/P

9 781783 084036